Praise for *The Means of Reproduction*
by Michelle Goldberg

"Surprisingly original . . . Goldberg defies expectations by making an argument that stands outside traditional liberal thinking about reproductive rights. . . . In her book, she presents nothing less than a new framework for advocates like herself." —*New York Observer*

"The sheer mass of information contained in [Goldberg's] new book, *The Means of Reproduction*, is stunning, but the real power is in her message—that the global battle for reproductive rights will continue to shape the world." —*Willamette Weekly*

"Goldberg's reporting toggles easily between the macroscopic geopolitical arguments and the remarkable personal stories of several men and women caught in the decades of crossfire. . . . [It's] a credit to Goldberg that she reports those aspects of the debate that push the boundaries of her own liberal sympathies." —*Democracy*

"[*The Means of Reproduction*] bring together so many crucial strands of recent history and current international politics, and in such a confident, sure-footed way. Plus, it's so well written! It should be required reading for anyone who wants to understand our world, from the proliferation of NGOs to the outbreak of fundamentalism around the world, including here in the U.S." —Katha Pollitt

"We know how to radically improve women's lives around the world: give them education, power, and the liberty to control of their own bodies. We also know something even more important: that improving women's lives in this way makes the whole world a better place—healthier, more prosperous, and more secure. Michelle Goldberg's sweeping saga about how this consensus came about, and the tragic impediments to putting it into practice, may be the most important book you'll ever read about the future of the human race." —Rick Perlstein, author of *Nixonland*

"Goldberg's book is more than a scrupulously researched chronicle of the brutalities inflicted on women throughout the underdeveloped world by the determination of antedeluvian religious institutions, and governments that protect them, to control female bodies. What this book demonstrates convincingly is that there can be no economic progress in any country that denies women basic human rights, and that women cannot exercise their human rights if they cannot determine when to have sex, whether or when to marry, and how many children they have. Ms. Goldberg's message is that the repression of women lies at the heart of all oppressive societies."

—Susan Jacoby, author of *The Age of American Unreason*

"*The Means of Reproduction* is a bold and vital book, a story about life and those who twist that word to front for agendas of sexual control around the world. We're lucky that we have Michelle Goldberg, a brilliant and clear-eyed journalist, to bring us news of how the struggle over reproductive rights has gone global, as the American Right teams up with reactionary forces abroad. Goldberg calls it one of the most important fights of our time; after you read *The Means of Reproduction*, you will, too. A landmark book."

—Jeff Sharlet, author of *The New York Times* bestseller *The Family*

"If you want to understand why women leaders the world over have challenged church, state and aid bureaucracies so that ordinary women can decide on when, whether and how to bring new life into the world, this book is a must-read. Goldberg brings to life the controversies that have shaped international public policy on population, reproduction and gender. Along the way she introduces us to the key actors, north and south, who put their lives on the line to give women the means to control their destiny."

—Frances Kissling, former president, Catholics for Choice

PENGUIN BOOKS

THE MEANS OF REPRODUCTION

Michelle Goldberg is a journalist and author based in Brooklyn. Her first book, the *New York Times* bestseller *Kingdom Coming: The Rise of Christian Nationalism*, was a finalist for the New York Public Library's Helen Bernstein Book Award for Excellence in Journalism. A senior correspondent for *The American Prospect* and a columnist for *The Daily Beast*, Goldberg's work has also appeared in *The New Republic, The Nation, Glamour, Rolling Stone, The Guardian* (UK), and many other publications. *The Means of Reproduction* won the 2008 J. Anthony Lukas Work-in-Progress Award.

THE **MEANS** OF **REPRODUCTION**

Sex, Power, and the Future of the World

MICHELLE **GOLDBERG**

PENGUIN BOOKS

PENGUIN BOOKS
Published by the Penguin Group
Penguin Group (USA) Inc., 375 Hudson Street, New York, New York 10014, U.S.A. • Penguin
Group (Canada), 90 Eglinton Avenue East, Suite 700, Toronto, Ontario, Canada M4P 2Y3
(a division of Pearson Penguin Canada Inc.) • Penguin Books Ltd, 80 Strand, London WC2R 0RL,
England • Penguin Ireland, 25 St Stephen's Green, Dublin 2, Ireland (a division of Penguin Books
Ltd) • Penguin Group (Australia), 250 Camberwell Road, Camberwell, Victoria 3124, Australia
(a division of Pearson Australia Group Pty Ltd) • Penguin Books India Pvt Ltd, 11 Community
Centre, Panchsheel Park, New Delhi – 110 017, India • Penguin Group (NZ), 67 Apollo
Drive, Rosedale, North Shore 0632, New Zealand (a division of Pearson New Zealand
Ltd) • Penguin Books (South Africa) (Pty) Ltd, 24 Sturdee Avenue, Rosebank,
Johannesburg 2196, South Africa

Penguin Books Ltd, Registered Offices: 80 Strand, London WC2R 0RL, England

First published in the United States of America by The Penguin Press,
a member of Penguin Group (USA) Inc. 2009
Published in Penguin Books 2010

3 5 7 9 10 8 6 4 2

Copyright © Michelle Goldberg, 2009
All rights reserved

ISBN 978-1-59420-208-7 (hc.)
ISBN 978-0-14-311688-2 (pbk.)
CIP data available

Printed in the United States of America
DESIGNED BY NICOLE LAROCHE

To Carolyn Goldberg and Binni Ipcar

CONTENTS

NOTE TO THE READER

This book is the product of both firsthand reporting and archival research. Often I would interview a person, sometimes several times, and then supplement what he or she told me with information gleaned from oral histories, news stories, journal articles, and books. All secondary sources have endnotes; things that I saw and heard myself do not.

INTRODUCTION: THE GLOBAL BATTLE FOR REPRODUCTIVE RIGHTS

Eunice Brookman-Amissah, the former health minister of Ghana, calls the death of her teenage patient Amina the beginning of her road to Damascus. The stepdaughter of an Anglican archbishop, Brookman-Amissah was brought up in a very conservative home, and those values stayed with her when she went to medical school. In the Accra teaching hospital where she trained in the late 1960s, young women who came in with botched abortions were put in a place called Chenard Ward. There were at least ten of them every day. "They were kept there bleeding and feverish and dirty until all the other cases were done—then it was time to do the evacuations," she told me. "They were kept on the floor. Even when there were beds, these women were put on the floor. People stepped on them and insulted them and called them names—this is how horrible it was!"

Brookman-Amissah did not, at the time, see all this as particularly outrageous. "We were brought up to think that women who had had unsafe abortions were criminals," she said. "They were bad women. They were the scum of this earth."

After graduating, Brookman-Amissah went into private practice. She looked after a poor Muslim family who lived very close by. Their daughter, Amina, was exceptionally bright. "Her parents were illiterate, but she was going to school," Brookman-Amissah said. Amina called her "Auntie Doctor," and liked to hang out at her clinic and talk to the nurses, saying she would be one herself one day.

In 1992, when Amina was fourteen, she came to the clinic one Friday. As Brookman-Amissah remembers it, she was agitated and had been crying.

A man in her compound, she said, had given her money to give to a doctor to make her period come. "My first reaction was one of outrage," said Brookman-Amissah. "'Amina, how dare you talk to me about that? Don't you know we don't do that here! Naughty girl!' That sort of thing." Brookman-Amissah asked Amina to send her mother on Monday so they could talk. "I can still see the look in her eyes," she said.

But on Monday, no one came. Nor on Tuesday. On Wednesday, she heard drumming and commotion outside. A nurse told Brookman-Amissah what it was. "Doctor," she said, "that's Amina. They've gone to bury her." The man who got her pregnant had taken her for an abortion over the weekend, and it had killed her.

"Was Amina really a criminal?" she remembers thinking. "Maybe I'm the criminal. That man, that older man, is a criminal. The whole society is liable for the death of an innocent young girl who didn't even know what was happening to her."

Brookman-Amissah began to alter her views. She got involved in training doctors in more humane postabortion care, and eventually became the representative in Ghana of Ipas, an international safe-abortion organization based in Chapel Hill, North Carolina. Ipas distributes manual, handheld abortion kits all over the world, which are also used to treat women whose backstreet abortions have gone wrong. Brookman-Amissah used to sit for hours outside the offices of the Ministry of Health, trying to donate the kits and to offer free training in their use. "I believe I was called the abortion lady," she said.

Yet while abortion remained illegal, the mood was changing among elites. Brookman-Amissah remembers that when she proposed programs to address complications from unsafe abortions, the woman who headed the government's office of reproductive health was unsure. Then the official went to a groundbreaking 1994 UN conference in Cairo, during which, much to the chagrin of an international network of religious fundamentalists, most of the world's countries pledged to commit themselves to reproductive health and rights. She came back clutching the conference's official program of action, which urged all countries "to deal with the health impact of unsafe abortion as a major public health concern and to reduce the recourse to abortion through expanded and improved family-planning services."

Soon Ipas and the Ghanaian government were collaborating on a program to train midwives to help women who'd suffered complications from illegal abortions. And then, in 1996, Brookman-Amissah became the minister of health herself. Later she would become Ghana's ambassador to The Netherlands, before rejoining Ipas as vice president for Africa. Abortion remains broadly illegal in her country, but the government is actively trying to educate workers in health care and law enforcement that there is an exception when a woman's health is at risk.

Promoting safe abortion in Africa is a monumental job. Thanks to the legal remnants of colonial constitutions, the procedure is severely restricted in most sub-Saharan African countries. According to the World Health Organization, of the forty-two million abortions performed in the world each year, twenty million are unsafe, and nowhere in the world are abortions more dangerous than in Africa. Botched abortions kill 36,000 African women each year, representing more than half of the global total of between 65,000 and 70,000 annual deaths.[1]

Worldwide, complications from unsafe abortions cause 13 percent of maternal deaths and account for a fifth of the "total mortality and disability burden due to pregnancy and childbirth," according to the WHO. Twenty-four million women have been rendered infertile by dangerous procedures, an especially crushing debility in parts of the world where childless women are reviled. Again, the toll is worst in Africa.[2]

The problem of unsafe abortion has been seriously exacerbated by contraceptive shortages caused by American policies hostile to birth control, as well as by the understandable diversion of scarce sexual health resources to fight HIV. Between 1995 and 2003, international donor support for family planning in the developing world fell from $560 million to $460 million, a shortfall that has hit Africa particularly hard. In Kenya, the World Health Organization reports, between 1998 and 2003, the number of births that mothers said were unwanted nearly doubled, from 11 percent to 21 percent.[3]

But it's not just the scale of the problem of unsafe abortion and lack of family planning that makes the work of reform so difficult. Cultural conservatism is deeply entrenched across Africa, as it is in most of the poor regions of the world. Religious revivals, Christian and Muslim alike, have caught fire, and they compete to condemn the destabilizing libertinism of the West. (During the American presidential campaign of 2008, the Ghanaian artist Blakk Rasta had a hit with the song "Barack Obama," which celebrated the candidate even as it promised that judgment would come to America for "legalizing abortion.")[4]

Churches in the global South "are by and large much more comfortable than their Northern neighbors in preaching a traditional role for women," wrote the religion scholar Philip Jenkins in *The Next Christendom: The Coming of Global Christianity.* "This is especially true in much of Africa, where Muslim notions exercise a powerful cultural influence. Although Christians do not accept the whole Islamic package of mores on this or any issue, they do imbibe a conservatism general to the whole community."[5]

The specific religious dynamics differ in other parts of the planet, but the conflation of women's rights with globalization or Westernization, and the concomitant desire to limit them in the name of national or cultural integrity, is nearly universal. Republicans in the United States, whether in Congress or the White House, have worked to bolster this conservatism by denying aid to groups that have anything to do with abortion, channeling funds to traditionalist faith-based groups, and using the country's diplomatic weight to thwart international efforts to improve reproductive rights.

American antiabortion pressure, said Brookman-Amissah, "has grown over the years. It started with resistance to the whole Cairo agenda, especially the reference to reproductive health and rights, a word they seem to be very allergic to. The fanaticism that is there about abortion, which is also threatening women in your country, this was translated onto the international scene."

Even as religious traditionalists in developing countries find support abroad—whether it comes from Saudi Arabia, American evangelicals, or the Vatican—they excoriate feminists and family planners as agents of Western cultural imperialism. Meanwhile, women's rights activists like Brookman-Amissah find bases for their work in international NGOs (nongovernmental organizations), and backing for their positions in statements of the United Nations and other international bodies. A global culture war is raging, and it's all about who controls women's fertility—and, more broadly, women themselves.

That is the subject of this book—the global battle for reproductive rights. It spans five decades and four continents, and it elucidates a multifaceted political and ideological fight that is one of the most important, if unsung, of our time.

All over the planet, conflicts between tradition and modernity are being fought on the terrain of women's bodies. Globalization is challenging traditional social arrangements. It is upsetting economic stability, bringing women into the workforce, and beaming images of Western individualism into the remotest villages while drawing more and more people into ever growing cities. All this spurs conservative backlashes, as right-wingers promise anxious, disoriented people that the chaos can be contained if only the old sexual order is enforced. Yet the subjugation of women is just making things worse, creating all manner of demographic, economic, and public health problems.

This is not just a story about abortion, though abortion tends to be a flashpoint. It is, rather, about how great international powers have worked to influence the rights of the world's women, and how, conversely, women's rights will ultimately shape the future.

The tale is much bigger than it might at first appear. For decades now the countries of the first world have been exporting family planning to the third world, for reasons that combine humanitarianism and national security realpolitik. With the West's help, governments worldwide concerned with overpopulation have tried to change the sexual and childbearing norms of their peoples. Feminists have fought, with a surprising if unheralded degree of success, to have reproductive rights recognized in international law. The United States has, depending on who is in charge, worked to bring safe abortion to poor countries, and worked with equal zeal to take it away. Imitating the organizing strategies of their opponents, fundamentalists have joined hands across national borders to stave off challenges to traditional gender hierarchies. And remarkably little of this hugely consequential story is understood by the American public, despite the country's crucial role in shaping the fate of women all over the planet.

Many of the roots of our current battles lie in the cold war, a time of widespread panic that overpopulation was going to lead to Malthusian doom and revolutionary upheavals. Back then, staunch anticommunists saw the mass diffusion of birth control as a key bulwark against anticapitalist chaos. A huge international family planning infrastructure was erected, and the idea that childbearing should be a matter of choice rather than fate spread throughout the world.

Not surprisingly, some countries saw this as a form of neocolonialism, a critique that has gained ever more salience in recent years, when it's been supported, ironically, by the American right. Nevertheless, in the second half of the twentieth century, a global consensus began emerging that overpopulation hindered development. As the concern grew, some countries started using coercion to bring down birth rates faster, resulting in outcries from both feminists and religious groups.

At certain points there was considerable hostility between those most concerned about women's rights and those most worried about overpopulation, groups whose aims now appear deeply intertwined. In the 1970s, though, a group of feminist-minded women who had come up through the ranks of the population-control movement decided to take it over from within. They argued that you couldn't treat women as mere means to a preferred demographic destiny; their rights and health had to be ends in themselves. If overpopulation was a problem, its root cause lay in women's subordination, which too often gave them little choice over how many children to have and almost no social value outside of reproduction. Women needed power, not just pills, and population programs could be harnessed to improve their health and status. Employing canny bureaucratic warfare, skillful organizing, and a solidarity that transcended borders, these women worked within emerging systems of global governance that, even today, few outsiders understand. As a result of their efforts, at the 1994 International Conference on Population and Development in Cairo, their once marginal views about the universal importance of reproductive rights became the official policy of the United Nations. It was a policy that was supported by every major donor country, including, at the time, the United States.

Religious conservatives in many regions were alarmed by this, and sometimes banded together across sectarian lines in opposition. At one point, as we'll see, Pope John Paul II even offered to help Libya achieve a rapprochement with Western governments in exchange for standing with the church against reproductive rights at the UN. When George W. Bush entered the White House in 2001, the fundamentalist alliance achieved an unprecedented level of power and influence. The global reproductive rights movement, though, had also grown strong, and found it could survive the defection of the United States, its original patron. Reproductive rights even entered the realm of international law when in several significant cases courts ruled in varied jurisdictions that women who had been denied abortions had had their human rights violated by their own countries.

Some of this might sound abstract. Debates in congressional hearings, foundation boardrooms, and international conferences can seem far removed from women's real lives. On the ground, though, the consequences have often been profound, determining, among other things, whether a woman has access to contraception and, if she needs it, an abortion; whether she can get an education before she starts her family and earn an income after; whether her government penalizes her for having what it deems too many children; and whether her genitals are left intact or ritually circumcised to encourage her chastity.

In reporting on controversies in Latin America, Africa, India, and Europe, I tried to portray women's stories in all their complexity, without attempting to tie up every ideological loose end. Unlike the brilliant philosopher Martha Nussbaum, I'm not attempting to create a universal framework of women's rights or to systematically disentangle transcendent values from culturally specific ones. If anything, I'm often trying to show how difficult it is to do just that. Real lives have a way of defying neat political categories, and of refusing to embody pat lessons. Grand plans to remake societies, no matter how well intentioned, usually have unintended effects. Nevertheless, ambitious efforts to improve the health and status of women have at times been quite successful, as have campaigns to roll them back.

Ultimately, one insight that I hope emerges from these stories is that feminists, liberals, and reformers have as much claim to cultural authenticity as conservatives do. To act as if only the most static and rigid parts of a culture are genuine, to treat other societies as less capable of dynamism and progress than we in the West believe ourselves to be, is deeply condescending to the women all around the world who are trying to effect change from within. I've been guided by the belief that we should show solidarity with people who aspire to be protected by the same universal human rights guarantees that we enjoy.

In almost every country on earth there are internal struggles over the role of women, fights that pit universalist claims for women's human rights against cultural relativist arguments for preserving traditional gender relationships. Indeed, women's rights are perhaps the most visible sign of modernity and thus an obvious bête noir for flourishing fundamentalist movements. In developing nations the situation is further complicated by the influence wielded by international donors, aid agencies, and UN bodies that work to promote reproductive rights, inevitably affecting sexual norms.

In 1984, the brash, flamboyant feminist Germaine Greer published *Sex & Destiny: The Politics of Human Fertility*, which is, among other things, a broadside against the ethnocentrism of the international family planning movement and a fetishization of traditional village life. "The majority of the world's women have not simply been entrapped into motherhood: in societies which have not undergone demographic transition, where children are a priceless resource, the role of mother is not a marginal one but central to social life and organization," Greer wrote.[6] This is absolutely correct, and it is the reason feminists once fought population controllers who ignored women's own hopes and desires.

Nevertheless, women everywhere do try, sometimes desperately, to limit their fertility, a fact borne out by their frequent recourse to abortion. In hymning traditional social arrangements, Greer moved so far to the left that she circled around to the right, treating every society but her own as a harmonious, homogenous system that could only be distorted by the malign influence of Western liberalism. Written at a time when she was herself struggling with infertility, Greer charged family planners with spreading the antichild ethos of a selfish, materialistic, and maladaptive modernity. Further, she defended the chador, extolled chastity over artificial contraception, and posited patriarchal peasant society as preferable to individualistic consumer capitalism. "One of the most insidious forms of pollution is the destruction of the integrity of one's culture by that of another, dominant, outsider group," she wrote, "and it is under such conditions of cultural resistance that adherence to cultural standards of purity becomes most important; it is part of taking the line of most resistance, whether to lipstick, Coca-Cola, opium, or oral contraceptives."[7]

As an observation, this is true enough; it's part of the reason that, for example, some humiliated Muslims have taken refuge in a medieval fundamentalism. Greer, however, wasn't just describing such cultural resistance; she was endorsing it. There was no place in her analysis for women who dissented from conservative forces in their own societies, women who longed for the freedoms she blithely dismissed. Writing about women taking up the veil after the 1979 Iranian revolution, she assumed that they had all done so willingly, as a sign of "liberation through self-discipline." Male domination is bad, she allowed, but the patriarchal family is preferable to the atomism of the "consumer economy." Wrote Greer, "To have rejected patriarchal authority within and without the self, however desirable in itself, is to have become vulnerable to much more insidious and degrading forms of control."[8]

Greer made a common error of the disillusioned Western radical, projecting onto other cultures all the authentic virtues she wished were in her own. In thinking about the situation of women in vastly different contexts, there are a number of dangers. One is assuming that Western ways are self-evidently superior and that all women would choose them, if only they could. But another is assuming that women in other cultures are so different from us that situations we would find intolerable—bearing child after child into grinding poverty; being utterly at the mercy of fathers, husbands, and brothers; having one's clitoris sliced off with a razor—do not also cause them great pain. The search for human commonality among vastly diverse people is tricky and elusive, but it is callous to surrender to relativism when so many women are clearly suffering.

For people living in the world's rich developed countries, it can be hard to grasp just how terribly women are treated in much of the world. Sexism and violence exist everywhere, but political correctness or condescending romanticism about exotic others should not obscure the fact that women in the third world often have it much, much worse.

In large parts of Asia girls are given less food and medical care than boys from infancy. Throughout Asia and Africa they are significantly less likely than boys to be enrolled in school. More than a third of girls worldwide are married off before they reach adulthood, often to much older men. Early pregnancy taxes their bodies; girls under fifteen are five times more likely to die during pregnancy and childbirth than women in their twenties.[9] Obscenely high rates of maternal mortality are a global scandal, taking more than half a million women each year, 99 percent of them in the developing world. One in twenty-six women in Africa will die of pregnancy-related causes.[10]

In many countries women have no rights to their husband's property, and should they be widowed, they can be either thrown out of their homes or inherited by their husband's brother. The lack of power that women have over their own bodies is directly responsible for the feminization of the AIDS epidemic, which in Africa is killing far more women than men. In 2004, when Ugandan feminists tried to pass a bill that would, among other things, ban spousal rape, men reacted with outrage. A member of the Ugandan parliament's legal affairs committee said the bill should address women's denial of sex, arguing, "Refusing to have sex is the most violent thing a spouse can do."[11] There are many parts of the world where domestic violence is the rule, not the exception: Seventy-one percent of women in one rural Ethiopian province, 69 percent in one rural province in Peru, and 62 percent in a province in Bangladesh say they've been abused by a partner.[12]

Writing about women's rights globally can be complicated for an American, since it can seem both condescending and like an alibi for imperialism. There is, after all, a long history of Western colonialists justifying themselves by promising to liberate benighted native women. In 1927, an American journalist named Katherine Mayo wrote a best-selling book called *Mother India* about the degraded position of females in that country. India's ills, she argued, had nothing to do with British rule and everything to do with child marriage and the oppression of women, which led sickly, ignorant mothers to raise devitalized, sexually perverse children. "The whole pyramid of the Hindu's woes," she wrote, "material and spiritual...rests upon a rock-bottom physical base. This base is, simply, his manner of getting into the world and his sex-life thenceforward."[13] At a time of mounting Indian nationalism she argued that the sexual organization of Indian society made self-rule impossible.

Mayo's book became a sensation in both England and the United States— there was a Broadway play based on it about a twelve-year-old Indian girl married off to an old man—while Indians so reviled it that some demanded it be banned.[14] Wrote one Indian historian, "Even today, few books—apart, perhaps, from Salman Rushdie's *Satanic Verses* (1989)—can match the scale of the international controversy generated by *Mother India*."[15]

Many decades later U.S. neoconservatives used Islamist abuses of women—which are, of course, quite real, as were many of the atrocities documented by Mayo—to justify American aggression in the Middle East. (Few, of course, suggest punishing friendly Saudi Arabia for its system of gender apartheid.) It is not surprising, then, that there is abundant suspicion in the developing world whenever Westerners begin cataloguing the ills visited on foreign women. However, that suspicion, and the history that gives rise to it, does not change the fact that the widespread, overwhelming abuse and devaluation of women, especially in poor countries, is the biggest human rights crisis in the world today.

Given the range of horrors to which women are subject, perhaps it's fair to ask why focus on reproductive rights at all. Access to contraception and abortion are obviously not all that's needed for equality. The right to work and go to school, to own land, to inherit, to live free from violence—these are life-and-death issues for many women in developing countries. They often have far more day-to-day salience than family planning.

Yet reproductive rights are the place where many of the crucial forces shaping and changing women's lives—religious authority, globalization, patriarchal tradition, demographics, American foreign policy, international law, environmentalism, and feminism—intersect. They are the ground on which major battles about women's status are being fought. And a woman's right to control her own body, to make her own decisions about childbearing, is closely bound up with other rights in myriad ways, as we'll see throughout this book.

For one thing, reproductive rights are intimately related to women's economic freedom. Having smaller families allows women to work. When they bring financial resources into the family, their power tends to increase and their daughters' welfare improves. When their daughters are educated, they also choose smaller families, which can be better cared for. As a paper by the World Health Organization put it, "The reproductive revolution—the shift from six births, of whom several might die, to around two births, nearly all of whom survive—represents the most important step toward achievement of gender equality by boosting women's opportunities for nondomestic activities."[16] That's part of the reason that Bangladesh's famed Nobel Peace Prize–winning Grameen Bank, which makes microloans to poor women, has borrowers pledge to "plan to keep our families small."[17]

At an even more elemental level, for far too many women pregnancy is either deadly or debilitating. Putting off childbearing until their bodies are mature enough protects mothers, as does spacing their pregnancies several years apart and having only as many children as they choose. Furthermore, it makes little sense to tackle maternal mortality and morbidity without paying attention to unsafe abortion, one of its major and most easily eradicated causes. Reproductive rights are not the whole of women's rights, but they are a precondition of them. They help women survive and allow them to transcend mere survival.

They are also powerfully symbolic, because women's reproductive role is often the justification for their subordination. International debates over family planning have as often as not become political battles over women's rights more generally, and even over women's humanity. Thus, reproductive rights, while being enormously consequential in and of themselves, also offer a lens through which to view even bigger questions of gender and power in a globalized but desperately unequal world.

From the anticommunist genesis of America's attempts to stem population growth in poor countries to the current worldwide attack on women's rights as a decadent Western imposition, the politics of sex and childbearing are woven into many of the great issues of our time. Underlying diverse conflicts—over demography, natural resources, human rights, and religious mores—is the question of who controls the means of reproduction. Women's intimate lives have become inextricably tied to global forces. At the same time, the fate of the planet has become inextricably tied to women's ability to control their own lives.

CHAPTER 1: SANDINISTA FAMILY VALUES

Eighteen-year-old Jazmina Bojorge, already the mother of a four-year-old boy, was five months pregnant when she arrived at Managua's Fernando Vélez Paiz Hospital in early November 2006. She was feverish, bleeding, and in pain, and she'd started having contractions. She was miscarrying, and under the circumstances the doctors should have given her a drug to speed the process. The reason they didn't remains unclear. Here's what is known: Just a week earlier Nicaragua's Asamblea Nacional voted to ban all abortions, even those meant to save a woman's life. In Bojorge's case, an ultrasound showed that her fetus was alive, and her doctors, ignoring medical protocols in order to try to rescue the pregnancy, gave Bojorge a drug to stop her contractions. She was kept on the medicine until tests a day later showed the fetus had died, at which point she was allowed to deliver. By then, though, her placenta had detached and her uterus had filled with blood. She went into shock and died.[1]

Feminists and human rights activists around the world called Jazmina Bojorge the first victim of an abortion ban that would soon claim many more, and the government promised an investigation. The director of the hospital insisted that the new law, which hadn't even officially gone into effect when Bojorge died, had nothing to do with his doctors' decisions. Many Managua gynecologists, though, spoke of the fear and confusion that had descended onto their practices, and said that they, too, might be forced to withhold help from pregnant women with complications like those of Bojorge. "They are between a wall and a sword," said Carmen Solórzano, an ob-gyn at Managua's bustling Hospital Militar, which serves around fifty thousand people in addition to soldiers and their families. Solórzano has short dark hair, high cheekbones, and a brisk, serious manner. Her office is a low-ceilinged room with peach-colored walls and a chugging air conditioner; outside in the waiting area dozens of chairs are set up like an overcrowded classroom, almost all of them taken. When I interviewed her in late November 2006, she'd seen a case just the day before not unlike that of Jazmina Bojorge and, apparently, like the doctors at Fernando Vélez Paiz, she'd felt forced to delay treatment.

A woman had arrived in the middle of a miscarriage. She was twelve weeks pregnant and bleeding, and her cervix was dilated. "When you have bleeding and you have a dilated cervix, you have to intervene," Solórzano said. In such cases the medical manuals recommend giving the patient Oxytocin to help her expel the fetus. But this woman's fetus was alive, and under the new law Solórzano couldn't do anything until it died. In the meantime, she said, the woman was at high risk of infection. The patient's mother pleaded with the doctor to end the pregnancy, saying she'd hire a lawyer if anyone decided to prosecute. But Solórzano had to make her wait. "If there is a heart beating, we can't intervene," she said. "We know the pro-life people are after the gynecologists." (The patient, thankfully, survived.)

Among many doctors there were rumors of coming persecutions. Dr. Ligia Altamirano, an exuberant, round woman with a high, lilting voice, is the former president of the Nicaraguan Society of Gynecologists and Obstetricians. She worked for twenty-three years in the Ministry of Health before leaving it "like a bad husband." "Undoubtedly women and doctors will go to jail," she said. "Doctors in El Salvador tell us that in the hospitals there are people from Pro-Vida"—the so-called pro-life movement—"who, when a woman comes in with any type of miscarriage they call the attorney general, and there is an investigation."

El Salvador is a frightening harbinger for Nicaragua's feminists. Conservative forces in the Catholic Church, often working with American pro-life groups, have long sought to bring Latin America, the world's most Catholic region, into line with Vatican teachings on abortion, and in El Salvador their triumph has been total. Since the late 1990s it's been a country where all abortion is criminalized; where women with ectopic pregnancies must wait for their fallopian tubes to burst, and where, as a *New York Times Magazine* article put it, "forensic vagina inspectors" treat women's bodies as potential homicide scenes.[2] El Salvador is not the world's only country where abortion is completely banned: Malta eliminated an exemption allowing for abortions to save a pregnant woman's life in 1981, and Augusto Pinochet's military dictatorship did the same in Chile in 1989. But El Salvador is the poorest such country, so many women there don't have the means to seek abortions elsewhere, and its legal system has proven the most zealously prosecutorial.

An intensified version of American-style abortion politics has come to Latin America, pitting the local religious hierarchy and its supporters in the United States and the Vatican against feminists and their allies in Europe and the United Nations. Nicaragua has had massive pro-life marches, TV airings of *The Silent Scream* (the famous antiabortion film), and in 2006 the first protests outside women's health clinics. The rhetoric of family values certainly isn't new in Nicaragua—Violeta Chamorro's 1990 presidential campaign, which led to her victory over the Sandinistas, was saturated with it. Nor did Nicaragua import its antiabortion ethos. Even before October 26, 2006, when the country's legislature voted to eliminate all legal abortions, the procedure wasn't easy to get. Only "therapeutic abortion," done to save a woman's life, was permitted, and the law required three medical professionals to sign off on each one. (In practice doctors would end ectopic pregnancies—in which the fertilized egg lodges in a fallopian tube, which bursts if left untreated—without first getting a committee's permission.) In the years before the ban fewer than ten therapeutic abortions annually had been approved in Nicaragua's public hospitals. By contrast, around twenty-two thousand underground abortions were performed in 2003 alone.[3]

Because legal abortion was so rare in the country, the intensity of the recent campaign against it seemed strange. The exemption for therapeutic abortions had been on the books for over one hundred years. Since it was already so narrow that the vast majority of women with unwanted pregnancies couldn't take advantage of it, why did the government feel compelled to close it altogether, even if that meant sentencing some women to death?

Part of the answer lay in domestic politics. Desperate for restoration, Sandinista leader Daniel Ortega—a man who has rarely hesitated to betray the revolution's feminist supporters—found Jesus and courted the church. By coming out in favor of the ban and instructing Sandinista lawmakers to vote for it, he ensured the law's passage and garnered religious support for his presidential bid.

But the battle over abortion in Nicaragua was never merely local. Countries such as Nicaragua have become the site of proxy fights in a much larger international culture war. Even as feminists have tried to expand reproductive rights there, conservative leaders in Nicaragua railed against what they describe as a kind of libertine social imperialism, and networks of foreign nonprofits and sympathetic governments support both sides. Abortion has come to symbolize broader anxieties among parts of the public, about familial chaos, declining religious authority, and the temptations and pressures of a louche, foreign pop culture.

Therapeutic abortion is increasingly accepted as a human right in international law—a remarkable, little understood development. That puts countries such as Nicaragua on a potential collision course with the United Nations and other multinational bodies tasked with upholding global agreements on women's rights. Thus, the same tensions highlighted by *Roe v. Wade*—between the liberties of the individual and the dominant mores of the community; between local sovereignty and central authority; between religion and science—are appearing all over the world.

In addition to Latin America, there are intense battles over abortion being played out in several countries in Africa and in Eastern Europe. Ethiopia, a country where one study showed that unsafe abortion was responsible for more than half of all maternal deaths,[4] was on the cusp of decriminalization in 2005 when an American-style evangelical antiabortion movement arose and thwarted some (though not all) of the reforms. In 2004, a national uproar over abortion in Kenya led to the railroading of a prominent gynecologist on murder charges, eventually dropped.[5] And the Protocol on the Rights of Women in Africa, the world's first treaty that specifically delineates a right to therapeutic abortion, has been ratified by a growing list of African nations, with Kenya poised to join them.

The fight over abortion has been internationalized in Europe, too. Abortion in Poland, freely available during Communist rule, was radically restricted in 1993, and the Catholic Church continues to seek a total ban. In 2007, Alicja Tysiąc, a Polish woman forced to continue a pregnancy despite warnings that it would destroy her already failing eyesight, won a judgment from the European Court of Human Rights in Strasbourg that her rights had been violated. Her government was ordered to pay her twenty-five thousand euros in damages.

Latin America, though, is where international pressure for liberalization has had the most repeated collisions with right-wing religion. The region has both the world's strictest abortion laws and the highest rate of clandestine abortion—four unsafe abortions for every ten births, according to the World Health Organization.[6] It's the site of a rearguard action by antiabortion forces: Even as reproductive rights expand throughout much of the world, they've contracted in several Latin American countries. (Mexico City, where abortion was decriminalized in 2007, is an important exception to the regional trend.) Several of the precedent-setting cases in international reproductive rights law come from Latin America, and by looking closely at it, we can see how individual women are affected by the all-ways tug-of-war between religious conservatives, feminist activists, international law, and nationalist politics.

In 2005, the UN Human Rights Committee decided its first abortion case, which dealt with a seventeen-year-old Peruvian girl who'd been forced to carry an anencephalic fetus—one missing most of its forebrain—to term, despite the fact that it had no chance of surviving more than a few days outside the womb. The committee ruled that Peru had "an obligation to take steps to ensure that similar violations do not occur in the future." The following year saw the resolution of a case before the Washington, D.C.–based Inter-American Commission on Human Rights involving a thirteen-year-old Mexican rape victim, Paulina Ramírez, who was prevented from having an abortion by public officials. The government of Mexico settled, agreeing to pay Ramírez, by then a nineteen-year-old single mother, forty thousand dollars plus a stipend for her son's high school education. It also pledged to force local authorities to comply with laws allowing abortion in cases of rape.

A couple of months later, Colombia's Supreme Court struck down that country's total abortion ban, citing both its own constitution and international law. The court ruled:

Various international treaties form the basis for the recognition and the protection of the reproductive rights of women, which derive from the protection of other fundamental rights such as the right to life, health, equality, the right to be free from discrimination, the right to liberty, bodily integrity and the right to be free from violence.... Sexual and reproductive rights of women have been finally recognized as human rights. As such, they have entered the realm of constitutional law, which is the fundamental ground of all democratic states.

Buttressing local conservatives, the American right has exerted powerful pressure in the other direction. Reinstituting a Republican policy first seen under Reagan, the George W. Bush administration famously cut off American family planning aid to groups that performed abortions, counseled pregnant women about where they could get abortions, or lobbied for the liberalization of abortion law.

Other Republican politicians got even more intimately involved in the abortion debate abroad. In 2004, when Uruguay moved to make abortion legal during the first trimester of pregnancy, the office of New Jersey congressman Chris Smith faxed a letter, cosigned by five other Republican representatives, to every member of that country's Senate, urging them to defeat the bill, saying it would "legalize the violent murder of unborn children and the exploitation of women through abortion up to the 12th week of pregnancy." (It lost by four votes.) That same year Smith attended a meeting of Latin American and Caribbean countries in Puerto Rico, where he urged several heads of state not to affirm international agreements on women's rights. "These documents contain direct attacks on the right to life, family rights and national sovereignty," the congressman wrote in a letter to the president and first lady of Guatemala.

Nicaragua's abortion ban was "a show of force by conservative forces in Latin America," said Luisa Cabal, director of the international legal program at the Center for Reproductive Rights and one of Ramírez's attorneys. "What we see now is a more concerted effort by antichoice groups.... My concern is that the antichoice groups will start pushing for reform in other countries." Cabal worries that similar legal changes could be afoot in the Dominican Republic and Panama, among other places.

The globalized conflicts over women's rights and religious authority that are playing out across the developing world have led to political realignments that complicate the simpler left/right divides of the cold war years. These days religious conservatives adopt the language of radical anticolonialism to attack the liberalism of the developed world. Just as in the United States, social progressives, especially feminists, are smeared as decadent elites, and reproductive rights are excoriated as an assault on the soul of nations. Denouncing groups that promote such rights, Dr. Rafael Cabrera, a Nicaraguan ob-gyn who emerged as a leader in the campaign against therapeutic abortion, called them "foreigners who do not represent Nicaraguans, feminist movements that promote lesbianism and organizations that promote sexual licentiousness and homosexuality."[7]

During the cold war the jagged divide between the economic left and right vastly overshadowed conflicts between cultural liberalism and fundamentalism. Indeed, ardent Catholics and Protestants were often on opposing sides. While evangelical conservatives in the United States raised money for the Nicaraguan Contras and for Efraín Ríos Montt, Guatemala's extravagantly zealous Pentecostal dictator, much of Latin America's Catholic Church, influenced by liberation theology, was an ally of revolution and a powerful force for social justice. Liberation theologians weren't liberal on sexual issues, but they focused more on repression and systematic injustice than on individual sexual sin. This brought out a kind of crude anticlericalism in their opponents. In El Salvador, militant reactionaries circulated leaflets saying "Be a patriot—kill a priest." A few years later a right-wing death squad did just that, by assassinating San Salvador's archbishop, Oscar Romero, as he celebrated mass at a small chapel in the capital. Roberto D'Aubuisson, a man with ties to American right-wing stalwarts like the late senator Jesse Helms, ordered the killing.[8]

Under Pope John Paul II the Vatican was deeply critical of liberation theology, and it moved to elevate more conservative clerics. (The head of the Congregation for the Doctrine of the Faith, Cardinal Joseph Ratzinger—now Pope Benedict XVI—was an especial opponent of the liberation theologians.) In the mid-1990s, Fernando Sáenz Lacalle, a member of the ultraconservative Catholic group Opus Dei and an ally of ARENA, the right-wing party originally founded by D'Aubuisson, became San Salvador's new archbishop.[9]

The conservative shift in the church heralded a new focus on sex and motherhood. Abortion was already severely restricted in El Salvador, but until the late 1990s there were legal exceptions for rape, severe fetal malformation, or danger to a mother's life. In the early 1990s, though, conservatives began agitating for a complete prohibition. Then, in 1995, the FMLN—the revolutionary movement turned left-wing political party—proposed a bill liberalizing the country's abortion law, turning up the heat on the issue even further. Two years later, when ARENA introduced a bill banning abortion totally, the archbishop, who compared legal abortion to Nazi genocide, backed it enthusiastically. Thousands of students from Catholic schools were organized to demonstrate on behalf of the law, and the country's leading pro-life group gathered a half million signatures supporting it. In an argument that would reappear in Nicaragua nearly a decade later, Julia Regina de Cardenal, head of the Yes to Life Foundation, insisted that medical advances had made therapeutic abortion unnecessary. In 1998, all exemptions to the abortion ban were struck from the penal code, and the next year, the country's constitution was amended to decree that life be protected from the moment of conception.

Between 2000 and 2003, 283 criminal investigations were initiated against women suspected of aborting.[10] Abortion remains common in El Salvador: Though exact figures are impossible to obtain, the World Health Organization estimates that there were thirty-four thousand illegal abortions in 2003.[11] Women with complications from such abortions take an enormous risk if they seek medical help, because, as the Center for Reproductive Rights has found, half of the women prosecuted for abortion were reported by their health care providers. Employees at public hospitals were more likely to report their patients than those at private hospitals, often because they felt legally bound to do so.[12]

D octors may come under similar pressure in Nicaragua. Harley Morales, a young ob-gyn at Berta Calderon, a public women's hospital in Managua, said that officials have told doctors there that police would soon be stationed in the emergency room to report women suspected of seeking help for complications from illegal abortions. Such complications are common, though they've become less so due to the spread of misoprostol, an ulcer medicine that can induce abortion at high doses. Though still risky and illegal, such abortions are safer than those performed manually.

"When I was in my sixth year as an intern, this room was filled with patients with complications from abortions," said Morales. We were sitting in a small, pink operating room with flimsy teal curtains. Before misoprostol, he said, women were more likely to use methods that were *"muy artesanal,"* or homemade—umbrella spokes, wood sticks, coat hangers. ("We could have had a museum of the things we took out of women's bodies," Ligia Altamirano told me.) The spread of the drug has cut down on such practices, and when women using it suffer complications, they can plausibly report them as miscarriages. Of the approximately ten women a day who come to Berta Calderon with miscarriages, Morales estimates that more than half are self-induced.

Even with misoprostol available, horrifying cases persist. The day I spoke with him Morales had a patient he'd first seen three weeks earlier, when she came in threatening to commit suicide because, already poor and raising one small child, she found herself pregnant again. The hospital sent her home. When she returned, she'd had an illegal abortion and was in septic shock, with a severe infection in her uterus. She had to have a hysterectomy and was in intensive care for a week. She was twenty-one.

Luckily—if "luck" isn't too perverse a word—the hospital didn't have to report her to the authorities. If Nicaragua follows El Salvador, though, that could change.

I n the waiting room of Dr. Cabrera's Managua office hangs a framed group photo taken at the Vatican, of him and a few others with Pope John Paul II. There's also a certificate of commendation from the pope, along with a huge fetal gestational chart. A father of six, Cabrera is stout, and has a sagging owlish face, thin hair, and round glasses. Earlier, when I had mentioned his name to Altamirano, she'd shuddered and crossed herself, but the man sitting before me doesn't look at all harsh or frightening. Rather, he appears both kindly and a little melancholy, and I imagine he would have a comforting bedside manner. When it comes to abortion, though, he is rigid and uncompromising. Asked about Jazmina Bojorge, he said only that her death was an "obstetric accident." Nor is he apologetic about the prospect of women who've had abortions being sent to prison. "If a person deliberately produces the death of another human being, the law says what should happen to them," he said. "The law is hard, but it is the law." (Of course, he was a driving force in crafting that law.)

Cabrera is the president of the Asociación Nicaragüense por la Vida, or Anprovida, the country's leading antiabortion group and an affiliate of the

Virginia-based Human Life International. He gave me a Spanish-language flier HLI had produced about the International Planned Parenthood Federation titled "Mortal deceit: The IPPF's Attack on Children, Families and National sovereignty." As he sees it, a network of promiscuity-promoting foreigners has been subverting Nicaragua's values for over twenty years, and the abortion ban is an attempt to beat them back.

"Since 1984, NGOs have started to organize here, backed by foreign agencies—IPPF, Ipas, Pathfinder, Marie Stopes, and others," he said. "They've started programs for women that include contraception, and many of them practice abortion." These groups, he said, manipulated the law by getting doctors working for them to sign off on abortions for women who could have carried their pregnancies to term. They tried to expand the term "therapeutic abortion" to include abortions in cases of rape, incest, fetal malformation, and poverty. By the 1990s, he said, they'd created clinics that practice abortion as a "business."

"All these abuses came to a peak in the case of the girl Rosa," he said.

The girl he's talking about, known throughout the country only by her pseudonymous first name, was the child of young Nicaraguan migrants working as coffee pickers in Costa Rica. Also called Rosita, the diminutive of Rosa, she was nearing her ninth birthday when she became pregnant. Her family claimed she'd been raped by a young man who lived nearby.

Rosa's story became the focus of a media circus in Nicaragua, and it was an international feminist cause célèbre. Indeed, one of the few things that both sides in Nicaragua's abortion debate agree upon is the role of the Rosa case in ratcheting up the conflict. "This case demystified the concept of abortion," said Violeta Delgado Sarmiento, a feminist who was deeply involved in the controversy. "Before the Rosita case even the women's movement didn't talk about abortion. But during that case, the media started an interesting debate, where they talked more deeply about abortion and about the conditions under which women have abortions."

It appears to an outsider like a strange case to galvanize pro-life forces, because in many ways the girl seemed like a poster child for legal abortion.

But fury over Rosa lingers, a sign both of the uncompromising absolutism of Nicaragua's antiabortion lobby and of the mistakes the women's movement made in its search for a story that would capture the world's attention.

Like Nicaragua, Costa Rica has very strict antiabortion laws, and abortion was never presented as an option to either Rosa or her mother, María Esquivel. Instead, Esquivel was told that Rosa would have to stay in the hospital until she delivered, and she was instructed not to tell Rosa's stepfather, Francisco Fletes. Some health officials believed Fletes had raped his stepdaughter, but the family insisted otherwise, and the neighbor Rosa identified as her rapist was eventually arrested, though he was never convicted. The girl didn't understand what was happening to her and asked her mother when she would be "cured."[13]

The sensational story of the pregnant nine-year-old soon hit the newspapers. That's how it came to the attention of a group of Nicaraguan feminists called Red de Mujeres Contra la Violencia, or the Network of Women Against Violence. A delegation of Nicaraguan activists, including Violeta Delgado Sarmiento and Marta María Blandón, head of the national branch of Ipas, traveled to Costa Rica, and by chance they met Esquivel and Fletes at the Nicaraguan embassy there. The couple had decided they wanted their daughter to have an abortion and were looking for help getting her out of the country. Dismissing suspicions about Fletes as unfounded prejudice against a poor and uneducated man, the Nicaraguan feminists became the family's champions.

As the case grew more politicized, with priests speaking out about Rosa during church services, officials tried to ensure that the pregnancy was brought to term. "We witnessed the highest authorities of the National Child Welfare Agency tell Rosita and her parents that they had been blessed by God, that what had happened was a blessing from heaven and they had to accept it, and that surely this baby was going to be someone very important, because it could be no random chance that Rosita had been chosen to experience the magnificent event of motherhood at such a young age," said Blandon.[14]

Rosa was in the hospital for nearly a month before the feminists succeeded in getting her released to the hotel where her parents were staying. Even then the Costa Rican office for children said they were going to block the family from leaving the country.[15] The girl and her mother had to sneak away in the middle of the night, driving with the women from Red de Mujeres and leaving all their meager possessions in Costa Rica.

In Nicaragua the situation was no less heated. By the time they got to Managua, Rosa was three and a half months pregnant. It also emerged, said Blandón, that she had two untreated venereal diseases. With the help of their advocates, Rosa's parents petitioned the Ministry of Health for a therapeutic abortion. Legally, the approval of three doctors was required, but Health Minister Lucia Salvo, a close ally of the Catholic hierarchy, appointed a sixteen-person committee instead, and put Rafael Cabrera in charge of it.

For Cabrera, Rosa's age made little difference. Speaking in *Rosita,* a 2005 documentary about the case, he said, "A nine-year-old child is perfectly able to have a normal pregnancy. Proof of this—another baby was born to a nine-year-old girl in El Salvador. If we follow history, in 1939 in Peru, a five-year-old child had a baby."[16]

Eventually, attorneys and activists working with Rosa's mother and stepfather were able to force the government to have her evaluated by three doctors instead of sixteen. But the doctors essentially punted. They waited until midnight to release their recommendation, and they said that Rosa's life would be equally endangered by giving birth or undergoing a late-term abortion. Following their determination, the Nicaraguan minister of the family announced that she wanted to remove Rosa from her parents' custody to prevent them from terminating the pregnancy.

For some in the government it was all about abortion, but for others it was more complicated. Throughout the entire ordeal, Carmen Largaespada, vice minister of the family (and a pro-choice feminist), was in contact with the Costa Rican minister of children's affairs. Her Costa Rican colleague told her that police there believed Fletes had impregnated Rosa. "They have a very strong and powerful children's protection system in Costa Rica," Largaespada said. She took their charges seriously. "That's quite common in Nicaragua— stepparents abusing their stepdaughters," she said. Largaespada blamed the NGOs for using Rosa to score political points, and insisted that, given all the time that had elapsed, an abortion would have been risky.

Nevertheless, once again Rosa and her mother decided to run in the middle of the night. The women from Red de Mujeres put the girl in a wheelchair and, with the help of a sympathetic nurse, snuck her out a back door. They were planning to take her to another hospital that had agreed to perform the abortion, but a journalist warned them that all hospitals had been ordered to detain Rosa if she showed up.

In the end, three gynecologists, all of whom insisted on remaining anonymous, performed the abortion in the home of one of Sarmiento and Blandón's colleagues. "The abortion was done in the same condition as the majority of abortions in this country—in a house," said Sarmiento. "The difference was, this was done by three of the best ob-gyns in Nicaragua."

The local media trumpeted the news of the abortion, and public opinion was firmly on the side of Rosa and her parents. There was an investigation, but it never went anywhere, and a few weeks after the abortion, the health minister resigned over the case.

The outcome left the Catholic Church outraged, and Nicaraguan cardinal Miguel Obando y Bravo announced the excommunication of Rosa's parents, the doctors who performed her abortion, and everyone who had helped them. It was a symbolic gesture, since unilateral excommunication was beyond the cardinal's authority, but his denunciation had the support of the hierarchy. Cardinal Alfonso Lopez Trujillo, president of the Vatican's Pontifical Council for the Family, told the BBC, "I am writing to the cardinal personally to express to him in all sincerity my support, because public opinion was quite confused with regard to that case. It did not spare a thought to defending the rights of unborn babies who are people who have a right to live."[17]

In response to this a feminist group in Spain presented a Vatican representative with a petition saying, "I also want to be excommunicated for collaborating in the interruption of the pregnancy and the saving of Rosa's life." There were over twenty-six thousand signatures.

Rosa would, for a time, disappear from the national scene, but the passions her ordeal stirred up still affect the country's politics. "They felt offended by the Rosa case and how it was resolved," Altamirano said of the antiabortion movement. For his part, Cabrera accused feminist groups of "kidnapping" Rosa. "The girl was taken out of the hospital by the back door, and twenty-four hours later they communicated that the night before she had an abortion in a private clinic," he said. "It originated a debate about whether the article of the law was being appropriately applied."

As the debate heated up, Daniel Ortega was getting religion. Since losing power in 1990, the Sandinista leader had made two failed runs for the presidency, and in 2006 circumstances were finally aligning in his favor. Through a power-sharing deal he'd struck with conservative president Arnoldo Alemán in 1999, the share of the vote necessary to win the election had been reduced from 45 percent to 35 percent. Shedding his past guerrilla trappings, Ortega ran on a platform of peace and reconciliation. He chose a former Contra leader as his running mate, and though traditional black and red Sandinista flags still festooned many barrios, his official campaign posters were a distinctly nonmartial bright pink. Perhaps most significant, he embraced the church, attending mass regularly and filling his speeches with talk of God. In 2005, he married the poet Rosario Murillo, his longtime *compañera,* in a church wedding. Cardinal Obando y Bravo presided.

With the conservative opposition divided between two candidates, Ortega's support of the abortion ban probably helped him get enough of the religious vote to push him over the top in the election. His stance disgusted Nicaraguan feminists, most of them former Sandinista militants, but it didn't surprise them. Women had played a major role in the revolution—some estimates say 30 percent of the combatants were female[18]—but they were shunted aside once the Sandinistas took over the government in 1979. In her memoir, *The Country Under My Skin,* Gioconda Belli, one of the most famous and mediagenic of the female Sandinistas, recalls how, not long after the uprising that brought the group to power, top army officials led by Ortega's brother, Humberto, "decided that from that point on women would only occupy administrative posts."[19] A little later Belli writes of encountering Murillo with Daniel Ortega in Cuba: "Rosario, who had always been such a strong woman, was now timid and frightened, a bag of nerves...following Daniel around like a faceless, sad little shadow."[20]

Women did make some crucial gains under the Sandinistas: The government replaced the sole legal authority men had enjoyed over their families with equal rights for mothers and fathers, and it ended discrimination against "illegitimate" children. Abortion laws weren't reformed, but they also weren't much enforced. Yet many Sandinista feminists felt marginalized and dismissed. "The priority was to win elections, not on women's problems," said former Sandinista Klemen Altamirano, the cofounder of a women's center in Masaya, a city near Managua. In 1987, Altamirano was part of a group of Sandinistas who drafted a declaration on sexual rights—including the decriminalization of abortion and access to contraception and sex education—that was presented to Ortega by hundreds of party women. According to Altamirano, the president told them to forget about it, "because we have to replace the fifty thousand martyrs of the revolution."

Still, until the Sandinistas were defeated by Violeta Chamorro in 1990, Nicaragua's feminists mostly worked within the party. Afterward, though, they developed an autonomous movement and put much of their energy into opening feminist health clinics like the one Klemen Altamirano runs. They offered birth control and sex education, and a few may have quietly performed abortions. This coincided with the growing emphasis on reproductive rights among American and European donors, and the clinics attracted significant international aid. Outside support was a mixed blessing. "Because of the reliance on external funding to support the clinics, there was the impression among some women activists that the women's movement was owned by the international development agencies," wrote Katherine Isbester, a scholar of Nicaraguan feminism.[21]

The clinics made a tempting target for populist demagoguery, and President Arnoldo Alemán, who succeeded Chamorro, fixated on them. He denounced them for corruption, accused several feminist NGOs of performing illegal abortions, and had his administration launch punitive, time-consuming audits. "In the campaign against the NGOs, Alemán united the church and state on one side, while he and his allies conflated foreigners and feminists on the other side," wrote the scholar Karen Kampwirth.[22] He even tried to pass a law banning Nicaraguan NGOs from requesting foreign funds without government permission.

The rift between the feminist movement and the Sandinistas grew further in 1998 when Ortega's stepdaughter, Zoilamérica Narváez, accused him of sexually abusing her as a child. Murillo, her mother, dismissed her as a "slut,"[23] but many leading Sandinista women took her side. "The woman's movement was with Zoilamérica," said Klemen Altamirano, "and the Sandinista movement looked for refuge in the church."

And not just in the Catholic Church. The newly pious Ortega, with his talk of making "spiritual revolution," also found support among Nicaragua's exponentially expanding population of *evangélicos*. In just the last three decades, the number of Nicaraguan evangelicals has exploded, from around 5 percent of the population to somewhere between 20 percent and 30 percent, and commentators estimated that as many as a third of them supported Ortega. As their numbers have grown, so has their political clout. "Evangelicals in Nicaragua were once overlooked as outcasts," the *Christian Science Monitor* reported before the election. "Now no political contender can afford to alienate them."[24] Ortega no doubt knew that when, a few months before the vote, he signed a declaration written by evangelical leaders that called therapeutic abortion "a pretext to legalize all abortions."[25]

In fierce competition for souls and stature, Nicaragua's Catholics and Protestants have yet to form anything like the united political front that's emerged in the United States. In 1992, Pope John Paul II compared Latin American evangelicals to "ravenous wolves" preying on the Catholic flock. Shortly after Nicaragua's abortion ban was passed, I went to a Sunday service at Hosanna, a U.S.-style megachurch in Managua, where the pastor spent most of the sermon railing against two things: sexual sin and the spiritual stasis of Nicaraguan Catholicism. "I know as you know that religion in Nicaragua for the last 514 years has been indulgent and permissive and flexible," he said. "It has been a conceptual faith in God, with nothing of practice, nothing of daily exercise.... People say, 'I believe in God, I believe in Mary, I believe in the saints, but I live in my own way.' This has been the traditional way to live religion in Nicaragua."

Yet even as they criticized each other, leaders of the two faiths have remarkably similar critiques of the religious laxity and moral decay they see in their country. "We see the world is changing, the values are changing," said Monsignor Miguel Mantica, the spokesman for the archdiocese of Managua. "There's a process of secularization, where people are losing their religious values, their family values." He continued: "There's a new way of religiosity. I would call it lite religion—like Pepsi Lite. You choose from the market [for] your religious needs, and maybe try to avoid what requires more commitment. That would be one of the explanations why people are flocking toward these different sects." By sects he means Pentecostal churches. "Our work is to attend to people's religious needs but without compromising the commitments of the gospel," he said.

Goaded in part by their own mutual antagonism, the two faiths are moving in a parallel direction toward ever greater social conservatism, as if to outdo each other in building bulwarks against the chaos of a changing world. In Nicaragua relations between Catholics and Protestants are strained enough that when the antiabortion movement planned a massive march in the capital in October 2006, the two groups started in different locations before converging on the National Assembly. Together, though, they mustered tens of thousands of people (one estimate suggested fifty thousand Catholics and twenty thousand Protestants)—an impressive show of force.[26]

Mantica was one of the organizers of that antiabortion march, and he said that working with evangelicals was "a little bit difficult because of the doctrinal differences." Still, he added, "when it comes to defending life we saw that we had the exact same position, and we saw that it was possible to have a collaboration with them."

Such cooperation portends a new kind of politics, with sexual conservatism creating fresh alliances and dividing moderates and modernizers from their more zealous, traditional brethren. "However unimaginable it may have appeared fifty years ago, not only is Christianity flourishing in the Third World, but so are distinctly Christian politics," writes Philip Jenkins. "If in fact Christianity is going to be growing so sharply in numbers and cultural influence in coming decades, we can reasonably ask whether the faith will also provide the guiding political ideology of much of the world."[27]

A belief in motherhood as a woman's primary and highest calling is at the center of the kind of Christian politics that have emerged in Nicaragua. "In the feminist movement there is a weakness," said Mantica. "If you read what they say, it's like it's a curse to be a mother, like it's something that puts women at a disadvantage. The struggle of the feminist movement should be to participate in society, but as women." At forty-three, Mantica is a relatively young man; he wears a black short-sleeve shirt with his clerical collar and has rimless glasses and salt-and-pepper hair. More than one woman told me with a sigh how attractive they found him. Sitting in his little fluorescent-lit office in the archbishop's curia, he speaks kindly and thoughtfully, and it's hard to tell how much he really understands about the actual implications of the abortion ban he worked so hard to pass. He insists that while all intentional abortions are illegal, medical interventions to save a woman's life—even if they have the secondary effect of killing an embryo or fetus—are permitted. Thus, he suggests that there's a kind of implicit exemption for doctors treating things like ectopic pregnancies. "There is no need for that term"—therapeutic abortion—"in order to preserve the lives of the mothers," he said.

It's tempting to think, then, that Mantica believes that the abortion ban doesn't actually imperil women at all, that he hasn't chosen to sacrifice mothers on the altar of motherhood. "This law comes to protect women," he insisted. "Therapeutic abortion made women believe that having an abortion was right, but after they would have psychological problems, very big ones, and also moral problems. Many gynecologists are not being honest. They don't say what the consequences of having an abortion are, what are the real risks, what are the side effects. In that sense, we think that the law is good for women."

Some women think so, too. Twenty-nine-year-old Linda Gutierrez marched in the October pro-life demonstration. She's a smart, articulate, single woman who speaks perfect English and vacations in New York City, where her sister works at the United Nations. Conservative but no prude, she has worked to raise awareness of HIV within the Catholic Church, holding seminars with priests and organizing HIV-awareness street fairs in each of Managua's parishes. While the American religious right tends to exalt heterosexual marriage with the dreamy breathlessness of bridal magazines, Gutierrez is rather more cynical: She says that if she gets married, she's going to assume that her husband, like most Nicaraguan men, will cheat on her. That way, if he doesn't, she'll be pleasantly surprised.

In recent years, she said, feminist groups had been trying to expand access to abortion by reading more into the therapeutic exemption than was intended, and the change in the law was meant simply to beat them back. "If a woman has cancer and they can't have a baby," she said, "obviously they need to have an abortion. I don't think the church has a problem with that, because we're saving a life." She simply didn't believe what most Nicaraguan doctors were saying about the ban's implications. "There is a lot of misinformation from the gynecologists who talk to the press," she said. "What I understood is that they were [saying] you can have an abortion in a free way, if I say or my gynecologist says. And the church said, 'Not correct, you are confusing people.'

"Now there is a penalization, but it doesn't mean they're going to let people die. Obviously that was not our intention," she said. Still, she believes that doctors shouldn't necessarily put the life of a woman above that of her fetus.

"They should do everything to save both lives. But if they can't, they should save the mother. Or the other way around—if the mother has less probability to live and the baby has more, they're going to save the baby, not the mother."

As we spoke, the conversation kept coming back to what Gutierrez saw as a kind of moral chaos that's descended on her country. The slide started, she said, when those who sought refuge in the United States during the Sandinista government returned after 1990, bringing American mores with them, and it's been exacerbated by cable and the Internet. Much of Managua, a sprawling, centerless city, is comprised of tin-roofed shacks crammed together on unpaved lanes, but there are also parts that feel like Los Angeles or Miami, with American chain restaurants as well as hip open-air cafés and bars. Casinos, some featuring strippers, have proliferated since the Sandinistas' 1990 defeat. (Managua is famous for its lack of street signs and marked addresses, and the names of gambling houses often serve as landmarks for taxi drivers.) The combination of widespread poverty with increasingly comfortable amenities for visitors with money has led to increasing sex tourism.[28] It's not hard to understand Gutierrez's vertigo.

"I definitely think we have changed," she said. "I just feel like there's no order. That's the only word I can find—there's no order. We lost that sense of the way we Nicaraguan people do things. The society right now is in redefinition. This thing about abortion is a product of that."

If the abortion ban was partly a reaction to globalization, it's now leading the country into a different kind of collision with the global order. Even before the ban was passed, a group of European, Canadian, and UN diplomats and development officials signed a letter to the president of the Nicaraguan Assembly reminding him of Nicaragua's international obligations to women and asking the legislature to "consult, discuss, and reflect profoundly and thoroughly before making its final decision." After it was signed into law, the Inter-American Commission on Human Rights sent a letter to Nicaragua's minister of foreign affairs arguing that banning therapeutic abortion violated international law. The German government called on Ortega to reverse the ban. All this further hardened the position of conservatives, who denounced international organizations for meddling in the affairs of a sovereign state. One legislator fumed that foreign critics were "sexual libertines and criminals."[29]

Such rhetoric is going to become more common, because Nicaragua could be charged with human rights violations before the Inter-American Commission on Human Rights. Created in 1959 by the Organization of American States, the commission investigates claims of human rights abuses in countries throughout the Western Hemisphere. Twenty-five countries, including Nicaragua, have ratified a 1969 treaty that recognizes its authority to hear complaints and "to take action on petitions and other communications pursuant to its authority." Its interventions can make a big difference: In the case of Paulina Ramírez, the Mexican rape victim, both local and national human rights bodies in Mexico had recommended restitution, but the state of Baja California ignored them. It took the commission on human rights to get the government to compensate Ramírez for her ordeal and to compel an admission of wrongdoing.

Feminist attorneys didn't have much chance of victory before Nicaragua's Supreme Court, because the judges are all loyal to parties that supported the abortion ban. Thus their hope rests on international redress. "When I came here I said, 'Don't be too upset, because the fact that [the ban] was so badly done, so shameful, will only give us more arguments and more strength and more attention to push toward the other side,'" said Monica Roa, a Colombian lawyer who went to Nicaragua to help draft the challenge to the law.

A beautiful woman in her early thirties, with long black ringlets, Roa, a graduate of NYU law school, may be the closest thing the world of international reproductive rights law has to a superstar. She was only twenty-eight when, working with the Spanish feminist group Women's Link Worldwide, she moved from New York City to her native Colombia to lead the charge against that country's abortion ban. As the face of the pro-choice movement there, she was subject to numerous death threats. During the trial someone broke into her apartment—which then doubled as Women's Link's Colombian headquarters—and stole her computer and files, leaving everything else of value. "We had cash in pesos, cash in dollars. They were clearly going after just one thing," she said. Roa's NGO still gets suspicious calls from people claiming to be her friends and asking for her home address. When she's in Colombia, the government provides her with full-time security.

Colombia's abortion law remains far from permissive—the court ruled only that abortion had to be decriminalized in cases of rape, severe fetal malformation, or when the life or health of the mother was endangered. But conservative Catholics fought hard against these exemptions. At one point, the local affiliate of Human Life International submitted thirty thousand antiabortion children's drawings—some by kids as young as three—as amicus briefs. Even with the 5 to 3 judicial victory, the fight is going to continue. "In the same way as it's been happening in the U.S., as the composition of the court changes, they'll try to push for more conservative judges," Roa says. Colombian Supreme Court judges serve eight-year terms. One judge who voted to strike down the abortion ban has already stepped down and been replaced by a judge who supported it.

Nevertheless, the court's ruling was an important victory, with implications for countries like Nicaragua. It affirmed that the vast body of international law is moving toward an understanding of reproductive rights as human rights. Besides various committees at the United Nations "you also have the European Court of Human Rights and the Inter-American system. They are all saying the same thing at the same time, and it sort of reinforces itself. The fact that we just did it at a national level in Colombia keeps reinforcing it," said Roa.

These days Roa spends much of her life on the road. "I've been giving presentations all over—Argentina, Spain, Italy, Jordan, Ireland," she said. Before Nicaragua she'd been collaborating with attorneys in Trinidad and Tobago. In Managua she worked on a laptop in the small back room of a local human rights center; above her hung a poster of a doll that said in Spanish, "All pregnant children have been raped. Therapeutic abortion is a right!"

"Most countries nowadays use the discourse of human rights, because that's what is politically correct, and because you need to say those kinds of things to get the approval of the international community," she said. "For example, the World Bank and the IMF include requirements to be respectful of human rights. Even if it's just lip service, all [countries] say, at least on paper, that they respect human rights." And by officially committing to human rights, countries create space for the kind of legal challenges Roa and her colleagues bring. "It opens up a big niche for all of us activists," she said.

By the summer of 2007, though, Nicaragua's feminist activists found themselves under attack, victims of their own high-stakes PR campaign. That August Rosa and her family reappeared in the news when María Esquivel,

Rosa's mother, filed a report accusing her husband of raping her daughter. The abuse, it emerged, had been going on for years. Rosa had gotten pregnant again not long after her abortion; by the time of her renewed notoriety she had a nineteen-month-old daughter. According to *El Nuevo Diario* it was an open secret in the neighborhood that the baby belonged to Francisco Fletes.[30]

Rosa's stepfather fled, but he was quickly apprehended, and in November 2007 Fletes was tried for rape and sentenced to thirty years in prison. During the trial Rosa begged for the forgiveness of the man she'd accused in Costa Rica. Equivel insisted she'd been unaware of the abuse until that year—Rosa had claimed a classmate fathered her daughter—but the Ministry of the Family believed she'd long known about it and was considering bringing criminal charges against her.[31]

The women who'd helped Rosa's family five years earlier were heartbroken by the revelations, and they now appeared under a cloud of complicity. The Red de Mujeres had stayed in touch with the family and had known about Rosa's second pregnancy, though they said they had believed her when she said the father was a boy near her own age. Some abortion rights activists had even brought Fletes and Esquivel to Chile to advocate for liberalization there. With Fletes revealed as a rapist, the dismissal of suspicions about him suddenly seemed inexcusable, and the antiabortion movement went on the offensive.

A Catholic human rights group petitioned the government to bring charges against several women in the Red de Mujeres, including Violeta Delgado Sarmiento and Marta María Blandón, accusing them of covering up for Fletes in order to further their political cause. An official investigation was opened. "It's the network's responsibility," the head of the Ministry of the Family told a Nicaraguan newspaper. "They knew what they were doing, and if they acted wrongly, there are laws to stop them from doing so."[32]

Outraged, feminists in Nicaragua charged that Ortega was seeking revenge for their support of his own stepdaughter when she accused him of rape. "We accused the president of abuse and his wife Rosario Murillo of being complicit," said one leading activist. "If anyone should be accused, it's not the Red de Mujeres or the people fighting for women's rights, but the president and his wife, who are sexual abusers and political abusers of the Nicaraguan people."[33] At the same time, human rights groups from around the world—especially Latin America—rallied to the women's defense, staging a letter-writing campaign accusing the government of waging a political persecution. In response, the government seemed to back off a bit, and it soon looked as if the case against the feminists might fizzle out.

Legally, when it came to Nicaragua's abortion ban, nothing had changed. Advocates still awaited the Supreme Court decision and discussed their next move. Taking the case to the Inter-American Commission on Human Rights was one option, said Lilian Sepulveda, the legal adviser for Latin America and the Caribbean at the Center for Reproductive Rights. Another possibility was appealing to the United Nations. But abortion controversies are always about more than the law, and the antiabortion movement momentarily appeared to have the moral high ground, at least in the public mind.

Meanwhile, in the year following the ban, government figures showed that maternal mortality in Nicaragua had doubled.[34] Human Rights Watch documented case after case in which women had died after being refused treatment for pregnancy complications. In April 2007, Olga María Reyes, a married law student in her early twenties, hemorrhaged to death in a hospital in the city of León because her ectopic pregnancy wasn't treated until hours after it ruptured her fallopian tube.[35] "Women are afraid of seeking treatment," said a UN employee in Nicaragua. "That's the first step....And doctors are afraid of providing treatment....It's the psychological factor....And the combination may have caused deaths."[36]

That autumn Pope Benedict XVI met with Nicaragua's new ambassador to the Holy See at the papal summer villa in Castel Gandolfo. "The pope said he wanted to express his appreciation to Nicaragua for its position on social issues," the *Catholic News Service* reported, " 'especially respect for life, in the face of considerable internal and international pressure.' "[37]

It remained to be seen which kind of international pressure would prevail.

CHAPTER 2: THE GREAT POPULATION PANIC, OR FIGHTING COMMUNISM WITH CONTRACEPTION

In the 1950s, before he became notorious, Harvey Karman was a psychology student at UCLA, attending on the GI bill. Writing a paper on the emotional impact of abortion led him into the abortion underground, where he helped a number of desperate coeds find ways to terminate their pregnancies. "It seemed like every guy who got a girlfriend pregnant, everyone who had remotely heard about me, said, 'This guy knows about abortion,'" he told *Ms.* magazine in 1975.[1] Often he'd help young women make their way to Mexico to end their pregnancies. Some of them came through the procedures fine, but some came home sick or injured, and Karman would take them to the school's medical center for treatment. Frustrated with this system, he eventually started performing abortions himself.

Much of Karman's early history is hazy, but one horrific incident stands out. In 1955, one of the women who sought Karman's help died of an infection, and he was charged with both murder and abortion. A court rejected his insistence that he was a mere middleman between the woman and a doctor, finding that he himself had tried to induce a miscarriage using a speculum and a nutcracker. Nevertheless, he was convicted only of the lesser charge, and after serving two years in prison, he emerged unfazed to resume the work that had become, for him, a kind of crusade.[2]

A man of the nascent counterculture, Karman dabbled in experimental films and worked with juvenile delinquents and at Head Start, but abortion remained his consuming passion.[3] A sympathetic doctor told him that if he could induce just a small bit of bleeding in a pregnant girl, she could be admitted to the hospital and her abortion could be completed legally, a technique he adopted. In fact, all around the world, in countries where abortion is restricted, that's often how it's done. According to Malcolm Potts, an Oxford-educated doctor who is one of the world's leading authorities on abortion, the "extralegal person is usually trying to produce uterine bleeding that will take the woman to the public hospital where she will be cleaned up."

However standard, this system struck Karman as crazy, and he started trying to devise something better. Karman "was a very dexterous person," said Potts, who later became his friend. "He used to make model airplanes when he was young. I once locked myself out of my car, and I'd never seen anybody break into a car as quickly as Harvey did. And he's pretty good at breaking into the uterus." As Potts recalled, Karman read the medical literature about abortion in Eastern Europe, where it had been legal since the 1950s. He wanted a method that was as painless as possible, allowing a woman to get up and walk away as soon as it was over. So he started experimenting in his kitchen. Karman cut the end off a large, plastic, handheld syringe, attached some polyethylene tubing to it, and soon came up with the prototype for the manual vacuum aspiration (MVA) syringe, a simple, hand-operated device that today is used all over the developing world. "It's probably done many millions of abortions since then," Potts said.[4]

Starting in the 1960s, Karman used his invention to perform illegal abortions out of a rented room next to a dentist's office in Los Angeles. Charismatic and swaggering, he was remembered by some in the nascent abortion rights movement as a hero, by some as a huckster. He added a Ph.D. to his name, though his degree came from a dubious Swiss diploma mill.[5] Without a doubt, there were abundant reasons to be suspicious of him, but he was no mercenary backroom butcher, and many recall him as more interested in spreading word of his discovery than in profiting from it, giving free demonstrations to interested doctors and health care workers. "I was most impressed... because of the safety for the women and because [the technique] made it possible to bring the price way down. And Harvey never charged a cent for his visits," one San Diego Planned Parenthood official told *Ms.*[6]

In 1972, Karman enlisted Potts to cowrite an article about the MVA syringe in *The Lancet,* the prestigious British medical journal. The first medical director of International Planned Parenthood, Potts had been fighting for safe, legal abortion since 1963, when, as a young obstetrician doing his internship, he had had to deal with botched or incomplete terminations nearly every night. He was familiar with the techniques used all over the world, and Karman's invention impressed him as a "very powerful technology." He showed it to Reimert Ravenholt, the head of population affairs at the U.S. Agency for International Development, whom he'd met at a family planning conference in what was then East Pakistan.

Ravenholt, a roguish figure gleefully dismissive of political sensitivities, had already decided that poor countries sorely needed abortion equipment that could be run without electricity. USAID was primarily focused on spreading contraception, but government officials knew that birth control was always going to fail for a certain percentage of people, especially in places where access was sporadic and use inconsistent. As a then classified 1974 government report on overpopulation would conclude, "[I]ncreasing numbers of women in the developing world have been resorting to abortion, usually under unsafe and often illegal conditions.... [A]bortion, legal and illegal, now has become the most widespread fertility control method in use in the world today."[7] To Ravenholt it seemed obvious that no comprehensive American program to bring family planning to the world could ignore abortion. Besides, after *Roe v. Wade* was decided at the beginning of 1973, the issue seemed to be settled. Abortion was legal in America. Why shouldn't American aid reflect that?

Agreeing with Potts about the potential of Karman's innovation, Ravenholt had USAID contract with the Battelle Corporation to reengineer it for mass production. Not long after the *Roe* decision came down, Battelle, at Ravenholt's urging, hired Karman, and soon they'd come up with a device that Ravenholt deemed "pretty ideal." It was a modified 50 cc syringe topped with a thin plastic tube, or cannula. When the plunger was pulled, a thumb-operated valve retained the vacuum. The abortionist would insert the cannula through the cervix, then gradually release the valve to suction out the uterus. "This was a very efficient way of terminating early pregnancies," said Ravenholt.

If there was a risk in putting an illegal abortionist to work, albeit indirectly, for the U.S. government, it seems not to have occurred to Ravenholt. "I knew what we needed, and Harvey had done something along that line, so what the hell?" he said. Through the U.S. government's General Services Administration, he ordered a thousand "menstrual regulation kits" that included a syringe, a dozen cannula, a speculum, and a plastic basin, and he supplied them to doctors all over the world. The feedback was positive, so he ordered ten thousand more. His staffers would bring suitcases full of them when they went on trips abroad. The technology has since been introduced in over one hundred countries.[8]

"I have a friend—a woman obstetrician-gynecologist in Malaysia—who, using one kit, with some replacement cannulae, did sixty-eight hundred pregnancy terminations," Ravenholt said, delighted and proud. "This was remarkably cost-effective. In fact, some women used it themselves, and nurses and midwives and others could use this with fair safety."[9]

It's hard to believe now, after years in which the United States has exported its antiabortion movement all over the globe, that the American government was once responsible for bringing safe abortion to great swaths of the developing world. Hard to believe, too, that support for distributing contraceptives to remote corners of the planet was once a solidly bipartisan undertaking. As George H. W. Bush wrote in 1973, "Success in the population field, under United Nations leadership, may, in turn, determine whether we can resolve successfully the other great questions of peace, prosperity, and individual rights that face the world."[10] (As a congressman, Bush earned the nickname "Rubbers" for his enthusiastic interest in family planning.)

Americans are used to thinking of birth control and abortion as thoroughly domestic issues, but reproductive politics have been global from the start. In the second decade of the twentieth century the American birth control movement created its clinic-based system on the groundbreaking model pioneered in the Netherlands, a country that remains in the vanguard of international family planning. Margaret Sanger, the glamorous dynamo who pioneered birth control access in America and around the world, was something of a hero in Japan; she was the first foreigner ever invited to address the Japanese parliament.[11] Abortion methods travel from country to country; the technique most often used in the United States today was pioneered by two doctors in the former Yugoslavia, a father and son team. The former had been the gynecologist to Yugoslavia's royal family before World War II, when illegal abortion was so common in that country it was called the white plague.[12]

Today abortion is broadly legal in the vast majority of the developed world and in Asian countries, including China and India; more than 60 percent of people live in countries with liberal abortion laws. Another 14 percent or so live in nations like Colombia and Ghana that allow abortion under certain circumstances. But in many poor countries, including large parts of Africa and Latin America and parts of Asia and the Middle East, abortion is either banned entirely or allowed only to save a woman's life. Twenty-six percent of the world's women and men live under such laws, which are largely the relics of colonial constitutions promulgated by European countries that have since abandoned such restrictions for themselves.[13]

Given that so many abortion bans are artifacts of colonialism, it is particularly ironic when the contemporary global antiabortion movement accuses reproductive rights activists of neoimperialism. Yet it's also true that realpolitik-driven fears of swelling third world population, more than humanitarianism, drove early efforts by the United States to bring family planning to poor countries. America's international commitment to birth control was intended to fight communism, not to liberate women. If it did the latter, that was at best a bonus. Eventually, the national security rationale would give way to a focus on women's rights, leaving birth control programs far more politically vulnerable to right-wing attacks, since nothing but women's lives was at stake.

The vicissitudes of the United States' policies on birth control and abortion have always had at least as much impact abroad as they do domestically. Americans don't pay much attention to what goes on beyond their borders, giving those working on issues of sexual health abroad a freer hand than at home, whether that means blanketing neighborhoods in other countries with packets of pills or channeling money to abstinence-promoting, condom-excoriating missionaries. American officials have introduced safe abortion into foreign countries, and they've interfered to make abortion more perilous. The United States pushed to create the United Nations Population Fund, the world's premier agency promoting reproductive health, in 1969. Decades later, the United States government tried to destroy it.

By then it was in some ways too late: The family planning infrastructure that America did so much to build had taken on a life and a legitimacy of its own. At the same time, the forces of cultural globalization—undermining sexual taboos and celebrating individual rights above community attachments—continue to be associated with Americanization. Thus a country like Nicaragua can pass abortion legislation that mirrors the position of the party then in power in the United States and still spin it as a blow against Northern imperialism.

The global spread of family planning has vastly changed the world. Even as the planet's population increased nearly fourfold in the twentieth century, from 1.6 billion to 6.1 billion people, fertility rates have declined sharply in most countries, and smaller families have become the norm. "In the 1950s, women in less developed regions had an average of six children," wrote UN demographer Joseph Chamie. "[T]oday's average is closer to three. By mid-century, the global fertility average is anticipated to be close to replacement levels of around two children per couple."[14] There are many reasons women are having fewer children, but many studies show that a substantial part of the decrease is due to increased access to contraception, now used by more than half the couples in the world.[15]

In some countries effective family planning programs have been a great boon to development. Falling birthrates, which for a time increase the percentage of working adults to dependent children in a society, create a window where a greater share of the population is productive. Demographers call this the "demographic dividend," and it can be a major spur to development. Harvard economists David Bloom, David Canning, and Jaypee Sevilla have argued that the demographic dividend created by East Asia's postwar embrace of family planning "was essential to East Asia's extraordinary economic achievements, accounting for as much as one-third of its 'economic miracle.' "[16] (The Philippines, conversely, is the only big East Asian country to eschew family planning, and the only one whose economy never took off.)

Perhaps most important, the global family planning movement has—often inadvertently, and in the face of great internal resistance—given rise to a new vision of universal women's rights that has changed both international law and individual lives. At the 1994 International Conference on Population and Development in Cairo, more than 180 countries adopted a program of action proclaiming, "Advancing gender equality and equity and the empowerment of women, and the elimination of all kinds of violence against women, and ensuring women's ability to control their own fertility, are cornerstones of population and development-related programs.... The full and equal participation of women in civil, cultural, economic, political and social life, at the national, regional and international levels, and the eradication of all forms of discrimination on grounds of sex, are priority objectives of the international community."[17]

This was a remarkable statement (and to some social conservatives an appalling one). Like most UN declarations it remains more a goal than a reality. Given the persistence of sexual oppression and even terror in much of the world, the half a million women who die due to pregnancy complications each year, the millions more who have their genitals cut in the name of purity, and the plague of illegal abortion that fills hospital wards from Nicaragua to Nigeria, the Cairo program of action can today seem like empty verbiage. But just as peacekeeping remains a crucial endeavor despite the endurance of war, and human rights law matters despite constant violations, the global commitment to reproductive rights represents an important attempt to unite humankind against an ageless scourge: the wholesale devaluation of women.

There have been setbacks and backlashes, some caused by right-wing forces in the United States, others by related movements in countries such as Nicaragua. In all likelihood there will be more, since fundamentalism and feminism are both spurred by the upheavals of globalization. Still, slowly, in frustrating fits and starts, a relatively new international ideal of women's rights as human rights is altering laws and societies in subtle but systematic ways, forcing changes to discriminatory inheritance laws and patterns of education, draconian abortion bans, child marriages, and other sources of female misery. The attempt to liberate half the world's people from the intertwined tyrannies of culture and biology is one of the least heralded but most ambitious global initiatives in history.

Margaret Sanger was well aware of the emancipatory potential of reproductive rights. "Women can attain freedom only by concrete, definite knowledge of themselves, a knowledge based on biology, physiology and psychology," she wrote in her aptly titled 1922 book *The Pivot of Civilization*. Birth control, she argued, "is no negative philosophy concerned solely with the number of children brought into this world. It is not merely a question of population. Primarily it is the instrument of liberation and human development."[18]

When international family planning entered the mainstream of American politics in the 1960s, though, liberation and human development were hardly foremost on the minds of its proponents. Some of the men—and they were mostly men—who created America's international population policy would develop decidedly feminist sympathies. But they were driven above all by a deep concern, sometimes shading into panic, about overpopulation. The international reproductive rights movement would extend and enrich the lives of millions of women around the world, but it began in a spirit of grim Malthusian fear.

P eril is imminent," warned Hugh Moore, the founder of the Dixie Cup Company and an early family planning activist, in his 1954 self-published booklet *The Population Bomb*. The cover of one version of *The Population Bomb* shows a globe so teeming with people that it resembles an orange with a fuzzy rot spreading over its rind. A fuse comes out of the top, but a giant scissors labeled "Population Control" is poised to snip it. On the inside cover were endorsements from Arthur Krock, the award-winning journalist known as "the dean of Washington newsmen," and famed judge Learned Hand. Moore distributed his pamphlet to ten thousand influential people whose names he took from *Who's Who*.

Like other advocates of population control, Moore was motivated by the anticommunist anxiety of his day. Under the heading "War, Communism and World Population," he wrote, "Hundreds of millions of people in the world are hungry. In their desperation they are increasingly susceptible to Communist propaganda and may be enticed into violent action." America's aid program, conceived as "a means of helping poor and hungry people, of combating Communism and of preserving peace, is doomed to failure as long as it disregards the present unprecedented world population explosion."[19]

This was a new spin on an old analysis, one that dates back to the British clergyman Thomas Robert Malthus. Writing in the late eighteenth and early nineteenth centuries, he warned that population growth would inevitably outstrip food production, resulting in widespread suffering and starvation. Should mankind's own vices, along with "sickly seasons, epidemics, pestilence, and plague," fail to kill enough, "gigantic inevitable famine stalks in the rear, and with one mighty blow levels the population with the food of the world."[20] The pious, conservative Malthus was no birth control supporter; instead, he argued for abstinence, late marriage, and the repeal of England's poor laws, which, by allowing the indigent to start families, "increase population without increasing the food for its support."[21]

Malthusian arguments would enjoy several vogues in the next hundred and fifty years, inspiring the earliest proponents of contraception. In the 1860s a group of birth control advocates founded the Neo-Malthusian League in London; they won the support of John Stuart Mill and, decades later, the psychologist Havelock Ellis, who would become Sanger's longtime lover. Neo-Malthusian ideas influenced the anarchist feminist Emma Goldman and Sanger herself, though both were always more concerned with women's individual rights.

Sanger was a complicated figure, a groundbreaking feminist who transcended some of the prejudices of her time while remaining mired in others. She operated in an era when eugenics, often a cousin of Matlhusian doctrine, was considered a respectable pursuit on both the left and the right, and rarely hesitated to invoke eugenic arguments for birth control, even going so far as to advocate coercive contraception for those with "gross" mental deficiencies.[22] Describing a conference she had convened in Zurich, she wrote that attendees were unanimous in the "cool scientific conviction" that contraception was on the way to being perfected "as an instrument in racial progress."[23] At another point, she spoke of birth control leading to the creation of "a race of thoroughbreds."[24]

It does not excuse such language to say that it sounded very different in Sanger's context than it does today. As Ellen Chesler, Sanger's sympathetic but not uncritical biographer, wrote, "As had happened briefly before World War I, eugenics became a popular craze in this country—promoted in newspapers and magazines as a kind of secular religion.... The great majority of American colleges and universities introduced formal courses in the subject, and sociologists who embraced it took on what one historian has called a 'priestly role.'[25] Liberal adherents included W. E. B. DuBois, John Maynard Keynes, and the American socialist and pacifist Norman Thomas.[26]

Many eugenicists opposed birth control, fearing that it would lead genetically desirable women to have too few children. Indeed, right-wing pronatalists were as apt to adopt eugenic rhetoric as left-wing proponents of contraception. In his book *Fatal Misconception: The Struggle to Control World Population,* the historian Matthew Connelly wrote of how one Catholic bishop, debating Sanger, warned that "the races from northern Europe," whom he called "the finest type of people," were "doomed to extinction, unless each family produces at least four children."[27] Nevertheless, as Chesler wrote, Sanger "deliberately courted the power of eugenically inclined academics and scientists to blunt the attacks of religious conservatives against her."[28] She was not, in fact, a racist, believing that inherent ability and intelligence varied among individuals rather than among ethnic groups, but at times she used dubious language that reeks of racism to modern ears.[29] Her words would provide rich fodder for the contemporary antiabortion movement, eager to tar family planning as a tool of genocide.

The stench of Nazism would eventually leave eugenics discredited among decent people. Ironically, though, in the aftermath of World War II, Malthus himself came to seem more prescient than ever. Thanks to immunizations, antibiotics, pesticides, and Western shipments of food and fertilizer to the developing world, "sickly seasons, epidemics, pestilence, and plague" were curtailed like never before. Death rates fell sharply, without a corresponding drop in births. World population grew at a rate no one had ever seen before—between 1930 and 1960 the number of people on earth increased by 50 percent, from two billion to three billion. Birthrates in Europe had been falling for centuries, but before World War II most population growth was nonetheless in the developed world. The postwar population boom was different; most of it took place in Asia, Africa, and Latin America.[30]

As the scope of the demographic change came into focus in the 1950s, overpopulation captured the attention of a number of highly influential figures. They were motivated by national security fears (too often tinged with racism) of rebellion in unruly, underfed nations, but some were also driven by compassion. They believed that the world's burgeoning numbers were making poor countries poorer and undermining the effectiveness of foreign aid.

John D. Rockefeller III, grandson of the legendary industrialist, was one of the altruistic ones. Rockefeller had a passion for Asia: As a naval officer, he worked on postwar policy concerning Japan and was later a cultural consultant to future secretary of state John Foster Dulles during the Japanese peace treaty negotiations. At the time a postwar baby boom had made overpopulation a major concern in that densely settled island nation. Unemployment was high, and illegal abortion was epidemic. (In an effort to stem the damage caused by these procedures, in 1948 Japan became the first nation to legalize abortion and sterilization.)[31] Rockefeller's experiences there and elsewhere in Asia convinced him that population growth was retarding development and exacerbating human suffering. In 1952 he founded the Population Council, a nonprofit organization that would eventually help build birth control programs throughout the world.

Rockefeller was a shy and modest man, known to travel coach on the train from New York to Washington, D.C. According to Joan Dunlop, who spent several years as his chief aid on population issues, he was deeply sympathetic to women. "[H]e used to say to me, 'You know, I go to all these dinners around the world, [with] heads of state, and I always sit next to the women, to the wives. And they always strike me as much more intelligent than their husbands. Much more interesting, much more intelligent,'" she recalled.[32]

General William Draper was at least as influential as Rockefeller in creating the international family planning movement, pushing both the United States and the United Nations to get involved in birth control programs all over the world, but the two men were profoundly different. Draper was brash and aggressive, a man's man. Dunlop, herself known for her sharp tongue and quick judgments, found him "boorish and arrogant and cavalier."[33] "Some people thought he pushed too hard," said Phyllis Piotrow, who worked as Draper's executive secretary. "John D. Rockefeller III, who was a very modest person and didn't push,...always thought Draper pushed too hard, should be more modest and so on. But you know, when you're John D. Rockefeller you can be modest and still get things done. When you're somebody like Draper, who is a self-made person, you have to be more aggressive to get things done."[34]

Get things done he did. By the late 1950s, Draper, a Harlem-born investment banker, had built a burnished, solidly establishment career. He had risen through the military during World War II, eventually serving as undersecretary of the army and supervising the occupations of Germany, Austria, and Japan. He was involved in organizing the Berlin airlift in 1948, and after the war he moved to Mexico to head the Mexican Light and Power Company. In 1958, when President Eisenhower convened a committee to review foreign aid priorities, he seemed a natural to lead it.

The day after the Draper Committee was established, the general received a wire from Hugh Moore, the Dixie Cup magnate. His message to Draper was this: "If your committee does not look into the impact and implications of the population explosion, you will be derelict in your duty."[35]

According to Piotrow, who later wrote an important account of the birth of U.S. population policy, Moore's message prompted chuckles among the committee members, but Draper took it seriously enough to learn more. Eisenhower himself nudged the general to delve into it further: In December 1958, Draper was invited to discuss the committee's work at the National Security Council, and as he was speaking the president said, "And Bill, don't forget the population problem, because that is very serious in some of these countries."[36]

He didn't forget, and as he traveled the world for the committee he became a true believer. "We found, the committee of ten, that in most of the developing countries their rate of population growth was such that it was interfering seriously with their economic development, particularly with any improvement in their per capita income," he said.[37] In 1959 he told the Senate Foreign Relations Committee, "The population problem, I'm afraid, is the greatest bar to our whole economic aid program and to the progress of the world."[38]

He also saw what family planning could do. Like Rockefeller, he'd spent time in postwar Japan. Returning a decade later, Piotrow wrote, "[H]e observed at first hand how, with legalized abortion and considerable publicity, the Japanese people had sharply reduced birth rates and achieved their 'economic miracle.'"[39]

The Draper Committee's final report, published in July 1959, concluded that population growth was reversing any gains that economic aid might offer poor countries. It recommended that the United States "assist those countries with which it is cooperating in economic aid programs, on request, in the formulation of their plans designed to deal with the problem of rapid population growth." It also urged the government to support population research within the United Nations.

By the end of the year population growth and birth control had become major public issues. In October 1959, Arthur Krock published a *New York Times* column headlined "The Most Dangerous Bomb of All." "In the rush of the great nations to produce nuclear weapons capable of agonizing mass destruction, and now to find means to turn them into the utilities of peace, their Governments have paid small attention to the limitation of a more dangerous instrument for the destruction of civilization that is swiftly being assembled," Krock wrote. "The social scientists have named this weapon 'the population bomb.'" He quoted the editor of the Princeton alumni weekly, who warned of "billions of half-alive, starving peasants, condemned to short, miserable lives of hatred and hunger."[40]

Leaders around the world had come to the same conclusion. At a 1959 conference of the International Planned Parenthood Federation in New Delhi, Prime Minister Jawaharlal Nehru warned that population growth portended a "tremendous crisis."[41] At the beginning of 1960, Reuters reported from Karachi, "Pakistan is preparing to open a campaign for population control that could mean the difference between life or death by starvation for many of its 87,000,000 people."[42] Sweden had begun helping some of its aid recipients implement birth control programs.

In the United States public discussion of birth control remained extremely difficult—its sale was still illegal in some states. Still, things were changing. Several Protestant denominations, including the United Presbyterian Church and the American Baptist Convention, endorsed family planning in 1959. A study group of the World Council of Churches, an ecumenical body that brought together representatives of major Christian denominations (though not Roman Catholics), published a report titled "Responsible Parenthood and the Population Problem." It strongly supported birth control and lamented that in the past "Christian thought has, especially in the area of the family and its relationships, often clung to tradition without taking into account new knowledge."[43]

The Catholic Church reacted to the emerging conventional wisdom with alarm. In a November 1959 statement the Catholic bishops in the United States decried the "terror technique phrase 'population explosion,'" calling it a "smoke screen behind which a moral evil may be foisted on the public." It attacked the "present attempts of some representatives of Christian bodies who endeavor to elaborate...a theological doctrine which envisages artificial birth prevention within the married state as the 'will of God.'" Further, it declared that American Catholics "will not support any public assistance, either at home or abroad, to promote artificial birth prevention, abortion or sterilization, whether through direct aid or by means of international organizations."

Protestant leaders criticized this stance; San Francisco Episcopal bishop James A. Pike said it would "condemn rapidly increasing millions of people in less fortunate parts of the world to starvation, bondage, misery and despair." In what seemed a clear provocation, he asked whether the Catholic bishops' policy was binding on Catholic politicians.[44]

"With that blunt inquiry, Bishop Pike inevitably dropped the problem at the doorstep of the nation's best-known Roman Catholic office seeker—Jack Kennedy," wrote *Time* toward the end of 1959.[45] The approaching election would be the first since 1928 to feature a Catholic candidate, making the burgeoning conflict over contraception even more heated. "The birth control issue was joined, and Jack Kennedy knew that the deep-rooted religious challenge to his presidential ambitions, newly burst into the open, could be hazardous indeed," concluded *Time*.

Kennedy was forced to walk a fine line. He opposed American support for international family planning programs, but he was anxious not to be seen as taking orders from the church. In a phone interview with James Reston of The *New York Times*, he attacked population control from the left, calling it "mean paternalism." "I think it would be the greatest psychological mistake for us to appear to advocate limitation of the black, or brown, or yellow peoples whose population is increasing no faster than the United States," he said. His position, he emphasized, preceded the bishop's statement and wasn't influenced by his Catholicism.[46]

Eisenhower was alarmed at the potential for a religious fissure in the United States, and he tried to make the issue go away. Despite his earlier concern about population, at a December 1959 press conference he decisively rejected Draper's family planning recommendations. "This government will not, as long as I am here, have a positive political doctrine in its program that has to do with the problem of birth control," he said. "That's not our business."

But the public movement was growing. "From the private organizations came a deluge of publicity and agitation," wrote Piotrow.[47] Newspapers all over the country published editorials calling for government action on overpopulation. Planned Parenthood collected the signatures of 179 world leaders from nineteen countries on "A Statement of Conviction About Overpopulation," which it published as an advertisement and presented to UN secretary-general Dag Hammarskjöld.[48] At the State Department a group of family planning advocates worked to change policy from the inside, while Draper made constant lobbying trips to Washington, D.C.

As the momentum built, Eisenhower came to regret his earlier capitulation. In 1963 he published a piece in the *Saturday Evening Post* titled "Let's Be Honest with Ourselves." "When I was President," he wrote, "I opposed the use of Federal funds to provide birth control information to countries we were aiding because I felt this would violate the deepest religious convictions of large groups of taxpayers. As I now look back, it may be that I carried that conviction too far. I still believe that as a national policy we should not make birth control programs a condition to our foreign aid, but we should tell receiving nations how population growth threatens them and what can be done about it."[49] In 1964, at Draper's invitation, both Eisenhower and Harry Truman became honorary chairmen of Planned Parenthood.

The taboos that had once made birth control an outré subject for public discussion were crumbling. The Food and Drug Administration approved the first oral contraceptives in 1960. In its 1965 decision *Griswold v. Connecticut* the Supreme Court ruled Connecticut's ban on contraceptives unconstitutional. When the Johnson administration took over, it worked, quietly but steadily, to expand access to family planning at home.[50]

Dean Rusk, the secretary of state under both Kennedy and Johnson, had previously been the president of the Rockefeller Foundation. After Johnson was elected in 1964, Rockefeller persuaded Rusk to try to insert a mention of population into the president's first State of the Union address.[51] He succeeded. Addressing the nation on January 4, 1965, Johnson said, "I will seek new ways to use our knowledge to help deal with the explosion in world population and the growing scarcity in world resources."

Soon Johnson was running with the issue. Six months after the State of the Union, in a speech on the twentieth anniversary of the United Nations, Johnson implored the world body to "face forthrightly the multiplying problems of our multiplying populations.... Let us act on the fact that less than $5 invested in population control is worth $100 invested in economic growth."[52]

He acted on his own advice, in one shameful instance using food aid as leverage to pressure India to adopt both agricultural reforms and family planning. Johnson "had put food-grain aid to India on a month-to-month basis because India, relying on the U.S., had neglected its rural economy and failed to promote family planning," wrote Joseph Califano Jr., one of the president's senior aides. "As the 1965–67 Indian drought and famine worsened, all the President's agricultural and foreign policy advisers urged him to expand food shipments to India immediately. But Johnson wanted India to take care of itself—improve its agricultural production, end food hoarding, and control its population."[53]

In October 1966, Johnson received the first Margaret Sanger Award in World Leadership, sending Labor secretary Willard Wirtz to accept it on his behalf. "It was a tribute no other President would have risked accepting," wrote Califano.[54]

Meanwhile, Congress was also taking initiative. Senator Ernest Gruening, a Democrat from Alaska, convened a series of subcommittee hearings on birth control and population growth. Eisenhower submitted written testimony, saying, "If we now ignore the plight of those unborn generations which, because of our unreadiness to take corrective action in controlling population growth, will be denied any expectation beyond abject poverty and suffering, then history will rightly condemn us."[55]

For a moment it even seemed as if the Catholic Church might come around. In 1962 the reformist Pope John XXIII called the Second Vatican Council, a historic convocation of bishops, cardinals, and superiors of men's religious orders, which met over four autumns. Vatican II, as it would be called, was revolutionary. It was meant to "open the windows" of the church to the modern world, in the pope's famous phrasing, and to cast off some of the church's insularity and authoritarianism. In many ways that is what it did. Vatican II brought a number of reforms, including the use of congregants' native tongues rather than Latin in the celebration of mass; an endorsement of religious freedom as opposed to state-mandated Catholicism; and, importantly, a rejection of anti-Semitism and the charge that the Jewish people are culpable for the killing of Christ.

At the time, birth control was an especially contentious issue among both Catholic theologians and the laity. Many of the faithful were chafing under the church's absolute ban on contraception, and some in the hierarchy were beginning to question traditional doctrine. In 1963, Dutch bishop William Bekkers, speaking on national television, said that couples alone should decide on the size of their families: "This is a matter for their own consciences with which nobody should interfere." Bekkers didn't endorse birth control, but he called for an open discussion. A few months later the rest of the country's Catholic hierarchy seconded these sentiments in a statement on the birth control pill.[56]

Meanwhile, many in the church were aware of the increasing salience of the population issue on the international stage, and the pope sought guidance in dealing with it at the United Nations. By most accounts neither Pope John XXIII nor his successor, Pope Paul VI, shared the kind of obsession with sex and fertility that marked the papacy of John Paul II. They were, however, hemmed in by church history. The church's hostility to contraception had been consistent for hundreds of years, though both the intensity of the opposition and the rationale for it have shifted considerably over time. And in 1930, in the encyclical *Casti Connubii,* Pope Pius XI did much to foreclose the possibility of a liberal evolution in Catholic doctrine.

That year, at the Lambeth Conference, the Anglican Church outraged the Vatican by becoming the first mainline Christian denomination to explicitly sanction contraception. A few months later the pope responded with *Casti Connubii,* which declared artificial contraception "intrinsically evil," something that could never be permitted for any reason. As author Robert McClory pointed out, even murder and theft aren't considered "intrinsically evil," since both could be justified by extenuating circumstances.[57]

Casti Connubii left later popes little flexibility. To amend the church's teachings on birth control it would have to admit that the encyclical had been in error, and to acknowledge that those who submitted to it did so needlessly. Yet many Catholics were desperate for licit ways to limit their families. In

1951, Pope Pius XII, speaking before a group of Italian midwives, gave his approbation to natural family planning, then often called the rhythm method, in which couples schedule intercourse to try to take advantage of the infertile days in a woman's menstrual cycle. It was a departure from previous doctrine, since it sanctioned nonprocreative sex. Still, couples often found natural family planning unreliable and anxiety provoking. And if it was acceptable to try to separate sex from reproduction, what sense did the ban on contraception make? John Rock, a Catholic Harvard Medical School professor who'd helped develop the birth control pill, argued that hormonal contraception should be acceptable to the church, since it simply mimicked nature in suppressing a woman's fertility. Some theologians agreed.[58]

Seeking a way out of this confusion, Pope John set up a secret six-man body, the Pontifical Commission for the Study of Population, Family, and Births—often called the papal birth control commission—to examine it. When he died in 1963, the commission was inherited by his successor, Pope Paul VI, who expanded it several times, so that it was eventually composed of seventy-two people, including, in a break from tradition, five women.

Commission members Pat and Patty Crowley, the married presidents of the Christian Family Movement, an international Catholic organization, presented statements from their members, all committed, pious believers. Wrote one father of six, "Rhythm destroys the meaning of the sex act; it turns it from a spontaneous expression of spiritual and physical love into a mere bodily sexual relief; it makes me obsessed with sex throughout the month." As the commission's work continued, the Crowleys organized a more extensive survey of their membership, which found widespread dissatisfaction with the rhythm method: Seventy-eight percent said that it had harmed their relationships. "Which is more pleasing to God," wrote one of their respondents, a mother of ten, "trusting in the miscalculations of rhythm or making a full, generous decision in holiness to have a child? Rhythm leads to self-seeking, promotes excess in infertile times and strain in fertile times. Is contraceptive sex irresponsible when I have already borne ten little responsibilities?"[59]

The more the members of the commission debated and learned, the more crucial change began to seem, at least to most of them. Worried by the commission's direction, apparently conservatives in the Vatican hierarchy maneuvered to have the commission members demoted to "advisers" and the commission itself reconstituted as a body of sixteen cardinals and bishops.[60] Yet the cardinals and bishops, hearing the same evidence that had convinced the previous commission members, eventually voted nine to three to change the church's position on contraception, with three abstentions. (One commission member, Karol Wojtyla of Poland—the future John Paul II—didn't attend the meeting where the vote was taken, out of solidarity with Polish cardinal Stefan Wysynski, who had been denied a travel visa by the Polish government.)[61]

In the summer of 1966, the commission's majority submitted a report of their conclusions to the Vatican. "The *regulation of conception* appears necessary for many couples who wish to achieve a responsible, open and reasonable parenthood in today's circumstances," it said. "If they are to observe and cultivate all the essential values of marriage, married people need decent and human means for the regulation of conception."[62]

Wrote historian Garry Wills, "The commission members left their work convinced that the Pope could no longer uphold a discredited teaching. When the report was leaked to the press, Catholics around the world took heart at the signs of change."[63]

In the end, of course, there was no change. Conservatives in the Vatican argued that the grandeur of church authority would be undermined if it admitted a previous error. One priest, wrote Wills, "said that if the church reversed itself now, it would prove that the Holy Spirit had been with the Anglicans at Lambeth, not with the Pope in Rome."[64] A Spanish Jesuit had exclaimed during the birth control commission's deliberations, "What then with the millions we have sent to hell, if these norms were not valid?"[65]

Pope Paul feared that any change would make it seem as if the church had imposed unreasonable burdens on its people. "Any attenuation of the law," he said in an interview, "would have the effect of calling morality into question and showing the fallibility of the Church.... Theology would then become the servant of science.... [T]he whole moral edifice would collapse."[66]

And so in 1968, ignoring the advice of his commission, Pope Paul issued *Humanae Vitae,* which reiterated the church's absolute ban on contraception. Around the world there was an unprecedented rebellion among the faithful. "Polls registered an instant noncompliance with the encyclical," Wills wrote. In a profound break with tradition many bishops told believers that, while they should take the pope's words seriously, they could follow their own consciences.[67]

In 1978, when Karol Wojtyla, a zealous supporter of *Humanae Vitae,* became Pope John Paul II, he moved to check such rebellion. McClory, whose book *Turning Point* chronicled the history of the papal birth control commission, wrote that the encyclical was practically "the foundation stone of his papacy.... Full and explicit agreement with *Humanae Vitae* (as well as opposition to women's ordination) became a prerequisite for anyone nominated to become a bishop." The church would go on to play a consistently intransigent role on questions of population policy, contraception, and, eventually, HIV prevention worldwide.

Yet in the early and mid-1960s it looked as if the last, most monumental bastion of resistance to birth control was beginning to give way. For supporters of international family planning, everything seemed to be falling into place.

In 1965, Reimert Ravenholt, an epidemiologist and professor at the University of Washington medical school, became convinced that there was a link between smoking and cancer, and he threw himself into researching it. His superiors were not encouraging. He was accused of overstepping his expertise; the head of one department, convinced that all cancers were caused by viruses, objected to Ravenholt presenting a paper arguing otherwise. Frustrated, Ravenholt complained to a friend that the university was stifling him. His friend, who worked at USAID, suggested that he try something new. Ravenholt, he said, should come to Washington, D.C., to head a new program on global population and family planning.

Ravenholt accepted, and as soon as he arrived in the capital he decided he'd made an enormous mistake. "President Lyndon Johnson was speaking loudly, [giving] very powerful messages about the importance of the world population explosion and doing something about it," he recalled. "In my naïveté, I expected I would have the resources to run a meaningful program." Instead, he was given a fifteen-square-foot office in the State Department, no staff except for a secretary, and no money. "With that I was supposed to drop the birthrate of the world," he said.[68]

That year the Vietnam War would increasingly consume the president's energy and political capital. The Johnson administration's will to act on population and risk antagonizing faithful Catholics, a loyal block of Democratic voters, vanished. Ravenholt was tempted to turn around and go home. "But my pride wouldn't let me just admit that—tell everybody and immediately say goodbye," he said. "In penance to myself I decided to stay and work a year. Teach me to be more careful in the future."[69]

Eventually, though, Ravenholt was able to assemble a small staff. And he found an important friend in William Draper, who had recently retired from a job as chairman of New York's Combustion Engineering to devote himself fully to fighting overpopulation. In 1965, when Hugh Moore founded the Population Crisis Committee, Draper became its chairman, a job he performed without pay. Draper made it his mission to get Ravenholt the resources he needed, and by 1968 he'd convinced Arkansas senator William Fulbright, chairman of the Senate Foreign Relations Committee, to earmark $35 million for population programs within USAID. That increased to $50 million in 1969, and by 1972 it would be $125 million.

"So, by the beginning of '68 we had the policy we needed," said Ravenholt. "We had, not many people, but we had enough to get going with, and we had enough money to get going, so we could really, finally, seriously move toward making a program."[70]

From the start Ravenholt was a polarizing presence. He's a giant man, well over six feet, with broad shoulders and wild hair that stands up from his head, adding another few inches. He has small, merry blue eyes and a mischievous smile, though when challenged at work he could become enraged and even physically intimidating. Now in his eighties, his sun-drenched house on Seattle's Lake Washington is packed with books, including many volumes on Thomas Jefferson and Thomas Paine. Despite his long-standing interest in history, though, he operates with a scientist's single-minded empiricism, unwilling or perhaps unable to make concessions to political sensitivities or bureaucratic processes. He's compulsively flirtatious and likes to shock. Photos from his time at USAID show him with long sideburns, looking very much the 1970s libertine that, by all accounts, he was.

Ravenholt was born on a Wisconsin dairy farm in 1925, the middle of nine children. The grandson of Danish immigrants, he was raised in a Danish-speaking community. His family had neither running water nor electricity. "It was almost as though we were born in the nineteenth or even eighteenth century," he said.[71]

Rejected from the army because of a heart murmur, he worked his way through the University of Minnesota, finishing in three years and getting accepted to medical school. After graduation he got an internship at the U.S. Public Health Service hospital in San Francisco, and from there joined the Epidemic Intelligence Service of the CDC. He ended up tracking diphtheria in Appalachia, where he encountered conditions not unlike those he'd later see in the third world. The memory of one poor household stayed with him. The mother was nursing her ninth child and the father was sprawled on a couch watching a large TV, their only real possession. Everyone in the family had roundworm disease; the father had vomited up a footlong parasite.

The source of their troubles quickly became clear: They got their water from an indolent spring located between the house and the outhouse. "These experiences really shifted my gears from reparative medicine to preventive medicine," Ravenholt said. "I became immediately fascinated and challenged by how we could interrupt the development of these diseases, especially when one can apply some inexpensive, mass approaches like immunization and improved potability of water and so forth."[72]

Ravenholt went on to direct immunization programs in Seattle, "making immunizations so readily available that almost all children got immunized," he said.[73] Similarly, he said, with family planning, "as a public health physician, I knew to my core that the overpowering determinant was sheer availability." He would fight overpopulation the way he'd fought disease. What the developing world needed were massive amounts of contraceptives—free supplies of pills, which had only come on the market in 1960, and all the condoms people could use.

In addition to channeling money to groups like International Planned Parenthood—by the early 1970s USAID was providing over half the organization's budget—Ravenholt initiated programs that sent workers into villages to blanket neighborhoods with pills. "The principle involved in the household distribution of contraceptives can be demonstrated with Coca-Cola," he told the *Los Angeles Times* in 1979. "If one distributed an ample, free supply of Coca-Cola into each household, would not poor illiterate peasants drink as much Coca-Cola as the rich literate residents?"[74]

In the spring of 1973, Ravenholt threatened to withdraw USAID funding from family planning organizers in Egypt unless they would agree to distribute contraceptives door to door. Egyptian leader Gamal Abdel Nasser had made family planning a priority in the 1960s, calling population growth "the most dangerous obstacle that faces the Egyptian people" in their drive toward development.[75] But the government's program, which made birth control pills available in all public health clinics, was a terrible failure. Most women didn't respond, and those who did encountered confusion and disorganization. By the 1970s the program was only reaching around 3 percent of eligible rural women.[76]

To Ravenholt, the solution to Egypt's problem was simple. Initially, he said, local partners had "recoiled in horror" at his idea, but once they realized it was the only way to keep getting money, they "muscled up the courage." Here's how it worked: Two field-workers, a man and a woman, would go to each house in a given area and offer three months' worth of pills (which came in packets without Arabic instructions). They usually found women at home, and most of them accepted the pills, though they didn't necessarily start using them. "Right away," said Ravenholt, "a storm of discussion would begin among neighbors and between husbands and wives. Eventually, about half of the women who'd accepted the pills started taking them."

After three months those who stayed on the pill would, of course, run out. "Well, they're not going to go ten miles to get a pack when they know that Mrs. X, a neighbor, got some that she hasn't used," he said. "So the O.C. [oral contraceptive] user will go there and ask for her supply. And right then, a very important thing—a satisfied user, not pregnant, asking this person who didn't use O.C.s and may already be pregnant for her pills. We found that within a year between 15 and 20 percent of the young women were using oral contraceptives regularly."[77]

This, of course, was more than a health intervention—it was a way of changing some fundamental cultural patterns. In years to come such programs would spark charges of "contraceptive imperialism" from right and left alike. Some feminists would attack these schemes for foisting pills on women without telling them about side effects. Yet for a while, Ravenholt and his team were able to bulldoze through most resistance even as he made enemies for both his personal and his professional behavior.

Ravenholt was known for walking around with menstrual regulation syringes hanging out of his pants pockets, eager to show anyone who was interested how they worked. Joan Dunlop recalled his keeping a cannula in his front pocket and using it to stir his cocktails. She found his broad flirtatiousness deeply irritating; she and her female colleagues used to joke about the number of women he made passes at.[78] And, indeed, after his first marriage broke up, Ravenholt dated a number of women in the field, including Sharon Camp, now the head of the Guttmacher Institute, the world's leading sexual and reproductive health think tank. She's much more sympathetic than Dunlop. "I thought Rei was a special kind of genius," she said. "He had some really inspired ideas. He also had some very bad ideas. And he *loved* to pick fights. He often said things that got people riled up just because he loved a good fight. I think had Rei been a different personality, he probably wouldn't have created so much rough and tumble around the issue, but he might not also have accomplished nearly as much as he got done. He was a very powerful personality, and a lot of the people who worked for him were really enthralled with him and his ideas, and they worked hard."

Camp recalls a classic story about Ravenholt. It was at a conference on abortion, during a discussion on the use of anesthesia during first trimester terminations. "And Rei Ravenholt stood up and said, 'I think it should be two martinis, because that's the way she got pregnant to begin with!' And the feminists in the audience went wild!"

Asked about it now, Ravenholt laughs and says that while he doesn't recall the two-martini crack, it sounds like the kind of thing he'd say. "Oh," he said, "I had a barrel of fun!"

Richard Nixon's election in 1968 was a very good thing for the global population control movement. During the Kennedy administration he'd come out for American-supported birth control in the developing world, and once in office he made population issues more of a priority than any president before him. In July 1969 he released "A Special Message to the Congress on Problems of Population Growth," a document on which Ravenholt collaborated. Population growth, it said, "is a world problem which no country can ignore, whether it is moved by the narrowest perception of national self-interest or the widest vision of a common humanity." Increasing populations, Nixon argued, threatened to outstrip development in poor countries "so that quality of life actually worsens." Nixon called on the United Nations to take the lead in reducing high birthrates, while promising increased U.S. support. He also asked Congress to create the Commission on Population Growth and the American Future to further study the problem. It was formed in 1970, with a host of bipartisan worthies and Rockefeller as chairman; one newspaper columnist called it "the Establishment epitomized."[79]

Meanwhile, population issues were gaining more and more salience. "It was exactly like the global warming coverage you get today," said Potts. "A very, very important issue that educated and liberal people were sincerely worried about." In 1968, Paul Ehrlich, a biologist who had previously specialized in butterflies, published his bestseller *The Population Bomb,* which became a sensation. The alarming prologue began, "The battle to feed all of humanity is over. In the 1970s the world will undergo famines—hundreds of millions of people are going to starve to death in spite of any crash programs embarked upon now."[80]

These were heady days in the field. "There was a spree that has never been recaptured," said Duff Gillespie, who began a long career at USAID as one of Ravenholt's researchers. "I mean we did crazy stuff and everything was kind of new."[81]

The condoms available when Ravenholt got started were gray and unlubricated; his office obtained lubricated ones, and then, in 1972, the first multicolored condoms—red, green, blue, and black—produced in the United States. "[T]hat helped to break the ice, because whenever I introduced a bunch of multicolored condoms to a new audience they couldn't help laughing," Ravenholt said.[82]

Logistics were always a problem, so people in Ravenholt's offices sometimes doubled as couriers. "I used to carry two suitcases with me when I went overseas," said Gillespie. One had his clothes, and the other was filled with condoms, birth control pills, and vacuum aspiration kits. "Basically, we were smuggling in contraband for a U.S. government program."

Gillespie recalls one trip to Tunisia. Worried about taking a suitcase full of condoms through customs, he asked someone at the local USAID mission for advice. "Just tell them it's your personal stuff and they won't even open up the suitcases," the staffer told him.

Arriving, he did just that, but the customs official opened his suitcases anyway. One was full of condoms—at least five hundred of them. "So this is for your personal use?" he asked. Gillespie kept a straight face and said, "Yes, it is."

After a tense moment the man burst out laughing, then called his friends over. Gillespie handed out condoms to all of them.[83]

To Gillespie, Ravenholt was a great man. "I'd say three fourths of the ideas that Rei came up with were totally outlandish and in some cases comical," he said. "But the other fourth was absolutely brilliant. He did things that other people hadn't even thought about and are now sort of standard operating procedures for international public health."[84]

Birth control pills, for example, had been sold in packages of twenty-one; women were supposed to count seven days before starting a new one. In poor countries, where few people had calendars, it was hard for users to stay on schedule. So Ravenholt added seven iron tablets, making the transition between packs seamless and treating widespread anemia at the same time.

For all their audacity, it was clear to Ravenholt and other leaders of the population field that if the most visible face of the family planning movement remained American, a backlash would be likely. Already there was significant leftist opposition to birth control programs. At home black militants decried government-funded contraception as a tool of genocide. Communist countries argued that population control was a way of avoiding more pertinent issues of development and economic redistribution. Mired in Vietnam, the United States, the global Santa Claus of birth control, was ever more unpopular.

It "was important to get a multilateral action going, because if it were just the United States pushing birth control, no doubt there would be political reaction to that," said Ravenholt.[85] American leaders wanted to see the United Nations take the lead.

Despite the opposition of Marxists and Catholics alike, the major international organizations were growing ever more receptive to population programs. Robert S. McNamara, who had resigned as defense secretary in 1967 to become president of the World Bank, had become convinced that overpopulation was a major obstacle to development. At the United Nations, family planning was being discussed under the rubric of human rights. On Human Rights Day in 1966, UN secretary-general U Thant declared, "We must accord the right of parents to determine the number of their children a place of importance at this moment in man's history." In 1968 the International Conference on Human Rights in Teheran affirmed that couples have the "basic human right to decide freely and responsibly on the number and spacing of their children." The affirmation of birth control as a basic human right would have profound consequences in the decades to come, but at the time it elicited neither much comment nor controversy.

For the UN to be effective, though, it needed to coordinate its family planning efforts. Together, Rockefeller and Draper worked to convince Thant to establish the United Nations Fund for Population Activities (UNFPA), later shortened to United Nations Population Fund, as a central source of money, resources, and information for family planning programs around the world. It supported both private groups and government initiatives, and would eventually work directly on the ground. At the start the United States agreed to provide $7.5 million in matching funds, and Draper lobbied European leaders tirelessly to contribute. Twenty-four countries pledged over $15 million in 1970, and the next year forty-six countries pledged almost $30 million.[86]

America's ardent support of the UNFPA seems ironic now, because Republican presidents since Ronald Reagan have consistently defunded, attacked, and undermined the agency. By the 1990s, right-wing operatives would be dogging UNFPA staffers in the field—sometimes putting the staffers' lives at risk. Echoing the seventies far left, they would spread rumors of the UNFPA's genocidal intent. During the era of George W. Bush, European countries would increase their support of the UNFPA in part to signal their defiance of the United States, the country that created it in the first place.

Even in the early 1970s, when the United States was the UNFPA's greatest champion, signs of the kind of abortion politics that would explode later in the decade were already emerging.

Rockefeller's Commission on Population Growth and the American Future finally released its recommendations in the election year of 1972, and they were revolutionary. His commission urged comprehensive sex education in the schools, stepped-up government funding for family planning, access to birth control for minors, liberalized abortion laws, government subsidies for abortion services, and the passage of the Equal Rights Amendment. (The suggestions weren't uniformly liberal—they also called for stringent limits on immigration and a crackdown on illegal aliens.)

"The majority of the commission believes that women should be free to determine their own fertility, that the matter of abortion should be left to the conscience of the individual concerned, in consultation with her physician, and that states should be encouraged to enact affirmative statutes creating a clear and positive framework for the practice of abortion on request," said the commission's report.

Several Protestant and Jewish groups signed a statement praising the report, but the Catholic bishops were predictably outraged, and Nixon rejected it decisively. He had built his electoral coalition on Middle American whites baffled and outraged by the social upheavals that had begun in the 1960s, and feminism and abortion rights were increasingly associated with countercultural mayhem. Unrestricted abortion policies would "demean human life," he said, and distributing contraception to minors would "do nothing to preserve and strengthen close family relationships."[87]

"It is hardly a secret that Nixon is making an all-out effort this year to capture the normally Democratic Catholic vote," wrote *Chicago Tribune* columnist Clayton Fritchey.[88] Indeed, after rejecting his commission's report, he wrote a letter to New York archbishop Terence Cardinal Cooke supporting the church's efforts to repeal the state's liberal abortion laws. Meanwhile, his supporters demonized George McGovern as the candidate of "acid, abortion, and amnesty," in the words of Senate Republican minority leader Hugh Scott. One *Washington Post* columnist characterized the 1972 race as "the first time in U.S. history that an incumbent president would, on the one hand, be running against his own advisers, and his rival, on the other hand, would be defending them."[89]

While Nixon inveighed against abortion to garner votes, within USAID Ravenholt was pushing forward with new abortion methods. Besides spearheading the development of the menstrual regulation syringe, he poured around $10 million into research to try to find a "nontoxic and completely effective substance which, when self-administered on a single occasion, would insure the non-pregnant state at the completion of a monthly cycle."[90] Ideally, Ravenholt hoped to see the development of a single pill that a woman could take whenever her period was late.

But not long after *Roe v. Wade* was decided, all this work was shut down. The decision, rather than signaling a new consensus as Ravenholt had hoped, motivated an entirely new level of antiabortion activism. As would happen repeatedly in the future, antiabortion politicians, unable to do much at home, turned their attention overseas. That year Republican senator Jesse Helms succeeded in passing an amendment to the Foreign Assistance Act banning USAID from funding abortion "as a method of family planning." Botched abortions would continue to strain hospital wards worldwide, but American family planning programs wouldn't be able to do much about it.

Just before the Helms amendment went into effect, Ravenholt organized a conference on abortion in Hawaii, where he distributed crates of menstrual regulation kits, paid for by the U.S. government, to health workers from all over the world. Then he organized another meeting of population groups and philanthropists to find someone to take over the production and distribution of the kits. That job went to a newly formed Chapel Hill, North Carolina–based group called International Pregnancy Advisory Service, or Ipas, funded with a half million dollars from one of the Scaife family's foundations. (While Richard Mellon Scaife is famous as the billionaire patron of the right wing, his more reclusive sister, Cordelia Scaife May, was a supporter of family planning and environmental causes.) Potts became Ipas's president and CEO.

Potts has called the Helms amendment the beginning of a "counterreformation" in family planning.[91] "I think if we hadn't had that, the world would literally look very different today," he said. "Helms has probably killed more women than most other people."

Still, for most of the 1970s, religious opposition to abortion and family planning on the right was outweighed by fears about mushrooming populations of poor potential converts to anti-American causes. In 1974, Henry Kissinger signed a classified national security study memorandum calling for a report on the impact of population growth "on U.S. security and overseas interests." The study, it said, "should focus on the international political and economic implications of population growth rather than its ecological, sociological or other aspects."[92] Eight months later the resulting document, also classified, was presented to President Gerald Ford, who had by then succeeded Nixon.

The study's executive summary began by declaring, "World Population growth since World War II is quantitatively and qualitatively different from any previous epoch in human history." The report's authors warned that the political consequences of rapid growth, including famines, internal and foreign migration, stagnating living standards, and increased urbanization, "are damaging to the internal stability and international relations of countries in whose advancement the U.S. is interested, thus creating political or even national security problems for the U.S."

"In a broader sense," it said, "there is a major risk of severe damage to world economic, political, and ecological systems and, as these systems begin to fail, to our humanitarian values."[93]

For the most part the report's recommendations tracked with what Ravenholt was already doing. It prevailed on the administration to try to assure full availability of birth control all over the world by 1980, and called for a substantial budget increase for population programs. It also urged support for expanded education and employment for women, and greater collaboration with the UN.

That was all very good, but the report made clear that not everyone thought voluntary programs sufficient. Under the heading "An Alternative View," the study explained the position, shared "by a growing number of experts...that the outlook is much harsher and far less tractable than commonly perceived.... The conclusion of this view is that mandatory programs may be needed and that we should be considering these possibilities now."[94]

Ultimately, though, the study's authors were aware that the perception of coercion would be harmful, and they recognized the danger that some developing country leaders would see pressure for family planning "as a form of economic or racial imperialism."[95] Indeed, to mollify world public opinion, it even recommended that the United States set an example and "announce a U.S. goal to maintain our present national average fertility no higher than replacement level and attain near stability by 2000."[96]

D espite this stance—and Ravenholt's own opposition to coercion—the reality on the ground could be murky at best. Faced with fertility goals and targets set from above, family planning workers from India to Indonesia cajoled, bribed, and sometimes forced people into accepting birth control, and even sterilization. All over the world birth control clinics were upgraded while other health facilities languished, dirty and run-down.

"I would visit these rural maternity clinics that were crumbling," recalled Sara Seims, who worked for USAID in Senegal. "And the only money I had was to refurbish one room for family planning. And the only medical personnel who had a nice clean uniform and equipment and electricity working was the family planning [practitioner]." The message to locals, she said, was that "the only thing we care about... is that you don't have so many babies."[97]

Seims saw how eager many women were for family planning. She'd ask some of them why they wanted to use birth control. "[A]lmost all of them said because they were tired," she said. "And I remember one woman pointing to her worn-out sandals, and she said to me in French, 'I feel like these shoes.'"[98]

Yet these women needed many other things as well, and programs that ignored those needs felt both callous and counterproductive. "[O]ne of the most important things I learned is, if you cared about women's reproductive health, you had to recognize that women didn't exist in a vacuum," she said. "They existed in a culture. They had families. You also had to care about the health of their children. You had to care about the health of their husbands, because 8 percent of the women in the villages we saw had gonorrhea."[99] Excessive fertility was a problem for many, but others were plagued by infertility wrought by rampant venereal disease. How could you ethically address one while ignoring the other?

All over the world women working in population control programs were having similar insights, and soon they would radically transform the field into one that attempted to change power relations as well as demographics. For a while the fiercest fight in global reproductive health wasn't between family planners and religious conservatives, but between those hewing to the population control paradigm and those for whom women's rights were paramount. Then a tide of religious opposition would shock both factions and push them back into an uneasy alliance.

CHAPTER 3: SISTERHOOD IS INTERNATIONAL

During the sweltering summer of 1970 a young woman named Adrienne Germain moved from Berkeley, California, where she'd been working toward a Ph.D. in sociology, to join her then husband in New York. Needing a job, she landed interviews at the Ford Foundation and Rockefeller's Population Council. At Ford she was told her marriage disqualified her. "You'll just work with us for a year or two and then you'll go and have babies," her interviewer said.[1] She had better luck at the Population Council, where she became a researcher in the field that she would eventually turn upside down.

Germain must have seemed like a natural fit for her new job. At Berkeley she'd been part of the Zero Population Growth movement, meeting at Stanford professor Paul Ehrlich's home for strategy sessions and giving speeches at schools and community centers. But population control had never been the point for her. As an undergraduate at Wellesley, where she was a classmate of Hillary Clinton's, Germain had spent six months working as a researcher on a study of urban growth in Lima, Peru. It was her first time out of the country, and it seared her. She'd rented a room in the house of a poor family whose father was so violent she had to barricade her door at night. The women she met in the country impressed her with their strength, but they were aged before their time, often subject to spousal rape and relentless battery. Many had suffered botched abortions. "[T]hey were going through the tortures of the damned as far as I could tell," she said. "And they weren't getting any family planning, that's for sure. I mean, it was a very strict Roman Catholic country. What options did they have? They had no health care for themselves and almost none for their kids, and that was just not fair. They were doing whatever they could to earn what little income they had."[2]

When she moved to Berkeley for graduate school, she quickly learned that the main source of international aid that might reach women like her Peruvian friends was population money, so she joined the movement. But she was always more interested in women's rights than in mere demographics, and at the Population Council she realized how much her agenda differed from that of her colleagues, who were almost all men. They never seemed to talk about women as people: They were always "contraceptive acceptors" or "postpartum cases." Not trusting women to use birth control correctly, they stressed long-term methods like IUDs and sterilization that took day-to-day decision making out of the clients' hands.

Other things angered her as well. There were good reasons for women in traditional societies to have lots of kids: They were sources of labor and insurance in old age. They could offer a woman pride and meaning, especially when nothing else did. Besides, even if women wanted smaller families—and some surely did, as evidenced by widespread illegal abortion—the ultimate decision often lay with their husbands. If they were going to control their fertility, they didn't just need contraceptives. They needed power.

Germain worried about the side effects of the IUD and birth control pills, which then used much higher doses of hormones than they do today, and were given without much thought to follow-up care. She hated the fact that the programs by their very nature did nothing to help women who were unable to have children. Infertility, after all, is a soul-crushing malady in countries where women's whole identity is bound up with motherhood, and one that is epidemic in some countries with poor health care and widespread sexually transmitted disease.

She also thought family planning programs should be offering access to safe abortion. "From my point of view," she said, "how could we morally ask women to take the risk of using contraception, of having fewer children, when clearly their life circumstances demanded that they have as many children [as] they could bear, and not enable a woman who had an unwanted pregnancy to end it?"[3]

Her argument points to a complicated, contentious issue in family planning. In societies where childbearing has never been regarded as a choice, where procreation is something to be celebrated or fatalistically accepted—but not controlled—introducing contraception is more than just a technological intervention. To be successful it entails a giant paradigm shift, a whole new conception of both human agency and ideal family size.

Thus, population programs always aimed to change culture as well as demographics. They produced posters featuring well-fed, well-dressed two-child families alongside bigger clans of scrawny paupers. In 1967, Walt Disney made a ten-minute animated family planning cartoon for the Population Council featuring Donald Duck, cheerful orchestra music, and a calmly authoritative voice explaining that "modern science has given us a tool that makes possible a new kind of personal freedom: family planning!" Translated into twenty-five languages, it first showed a happy farming family of five with enough to eat "and even a little left over, to provide money for some comforts and modern conveniences," symbolized by a picture of a radio. Then the same family appeared with six children, skinny and drawn, sitting miserably around a near empty bowl. The radio vanished from the screen. In such a family, said the narrator, "the children will be sickly and unhappy, with little hope for the future. And when the sons grow up the land will have to be divided into so many small pieces that no one will have enough."[4]

Such pop culture overtures continued for decades. In the 1980s one U.S.-funded agency, Population Communication Services, commissioned musicians—including Nigeria's King Sunny Ade—to sing songs celebrating family planning.[5] The organization got a Menudo-era Ricky Martin to perform in a video in the Philippines promoting an adolescent sex information hotline.

"The early family planning programs in the sixties and seventies especially did a lot of that public educational stuff," said Germain. "They trained journalists, they had billboards, they did all this media work—huge investments, actually. It was a massive social and behavioral change investment of a kind we had never before seen." Indeed, she pointed out, international family planning programs, especially those in Asia, became a paradigm of successful social engineering that would be studied in both university classrooms and on Madison Avenue.

But even as norms were changing and more women sought to have fewer children, contraceptives remained far from perfect. Having decided on smaller families, women were less inclined to simply accept unwanted pregnancies.

Thus, in some countries, the demand for abortion increased even as birth control became more popular. "[W]ithin particular populations, contraceptive prevalence and the incidence of induced abortion can and, indeed, often do rise in parallel, contrary to what one would expect," concluded an article in the journal *International Family Planning Perspectives*.

According to researchers Cicely Marston and John Cleland, in societies "that have not yet entered the fertility transition," people either want big families or don't consider childbearing "within the calculus of conscious choice," meaning there's little concept of "unwanted" pregnancies. They may have been overstating the case, since folk methods of contraception, as well as abortion and infanticide, have existed in many premodern cultures, suggesting a common desire to limit childbearing. Nevertheless, such control is imperfect at best, leading to a degree of fatalism about family size.

The introduction of modern contraception with its ideals of family planning tends to upend this resigned acceptance, spurring people to actively try and exert more control over their reproduction. "Thus," Marston and Cleland wrote, "as contraceptive prevalence rises and fertility starts to fall, an increasing proportion of couples want no more children (or want an appreciable delay before the next child), and exposure to the risk of unintended pregnancy also increases as a result."[6]

As the article showed, this correlation is only temporary; in most societies the use of effective birth control eventually becomes widespread enough to send abortion rates down. Nevertheless, in their early stages family planning programs weren't there for many women with unintended pregnancies—even though the very concept of an unintended pregnancy was one they'd help establish. (Not surprisingly, this isn't something most family planners like to discuss, since it seems to play right into the hands of their right-wing critics.)

Germain's frustration at the Population Council kept building, so when, in 1972, she got a recruiting call from the Ford Foundation—the same place that had written her off just two years earlier—she jumped at it. (The man who'd rejected her because she was married was still there. Ironically, she'd since been divorced.) At the time the Ford Foundation was one of the leading funders of international family planning programs, and once she was hired she wrote a memo critiquing the foundation's lack of attention to the circumstances of women's lives. Poor women, she argued, have very good reasons for having big families. If you want them to have fewer children, you need to give them more than contraception—you need to give them options, including education and employment. Her memo so impressed her bosses that they gave her a new job as a project specialist tasked with figuring out how to make the foundation's programs support women.

In 1973—the year she turned twenty-six—Germain used her own money and vacation time to travel to the Philippines and Pakistan to check out Ford Foundation programs. Filipino strongman Ferdinand Marcos had made population control a major priority, and officials at Ford were considering supporting a scheme that would financially reward plantation workers in Mindanao, a Muslim separatist community under military occupation, for having smaller families, and penalize them for having larger ones.

Such ideas had been in vogue for the previous few years. In 1969, Bernard Berelson, president of the Population Council, had published an influential article titled "Beyond Family Planning," which surveyed proposals for new approaches to reducing birthrates, including incentives, antinatalist taxes, and compulsory sterilization. Berelson rejected the more extreme ideas, although rather wanly: "The 'heavy' measures—involuntary means and political pressures—may be put aside for the time being, if not forever."[7]

Germain had been a strong critic of Berelson's piece, but the local Ford office didn't know that. Assuming she was onboard with her old boss's ideas, they arranged for her to be taken, with a military escort, to Mindanao in order to assess the feasibility of a proposed incentive scheme. She was driven around by a commander who was "just sexist, outright," she recalled, through an area where most people were living in a condition close to serfdom. The idea of bribing a captive minority population into having fewer children—and punishing them for having more—shocked her. "I was just so taken aback that anybody would even *think* of doing this kind of work in that kind of circumstance," she said. (In the end, Ford didn't get involved.)

"[T]hese scenes were to repeat themselves across my work life—in the northeast part of Brazil, which is one of the most impoverished areas of the world, actually, especially in those days, and of course in India and other countries," she said. "And again, I didn't have a problem with providing family planning to women, or even a problem with thinking about population growth as an issue, but I did feel very strongly that you could not treat any human beings in this way."[8]

From the Philippines she went to Pakistan. Trying to be culturally sensitive, she wore a burqa, which suffocated her. "You can't breathe, but more important than that, you have no peripheral vision, and what little you can see through the embroidered screen is such a distorted view of the world," she said. "And it became an image for me, a very physical, tangible image, of how restricted and constrained women's views and opportunities and voices are."[9]

R eturning to New York, Germain tried to pull her experiences together in an article; it was eventually published as an op-ed in the *New York Times* in August 1975. Titled "A Major Resource Awaiting Development: Women in the Third World," it began, "Who does the major part of the work in poor countries? Women do. Yet they are probably the most underrated economic resource in 'resource-poor' third world countries." Germain argued that helping women improve their economic productivity is key to fighting poverty. First-world governments and international organizations, she said, should "support women's organizations as a focal point for work, a source of credit, training, information and community power." They should "develop and distribute work-saving devices (such as wheelbarrows) to lighten the burden of work, and organize training programs in simple accounting, for example, to increase women's productivity."[10]

It's now conventional wisdom in development circles that the economic empowerment of women is key to fighting poverty and child mortality—and, in sub-Saharan Africa, to fighting HIV. At the time, though, these were radical ideas. The pioneering Danish economist Ester Boserup had published *Women's Role in Economic Development* in 1970, but much more needed to be learned. One of the tasks Germain set herself at Ford was generating just such research, contributing to the burgeoning new field of feminist economics. "We first documented that 80 percent of the agricultural production in sub-Saharan Africa comes from women, and they own 1 percent of the land," she said. "All those findings were generated in the 1970s."

In the years to come such work would contribute to fresh ways of looking at the distribution of resources within families. In the 1980s and 1990s new research on intrafamily economics would reveal that, contrary to conservative shibboleths, households aren't single economic units, with each member working toward the collective good. Instead, they're full of power struggles and competing interests, with the relative prestige of men and women determining whose needs will be met. When men control all the resources in a household, both their wives and their children tend to suffer. Women who can make financial decisions spend most of their money on their families, Germain explained, "whereas the expenditure surveys with men clearly document the leisure time, the cigarettes, the alcohol, the unnecessary clothes, like western-style shirts."[11]

Furthermore, women who work outside the home increase their status and their decision-making power *inside* it, as economists would make clear in the ensuing decades. "While women work long hours every day at home, since this work does not produce a remuneration it is often ignored in the accounting of the respective contributions of women and men in the family's joint prosperity," wrote the Nobel Prize–winning economist Amartya Sen in his 1999 book *Development as Freedom*. "When, however, the work is done outside the home and the employed woman earns a wage, her contribution to the family's prosperity is more visible. She also has more voice, because of being less dependent on others. The higher status of women even affects, it appears, ideas on the female child's 'due.'"[12]

Thus, the more agency women have, the more likely their children are to be taken care of, something clearly seen in the correlation between child survival and female literacy. "The extent to which maternal education has been identified as a major—or even the major—factor in determining child mortality is astonishing, although even this finding merely provides clues to the forces at work rather than a simple answer," the demographer John C. Caldwell wrote in 1990.[13] Common sense suggests that women who've been to school would have higher incomes and better access to health care information, but the effect of female education on children's health appears to go far beyond that. "There is compelling evidence that the impact of maternal education on child survival is not merely a case of learning more about health," Caldwell found. "The most important evidence is that it occurs everywhere: in good schools with good teachers who do teach about health and in poor schools with underqualified teachers who devote no time to the subject, as well as in every part of the Third World."

Caldwell's explanation for this is cultural as much as material. Women who have some education are more likely to demand family resources for their children, to have the confidence to take action when their children are sick, and to persist as long as the illness continues. If an uneducated woman does take her child to a doctor but doesn't see any subsequent improvement, she often won't report the problem to him, "partly on the grounds that she cannot tell an important man he has failed," Caldwell wrote.[14]

And, of course, educated women are more likely to use family planning, itself strongly correlated with declines in child mortality.[15] "In terms of policy analysis, there is much evidence now, based on intercountry comparisons as well as interregional contrasts within a large country, that women's empowerment (including female education, female employment opportunities and female property rights) and other social changes (such as mortality reduction) have a very strong effect in reducing fertility rate[s]," wrote Sen.[16]

Thus, the research Germain was involved in led to a new way of thinking about overpopulation—one that saw it as the symptom of women's oppression rather than as a crisis that trumped individual women's rights. Give women what they need to thrive, the new findings suggested, and they'd solve some of the world's most pressing problems.

While Germain was doing this work at Ford, Joan Dunlop was undertaking a similar investigation for John D. Rockefeller III. Raised outside of London, Dunlop was the rebellious daughter of a wealthy family. At twenty-one she ran away to the United States, living for a time in a Manhattan Salvation Army hostel, where she shared a room with the daughter of a Mississippi chicken farmer.[17] She never went to college, but, starting as a secretary at the Ford Foundation, she worked her way up through the public policy world, eventually serving in the administration of New York City mayor John Lindsay. In 1972 she was working as the assistant director of a small New York foundation when she got a call from Rockefeller's office asking her to lunch with him at the Algonquin.

It was the beginning of five months of interviews, after which Dunlop—

despite her total lack of experience in family planning, demographics, or international issues—was hired to head up Rockefeller's population interests. Why her? She's still not quite sure. "What he always said to me is, 'I wanted somebody outside the field, because the field needs new blood,'" she said. He had a sense that something was wrong in the population world but wasn't sure what it was.

He was also looking for someone who would care as much as he did about safe abortion. "When we talked about abortion he said, 'You won't fail me, will you?'" Dunlop recalled. "Meaning, you won't be equivocal about the abortion issue. And I then said there's no way, because I've had an illegal abortion, and let me tell you what it was about. And that point, I felt, was the deciding point for him."

She later found out that she almost didn't get the job because her bleached hair was considered too brassy. Nevertheless, once she was hired she was treated with deep respect. Her first week on the job, Rockefeller's wife visited her in her new office. "'I'm very glad to see you here,'" Dunlop recalled her saying. "'I've wanted him to have a woman on his staff for many, many years, for a long time. But I want to say to you that you must tell him the truth. He's not being told the truth. And in order for you to tell him the truth, you must consider yourself to be his equal.'"[18]

For her first assignment Rockefeller asked Dunlop to spend a year immersing herself in the population milieu in order to figure out what was wrong with it. She was to talk to everyone, go to all the meetings she could, read the literature. Once women in the field realized what Dunlop was doing, they started sending her anonymous notes telling her about the sexism they encountered at work. "It just reconfirmed for me that the personal was political," she said. Meanwhile, when Dunlop listened to Population Council technocrats talk, she was aghast at the way women were reduced to their wombs. Women's lives, she said, "why women have children, or what the rationale for it [may be], or what they felt, or were their concerns, never came into it at all, ever."[19]

Soon Dunlop heard about a young woman at the Ford Foundation with similar interests, and she invited Adrienne Germain out for Chinese food. Germain impressed her deeply. "She had her finger right on it, as far as I was concerned," said Dunlop. "And then I went back to Mr. Rockefeller, and I said, 'There's a problem. This is the problem. The [population] field was shot through with unintended sexism and racism, and there was a stranglehold on money and ideas, and it's held by six people.'" Chief among the culprits was Rei Ravenholt, who controlled more money than anyone else.[20]

Part of Dunlop's problem with Ravenholt was personal. His lascivious sense of humor alternately exasperated and enraged many of his female colleagues. "I mean, I found Rei Ravenholt totally unacceptable, as an American, as somebody who was representing the United States in the international arena," Dunlop said several decades later. "In villages, I mean, forget it. This was the Ugly American, as far as I was concerned. And to me it seemed so defeating. Here we were trying to help—we were trying to do something about development. And we had this man who was in such a powerful position who was such an embarrassment.... These guys had no respect for women. None. At least, that's how I felt at the time.... In retrospect, I'm sure that wasn't fair."[21]

The dispute went deeper than Ravenholt's personal style, though. Dunlop and Germain objected to what they saw as his agency's single-minded focus on preventing births. At the time one focus of USAID's programs was offering IUDs to women who had just delivered babies in hospitals. That might sound reasonable: Such women are obviously sexually active, probably didn't want to get pregnant again right away, and may have no other contact with the health system.

But imagining herself in the women's place, Germain was disturbed. Most women in poor countries don't go to public health facilities when they're in labor unless something has gone horribly wrong. After going through a hellish experience, these women needed attention to their immediate health and that of their newborn, if he or she had survived. Inserting an IUD immediately after a difficult labor seemed unthinkable. "Anybody with any common sense, knowing what birth is about, would think, you know, the IUD probably isn't appropriate," Germaine said. "What maybe they should try to do would be to ensure that she came back for one-month and three-month checkups, and at the three-month checkup, or maybe even one month, you could talk to her and say, 'Look, if you don't want to conceive again soon, then don't count on amenorrhea to protect you. We can give you condoms. We can give you whatever if you're still breastfeeding.'"[22]

There were other general problems with IUD programs. Women suffering side effects, including heavy bleeding and cramps, sometimes had trouble getting their IUDs removed, either because of the resistance of target-obsessed family planning workers or because they simply didn't have access to professional health care after the initial insertion. Others left them in past the five-year expiration mark for similar reasons.

In the early 1970s USAID distributed Dalkon Shield IUDs, devices that were later shown to slice through the uterine wall and conduct dangerous bacteria into the uterus, to dozens of countries. A *Mother Jones* investigation documented how in 1972 Dalkon Shield manufacturer A. H. Robins Company arranged to sell bulk, unsterilized packages of the IUDs to USAID just as the company was learning how hazardous they were. Eventually, after contentious FDA hearings—and the deaths of seventeen American women—domestic sales of the Dalkon Shield were suspended, and USAID issued an international recall.

There was, of course, no way to get the word out to remote villages. "When the recall order was issued in 1975, AID could hope to recover stocks of unused devices from the warehouses and storage rooms of major international agencies, like the International Planned Parenthood Federation," wrote *Mother Jones* reporters Barbara Ehrenreich, Mark Dowie, and Stephen Minkin. "But it could not, despite any number of memos, recall the AID-supplied Shields from the approximately 440,000 women already using the device. Nor could it hope to recover the thousands of Shields lying in the drawers of countless private practitioners and tiny rural family planning clinics."

In 1979, when the *Mother Jones* article came out, Ravenholt was still defending A. H. Robins Company. "Robins didn't know there was any problem with it in 1972," he told the magazine, dismissing early reports of adverse reactions. "You don't really know anything until you have a very, very large number of people who have used it. You might have one kind of impression from 10,000 people, another from 100,000. You might need a million—10 million—before you really know."

Ehrenreich, Dowie, and Minkin noted acidly, "You might, in other words, need a few medium-size nations to experiment on."[23]

Ravenholt and his allies weren't entirely callous, but to them the macro-scale specter of overpopulation obscured concern about individuals. As they understood it, family planning had the potential to save millions of lives—more lives than any other intervention they could imagine. It had to be done as economically and on as wide a scale as possible. People in the field, said Malcolm Potts, fall into two groups: "There's one group which is sincerely regulated by human beings' sufferings, and talks about rights and individuals' stories, and another group, to which Rei Ravenholt and I and other people belong, . . . that has a sense of scale, that says a million people suffering is worse than a thousand people suffering."

It was precisely this kind of cold demographic utilitarianism that would come under increasing attack in the years to come. Rockefeller, erstwhile stalwart of the population control movement, fired one of the first salvos.

Launching a drive to raise awareness of overpopulation worldwide, the United Nations declared 1974 World Population Year. The highlight was to be a world conference on population, to be held in Bucharest, Romania, that August.* As U.S. representative at the UN, George H. W. Bush encouraged both initiatives. The United States hoped the Bucharest meeting, the largest UN gathering ever convened, would convince recalcitrant nations of the urgency of population control. Diplomats were unprepared for the fierce skepticism of developing countries, though perhaps they shouldn't have been—this was, after all, a period of powerful third world solidarity, in many ways the first iteration of the anti-globalization movement. Led by Algeria and Argentina, poor countries banded together and argued that if there was a looming demographic problem, its root cause was an unjust global economic order. China called the idea of a population explosion a "false alarm" designed to foster imperial exploitation.[24] Brazil insisted that rapid population growth was necessary to transform itself into a world power.[25] Other countries rallied around the slogan "development is the best contraceptive," and tried to use the meeting to press for economic concessions from the United States and Europe. Even India, a country long concerned about its own population growth, sided with the developing nations. The *New York Times* characterized the struggle as one of "Marx vs. Malthus."[26]

In addition to the main conference, a parallel "Population Tribune" gathered nine hundred activists, students, academics, feminists, NGO representatives,

---

* Romania was a brutally ironic choice for a host country. Under the dictator Nicolae Ceausescu, who outlawed abortion and contraception in 1966, it was a kind of pronatalist police state, where women were subject to random gynecological exams and all miscarriages were investigated. According to scholars Barbara Crane and Jason Finkle, the United Nations hoped that holding the conference in a communist country would help to win over the nations of the Eastern bloc.

and miscellaneous gadflies in a sweltering university building nearby. (Such parallel meetings would become the norm at future UN conferences, turning them, in the words of one diplomat, into latter-day medieval trade fairs.) Betty Friedan showed up, as did Margaret Mead and Germaine Greer, who would eventually become one of the fiercest feminist critics of population programs. (The World Plan of Action, Greer announced, regarded women as baby factories, the only difference from other factories being that they were being asked to cease production.[27])

Rockefeller spoke to the tribune on the conference's seventh day. Many were expecting him to affirm the Malthusian American position. Instead, invoking his onetime belief in population control, he announced, "I have changed my mind.

"The evidence has been mounting, particularly in the last decade, that family planning alone is not adequate," he said. The old population establishment was shocked. He continued with a call for greater attention to social and economic development, especially for women.

> As long as the social status and economic security of women throughout the world depend largely on the number of children they have, as long as development programs that do reach women deal with them largely or solely in their roles as mothers, they will have good reason to continue having many children.... In my opinion, if we are to make genuine progress in economic and social development, if we are to make progress in achieving population goals, women increasingly must have greater freedom of choice in determining their roles in society.[28]

The speech, said Germain, was "world-shaking" in the population field. She was proud; she had written most of it. Charged with crafting Rockefeller's remarks, Dunlop had invited Germain and Germain's future husband, Steve Salyer, to collaborate. They'd penned draft and after draft and had countless meetings with Rockefeller, often over lunch at his Rainbow Room restaurant. During those meetings Germain spoke about the women she'd known in Peru and told Rockefeller about the problems she'd faced at the Population Council. All this made its way, indirectly, into the speech.

Ravenholt was in Bucharest, and he was livid. "The essence of that speech was that family planning had failed," he said. "Dunlop must have been quite persuasive for him to say that, because he really had much better sense than that. It was really sad, because his going along with Joan Dunlop and saying that was counter to everything he'd been doing for years."

But Ravenholt's time in the field would soon come to an end. A promiscuous maker of enemies, he'd managed the neat trick of enraging both the Catholic right and the feminist left, and when the Carter administration took over in 1976, he soon found himself isolated. His strategy of contraceptive inundation, while showing success in some parts of the world, had already been judged a spectacular failure in Pakistan. "Small children here have discovered that condoms paid for by the U.S. government make wonderful holiday balloons," began a 1978 *Washington Post* story. "It's about the only use they're put to." Despite millions of dollars and a flood of contraceptives, the story reported, Pakistan's birthrate had *increased* since 1960. A USAID official quoted in the piece said, "There's never been a failure in population as large as this one."[29]

So Ravenholt was vulnerable. When Carter came in, he made Sander Levin the assistant administrator at USAID. Those who worked with Levin sensed that he had orders to get rid of Ravenholt, who had no intention of going meekly.[30] Levin asked for his resignation, Ravenholt refused, and several years of bureaucratic warfare ensued. Eventually Ravenholt was demoted. He fought hard against losing control of his program, spending upward of fifty thousand dollars on a legal challenge before the government's Merit System Protection Board before finally giving up and taking a job in the Centers for Disease Control. Soon he went to the National Institute on Drug Abuse to pursue his early interest in the dangers of smoking.

An even greater blow to the population control orthodoxy came from reports of terrible abuses in India and China. First was the revelation of widespread compulsory sterilization during the Indian "emergency" that began in 1975, when civil liberties were suspended and Prime Minister Indira Gandhi ruled by decree. The horrors of the mass vasectomy campaign organized by Gandhi's younger son, Sanjay Gandhi, are well known, their trauma immortalized in novels such as Salman Rushdie's *Midnight's Children* and

Rohinton Mistry's *A Fine Balance*. Obsessed with overpopulation and modernization, thirty-year-old Sanjay Gandhi mobilized all levels of government to meet ever-escalating sterilization targets. Uttar Pradesh's chief secretary telegraphed his subordinates: "Inform everybody that failure to achieve monthly targets will not only result in the stoppage of salaries but also suspension and severest penalties. Galvanise entire administrative machinery forthwith repeat forthwith and continue to report daily progress by crash wireless to me and secretary to Chief Minister."[31]

Millions of men were bribed, threatened, or physically forced into vasectomy camps. One story in the *Indian Express* described what happened to a Muslim village that resisted: "At 3 a.m. on November 6, the villagers of Uttawar were shaken from their sleep by loudspeakers ordering the menfolk—all above 15—to assemble at the bus-stop on the main NuhHodol road. When they emerged, they found the whole village surrounded by the police. With the menfolk on the road, the police went into the village to see if anyone was hiding....As the villagers tell it, the men on the road were sorted out into eligible cases...and about 400 were taken...to clinics to be sterilized."[32]

When democracy returned to India in 1977, such abuses led Indians to sweep Gandhi's Congress Party from power for the first time since independence.

In the following decade still worse abuses would be reported in China. Though some still refused to see it, it was becoming clear that demographic targets, once blandly accepted by pillars of the American establishment, could be tools of tyranny. The emergency, said Germain, was "a profound indicator of what can go so wrong if you only look at demographic control goals and don't understand the human dimensions."

Plenty of people continued to do exactly that. Still, in the United States, the family planning field was slowly being remade in Dunlop and Germain's image. In 1976, the Population Council needed a new president, and at Dunlop's suggestion Rockefeller chose George Zeidenstein, the former head of the Peace Corps in South Asia and someone who was onboard with the feminist critique of population control. Franklin Thomas, a liberal-minded man raised in poverty by a widowed mother from the West Indies, became the new president at the Ford Foundation, and he ordered a massive review of the way the foundation's programs affected women. Soon there was a specific budget for women's programs and staffers specializing in women's issues in country offices. And in 1981 Germain, then thirty-two, was sent to run the Ford Foundation's office in Bangladesh.

Right away Germain started making grants to groups that were getting family planning money from USAID but needed additional resources to give pregnant women and their children other kinds of care. After several months she got an infuriating letter from someone in the USAID mission asking her to stop, apparently because he felt the new programs were distracting NGO workers from the more important work of birth control.

Germain didn't limit herself to health care; she also overhauled the agriculture program to make it more supportive of women. Most donors were pouring money into staple grains like rice and wheat, and Germain saw that no one was supporting the women who processed the food, grew secondary crops in their home gardens, and raised chickens. Several years earlier she'd gotten to know Muhammad Yunus, the Bangladeshi economist who would win the Nobel Prize in 2006. In her new posting she helped him get an eight-hundred-thousand-dollar Ford grant to expand his nascent Grameen Bank, which would become famous for demonstrating the symbiotic relationship between women's economic power, their rights, and the development of their communities.

Yunus had recognized the connection between women's oppression and poverty. When he started Grameen Bank, women made up less than 1 percent of bank borrowers. "The banking system was created for men," he said.[33] He set an ambitious goal: He wanted half of Grameen's clients to be women. This focus had a great deal to do with his success. "The more money we lent to poor women, the more I realized that credit given to a woman brings about change faster than when given to a man," he wrote.[34] He found that women worked harder, spent more of their earnings on their children, and repaid loans more reliably. By 2007, 97 percent of the bank's 7.27 million borrowers were women.

Family planning is part of the Grameen Bank credo. Though it is motivated by women's well-being rather than by population control, it has proven to be far more successful at the latter than the neo-Malthusian policies of previous decades. Women involved with the bank use family planning at twice the national rate, and their birthrate is well below the national average. "Once they have increased their incomes through self-employment, Grameen borrowers show remarkable determination to have fewer children, educate the ones they have, and participate actively in our democracy," wrote Yunus.[35]

Unlike Pakistan, Bangladesh as a whole has experienced a sharp drop in fertility, from 6.3 children per woman in the early 1970s to 3.3 in the mid-nineties.[36] During that time contraceptive use increased dramatically, from 3 percent of married women to 40 percent.[37] Amartya Sen connects these trends to such organizations as the Grameen Bank and the Bangladesh Rural Advancement Committee, or BRAC, another microlender with a focus on female empowerment. "[T]he sharp decline in fertility rate that has occurred in Bangladesh in recent years seems to have clear connections with the increasingly higher involvement of women in social and economic affairs, in addition to much greater availability of family planning facilities, even in rural Bangladesh," he wote.[38]

None of this means that contraceptive supply—Ravenholt's obsession—doesn't matter. It just means that supply alone is not enough. Indeed, for all her differences with Ravenholt, Germain will always be grateful to him for developing the manual vacuum aspiration syringe and for getting birth control commodities into the developing world. "Even though I had criticisms about the way he made them available, the fact was that AID leadership in getting contraceptives out was enormous," she said. The MVA syringe proved especially important in Bangladesh, where Germain helped support a pioneering abortion clinic run by Sandra Kabir, who would become a major figure in the global reproductive health movement.

Like many countries in the developing world, Bangladesh's government took a deliberately ambiguous approach to abortion rights. It retained the British colonial law banning abortion, but it allowed a procedure widely called menstrual regulation. Performed with an MVA kit, menstrual regulation is essentially an early abortion, but it's spoken of as a cure for a late period or, in the local vernacular, as a "wash." No pregnancy test is done.

The practice was first introduced in 1972, in the aftermath of the civil war that led to Bangladesh's independence. The Pakistani army had used mass rape as a weapon of war against Bangladesh; hundreds of thousands of women were systematically violated in a campaign the feminist writer Susan Brownmiller has compared to the Rape of Nanking. "Girls of eight and grandmothers of seventy-five had been sexually assaulted during the nine-month repression," she wrote in her classic history of rape, *Against Our Will*. "Pakistani soldiers had not only violated Bengali women on the spot; they abducted tens of hundreds and held them by force in their military barracks for nightly use. The women were kept naked to prevent their escape. In some of the camps, pornographic movies were shown to the soldiers, 'in an obvious attempt to work the men up,' one Indian writer reported.' "[39]

This rape offensive left around twenty-five thousand women pregnant. Their revulsion at their pregnancies was compounded by the certainty that if they gave birth both they and their children would be ostracized. Mother Teresa opened her convent's doors to those who wanted to put their babies up for adoption, but few were interested. Instead, many resorted to crude self-administered abortions, suicide, or infanticide.[40]

These atrocities marked the first time that systematic rape in war received widespread international attention. Merle Goldberg, an American journalist turned abortion rights activist—she had opened one of the first legal outpatient abortion clinics in the United States, in New York City, a couple of years earlier, and was close to Harvey Karman—wanted to do something. At her instigation the International Planned Parenthood Federation arranged to send a team, including Karman and Malcolm Potts, to Bangladesh to perform abortions and train local medical workers to do them as well. At the time Karman was free on bail in the United States, having been arrested for performing illegal abortions in California, but Bangladeshi prime minister Mujibur Rahman welcomed him and publicly urged women to take advantage of his services.[41]

Karman's team set up a temporary clinic in an abandoned house in Dhaka, and women came from as far as two hundred miles away seeking help.[42] Using a Red Cross helicopter the providers traveled all over the country, distributing thousands of MVA kits and teaching health workers how to use them. At one point Mother Teresa showed up at Karman's hotel room to lecture him, but he and his colleagues were otherwise received with gratitude. Some patients at the Dhaka clinic even trained to become providers themselves.[43]

Goldberg went on to coordinate a similar effort in Cyprus, responding to the widespread rape accompanying the Turkish invasion in 1974. A few years later she turned her attention back to Bangladesh, traveling to Dhaka to investigate the possibility of opening menstrual regulation clinics in the country. She was staying at the Ford Foundation guesthouse in Dhaka when she met Sandra Kabir, who would later describe her as "an older sister and a mother rolled in one."[44]

The daughter of a Bangladeshi father and an English mother, Kabir was raised in England until she was thirteen, and she had never adjusted to the passivity that was expected of women in her father's country. Headstrong and passionate, she eloped as a teenager, only to find herself trapped in a conservative Muslim family in a provincial town; the young man she'd been madly in love with was revealed as a violent and domineering thug. After nine terrible years she was finally ready to leave her husband when she found herself pregnant. She went to a government-funded model clinic, had a termination, and emerged as a fierce advocate for choice. That same year she joined Family Planning International Assistance (FPIA), a USAID-funded arm of Planned Parenthood, as an administrative assistant. Within a couple of months she was promoted to program officer.

Yet even before Reagan came to power, political forces in the United States were pushing USAID to cut off funding for agencies that performed abortions. Unlike Catholics, most evangelicals had not initially been much concerned with abortion (Jesse Helms was an exception). The origin myth of the Christian right holds that it rose up in outrage over *Roe v. Wade*, but as Columbia historian Randall Balmer has shown, that story isn't true. Conservative evangelicals first started organizing politically in the early 1970s in response to government efforts to revoke the tax-exempt status of private, whites-only Christian schools. When *Roe* was decided, wrote Balmer, "the vast majority of evangelical leaders said virtually nothing about it; many of those who did comment actually applauded the decision."[45]

As the 1970s progressed, though, and the feminist movement became more powerful in the United States, abortion emerged as a tangible symbol of women's emancipation and the declining authority of the patriarchal family.

The Protestant right developed a deep concern for fetal life and formed an alliance with Catholic conservatives that would shape American politics for the next three decades. As a synecdoche for American social chaos, abortion was a powerful political motivator. With *Roe* the law of the land, though, there was little that politicians could do for their pro-life constituents at home (though eventually some would figure out ways to chip away at abortion rights through various regulations and restrictions).

Internationally, however, there was more scope for action. By 1979, congressional restrictions forced USAID to stop supporting NGOs involved in menstrual regulation. "Even if it was a referral, they would no longer get USAID funding. And that *outraged* me," Kabir said.[46] Such a restriction would be unconstitutional in the United States, since it would interfere with free speech, but Bangladeshi women weren't protected by the American constitution.

Angry as she was, it fell to Kabir to implement the new policy, making sure that no organization getting grants from her group had anything to do with menstrual regulation. Soon there wasn't a single NGO performing safe abortions in the whole country.

One day, as Kabir was railing against the new American policy, Goldberg suggested that she start her own clinic. "I said yeah, where's the money coming from?" Kabir recalled. "She said, 'I'll get it for you.'" Goldberg went to the Population Crisis Committee, which agreed to support the new venture for the first year.

There were several hundred manual abortion kits at Kabir's old office, and the staff there was desperate to get rid of them lest an auditor spot them and report them to Washington. So Kabir took them, and with Goldberg's help she set up shop opposite one of the most prominent USAID-funded family planning clinics in Dhaka, which made surreptitious referrals. She called her clinic the Bangladesh Women's Health Coalition, after a group Goldberg had formed in the United States called the National Women's Health Coalition (later changed to the International Women's Health Coalition). Soon Kabir's organization was training government health workers to provide safe abortions at the local level all over the country. As so many women worldwide would, she was able to take American population-control resources and turn them into instruments of liberation.

Bangladeshi women, of course, needed much more than reproductive rights. "Women were telling us, look, you're providing us safe abortion services, you're providing us family planning, what about the basic health of our children? We want our children to be immunized," Kabir said.[47] So the Bangladesh Women's Health Coalition started an immunization program. Her clients told her how humiliated they were when they had to sign documents with a thumbprint, so she started adult literacy classes. Many of the women wanted to start small businesses, so she referred them to the Grameen Bank and other microfinance groups. They were eager to know what their rights were, so the coalition started legal aid services and legal education classes. "Whatever program the coalition did was because women wanted it," she said.[48] Within a year she opened a second clinic in the capital. More than a dozen more followed throughout the country.

Clients paid on a sliding scale. For many of them, their experience at the clinic was the first time anyone had ever offered them attention as individuals. Indeed, often the women were so used to being referred to simply as someone's daughter, wife, or mother that they had to think for a moment when asked their own names. "If you look at women in Bangladesh, it's such an enlightenment for them to have time alone with someone who is focused on them, who cares about their concerns, who is helping them," said Kabir. "You can actually literally see the self-confidence rise in these women. For them to understand and accept that they are an individual who has value. Because so often they didn't see that. They thought they were an appendage of their father or their husband."

Eventually, after a Ford Foundation survey found that botched abortions were responsible for almost 40 percent of maternal deaths in Bangladesh, Germain convinced her superiors to allocate $750,000 to support menstrual regulation in that country. The Swedish government contributed as well. The Bangladesh program, Germain said, "became a lasting example of how countries with very strict abortion laws can nonetheless recognize women's need for this service and find a way to provide it through a government system, including through mid-level health care workers who are not medical doctors."[49]

John D. Rockefeller III was killed in a car accident in upstate New York in July 1978. For Dunlop it was the greatest heartbreak of her life, and it cast her adrift professionally, since she was widely distrusted as a radical within the population field. Another blow followed—she was diagnosed with breast cancer. She spent a year fighting it; then, looking for a job that was "nontoxic" and free of the controversy and competition of the population world, she went to work for the New York Public Library. Dunlop was happy there, but after two years her mounting rage at the Reagan administration began impelling her to rejoin the fray.

Just then she got a call from Anne Murray, a grant-maker at the Northern California–based William and Flora Hewlett Foundation, which was giving away some of the fortune William Hewlett had amassed as a cofounder of the technology giant Hewlett-Packard. The Hewlett foundation had always been concerned with population and women's issues, and Murray saw the need for an organization to keep the issue of safe abortion alive internationally during Reagan's tenure. She wanted to channel the effort through Goldberg's International Women's Health Coalition, but only if Goldberg herself—an "impossible, energetic, and deeply committed maverick," in Dunlop's words, but a terrible manager—surrendered the reins. It was Murray's idea to bring in Dunlop, who agreed on the condition that Germain be brought back from Bangladesh to work with her. " 'I think we should go back to the coven, take over this organization, and see what we can do with it," Dunlop told her old friend.[50] Germain was coming up on four years in Dhaka, which was as long as most country officers stayed. She agreed to return to the United States in 1985.

The organization Dunlop inherited was a mess: There was no staff, no files, no accounting, and no money. She essentially had to create it from scratch, and as she proceeded it became clear that in addition to battling the old-fashioned population controllers, she'd have to learn to fight an entirely different antagonist. "It was then, for the first time in these international conferences, we began to see the right-to-life activity in opposition to our work," she said.[51]

R eagan's election had created a total turnaround in the politics of family planning. He won the presidency with the help of the religious right, which would now have more clout than ever before. As the movement gained in power throughout the 1970s, Carter, a born-again Christian who had been elected with the support of newly politicized evangelicals, had made some foreign policy concessions to antiabortion forces, but family planning itself retained broad bipartisan support. Serious opposition to population programs was mainly centered in the Vatican and the far left. That would all change when Reagan took over.

The new administration's hostility to international family planning programs came from two distinct ideological directions. Most obviously, Reagan was deeply enmeshed with an ascendant religious movement fiercely opposed to abortion and feminism and profoundly hostile to the United Nations, which had been long associated in evangelical lore with the anti-Christ. At the same time, while social conservatives provided the political impetus to reverse America's long-standing support of international family planning, a new breed of so-called supply-side demographers cloaked Reagan's population policy in intellectual legitimacy. These secular economic libertarians, many of whom were not actual demographers, objected to what they saw as the environmental hysteria and taste for social engineering underlying the whole population control project.

By the time Reagan was elected, the success of the "green revolution" had made the problem of rapid population growth seem less urgent. For several decades the Rockefeller and Ford foundations had poured money into developing high-yield crops for farmers in poor countries, an initiative that would revolutionize agriculture in Latin America and Asia. Combining new, more efficient breeds of wheat, rice, and corn with modern irrigation methods and chemical fertilizer, the green revolution vastly increased food output throughout the world. The Iowa-born agronomist Norman Borlaug, called the father of the green revolution, won the Nobel Peace Prize in 1970 for his work on the subcontinent, where his innovations led to dramatically enlarged harvests that staved off the mass starvation so many had feared.[52]

Thanks to these developments the alarming scenarios of the cold war neo-Malthusians never came to pass. Borlaug never believed that they made concern about overpopulation—what he called the "Population Monster"—obsolete. "[T]he frightening power of human reproduction must also be curbed; otherwise the success of the green revolution will be ephemeral only," he said in his Nobel lecture.[53] To the supply-side demographers, though, it seemed that human ingenuity would always outpace human need.

Perhaps the most well-known of these thinkers was Julian Simon, a polymathic professor of business administration and a fellow at the conservative Heritage Foundation. Simon's quirky oeuvre included books such as *How to Start and Operate a Mail-Order Business* and *Good Mood: The New Psychology of Overcoming Depression,* but it was his contrarian work on population that made him famous. In his 1981 best seller, *The Ultimate Resource,* he made the optimistic argument that population growth *increases* wealth by increasing the supply of human inventiveness. "It is a simple fact that the source of improvements in productivity is the human mind, and a human mind is seldom found apart from a human body," he wrote. "And because improvements—their invention and their adoption—come from people, it seems reasonable to assume that the amount of improvement depends on the number of people available to use their minds."[54]

Taking aim at one of the central premises of environmentalism, Simon argued that the earth's resources are essentially inexhaustible. One chapter was titled "Can the Supply of Natural Resources Really Be Infinite? Yes!" Another was "When Will We Run Out of Energy? Never!" His bête noir was Paul Ehrlich, with his predictions of imminent environmental doom. In 1980 the two men made a notorious bet. Simon wagered one thousand dollars that the price of five metals would be lower a decade hence, an indication that, contrary to what a Malthusian might predict, they weren't becoming scarce. To the infinite glee of conservatives, Ehrlich took him up on it, and ten years later had to send his nemesis a check.*

Yet while Simon was clearly right about a few things—and the hyperbolic Ehrlich wrong about a great many—much of what he wrote was technolibertarian sophistry. He made astounding arguments against the conservation of energy or ecosystems. "When we use resources, then, we ought to ask whether our present use is at the expense of future generations," he wrote. "The answer

---

* Ehrlich might have had his revenge had Simon agreed to a second bet. In 1995, Simon wrote in the *San Francisco Chronicle,* "Every measure of material and environmental welfare in the United States and in the world has improved rather than deteriorated. All long-run trends point in exactly the opposite direction from the projections of the doomsayers." He offered to stake one thousand dollars against "any wrong-headed doomster" on "any trend pertaining to material human welfare." Ehrlich and his Stanford colleague Stephen Schneider proposed a wager that global warming, greenhouse gases, fishery depletion, deforestation, AIDS deaths, and income inequality would all be worse within ten years. Going back on his challenge, Simon refused.

is a straightforward *no*. If the relative prices of natural resources can be expected to be lower for future generations than for us now…this implies that future generations will be faced by no greater economic scarcity than we are, but instead will have just as large or larger supplies of resources to tap, despite our present use of them."[55]

Such ideas were risible to the vast majority of experts, but members of the Reagan administration embraced them. Simon became an adviser to James Buckley, undersecretary of state for security assistance, science, and technology (and brother of conservative eminence William F. Buckley Jr.), who soon tried to zero out family planning assistance. Secretary of State Alexander Haig quickly killed that idea. "Do you all know why alligators stomp on their eggs?" Haig reportedly asked during one meeting. "Because otherwise they'd be up to their asses in alligators."[56] Soon Buckley was pushed out, and he went to work at Radio Free Europe in Germany.

Having failed in their frontal attack, right-wingers in the administration worked to undermine international family planning from within—a pattern that would repeat itself with even more intensity during the administration of George W. Bush. First, hard-liners seeded USAID and the State Department with ideological operatives hostile to both abortion and contraception, and they channeled family planning grants to religious groups that shared their views.

In 1983, a group called the Family of the Americas Foundation was brought in to brief foreign aid officials in the main State Department auditorium. The outfit was the American affiliate of WOOMB, or the World Organization of the Ovulation Method Billings, which advocates a method of natural family planning developed by married Australian doctors John and Evelyn Billings in which women measure changes in their cervical mucus to determine their fertile periods. At the State Department, the Family of the Americas Foundation proposed setting up billboards outside of third world capitals reading: "When you're wet, a baby you will get. When you're dry, the sperm they will die."

Attending officials were skeptical. One asked how the Billings method would work for women whose husbands came home drunk and demanded sex. The foundation's answer: The woman could try sleeping at her mother-in-law's house or, failing that, she could give her husband money to hire a prostitute.[57]

In June 1984, over the unanimous objection of the professional staff at USAID, the Family of the Americas Foundation received a grant of $1.1 million. It wasn't an enormous amount of money by USAID standards, but it represented the beginning of a shift toward faith-based rather than evidence-based population policy, which would reach critical mass during the George W. Bush administration.

Agency staffers tried to make the foundation adhere to their "informed choice" guidelines, which required providers to offer information about other forms of birth control and, if requested, to make referrals. Refusing to submit to the rules other grantees operated under, a number of right-wing Catholic groups launched vehement protests—the Catholic League for Religious and Civil Rights even threatened to sue. Responding to these complaints, White House public liaison director Faith Whittlesey wrote a letter to foreign aid director Peter McPherson complaining that the guidelines could "affect the president's credibility with the pro-life movement which has been so supportive." She urged him not to let any conflict develop between "the administration's pro-life policies and its population assistance policies."[58]

Soon after, McPherson got phone calls from Vice President George Bush and Secretary of State George Shultz. Mercedes Arzú Wilson, the flamboyant head of the Family of the Americas Foundation, had recently visited both of them. Congressman Henry Hyde, one of her patrons in the GOP, had accompanied her on her visit to see Bush.

A consultant to the Vatican's Pontifical Council for the Family, Wilson came from a powerful family in Guatemala: Her brother, Álvaro Arzú, became the country's president in 1996. "She would come in wearing about six pounds of gold and start talking about representing developing women of the world," recalled Duff Gillespie, who was then deputy director of the Office of Population. "She was crazy as hell," he said, and "would say things that were not only outrageous and untrue, but that were *so* outrageous and *so* untrue that any rational person she was talking to *knew* they were outrageous and untrue."

But she had the support of the White House. Under pressure from above, McPherson capitulated, exempting Wilson's group from the guidelines.

After a media uproar, Congress, then divided between a Democratic House and a Republican Senate, put an amendment in an appropriations bill reinstating informed choice. It was a small victory, but the Family of the Americas Foundation kept getting government grants. Meanwhile, USAID funded international antiabortion conferences in Paris and Caracas, where speakers from around the globe excoriated family planning, feminism, and secularism. Frank Ruddy, a Texas antiabortion activist whom Reagan made assistant USAID administrator for Africa, sent the Billingses on a taxpayer-funded speaking tour of the continent. On a Tanzania radio show they warned listeners that anyone using contraception would go "straight to hell."[59]

Pro–family planning officials in Washington were systematically harassed. Richard Benedick, the State Department's coordinator for population affairs, suspected one political appointee of stealing documents out of his secretary's printer and leaking them to right-wing pressure groups. The personal campaign against Benedick was particularly vicious. He was a career foreign service official who considered himself a conservative in the old, antiradical sense of the word. A graduate of Harvard Business School, he'd been posted to both Iran and Pakistan, where he worked on economic policy. One day in 1984, when he was back in D.C., someone handed him a photocopied article published by the American Life Lobby, a grassroots, militant antiabortion group, headlined, "SPECIAL WARNING TO ALL ISLAMIC PRO-LIFERS: *These men are dangerous to your health!*" Benedick, it said, was probably "the single most dangerous anti-life official in the Reagan administration.... A career foreign service officer, he served in the U.S. Embassy in Tehran during the reign of the late Shah, whose imposition of U.S.-devised population control schemes upon the Iranian people was a major grievance in his downfall."

"This was 1984, when people were being kidnapped in Beirut," Benedick said. He asked for an armed escort from the State Department and spoke to a lawyer about suing for libel. He was told that as a public figure he didn't have much of a chance.

At the time, Benedick was preparing for the 1984 International Conference on Population in Mexico City, the follow-up to the Bucharest meeting a decade earlier, where Rockefeller had spoken so eloquently about the central importance of women's rights. The American Life Lobby article ended by warning that sending him as part of the U.S. delegation "would be like sending Adolph [sic] Eichmann to a holocaust memorial gathering."[60] It was not particularly surprising, of course, that the antiabortion movement was comparing family planning to genocide. It was surprising, though, that they singled out Benedick, an otherwise fairly obscure figure, showing just how fixated they were on even the arcane details of American population policy.

As it happened, the American Life Lobby got its wish. Ronald Reagan always met with antiabortion groups on the anniversary of *Roe v. Wade,* and in 1983 they added a new demand to their customary list: They wanted the White House to send a "pro-life" delegation to the Population Conference. Reagan was happy to comply. Benedick was kept off the delegation, and, humiliated, he left the department.[61]

Seeking a leader for the American team, the administration tapped James Buckley—a "distinguished Catholic layman and abortion hater," in the words of conservative columnists Rowland Evans and Robert Novak.[62] The ultraconservative Alan Keyes, then the American ambassador to the United Nations Economic and Social Council, was picked to back him up. (Years later, Keyes would run a disastrous campaign for the U.S. Senate against Barack Obama, based on railing against abortion, gay rights, and "America's moral crisis.")[63] William Draper rounded out the trio of official U.S. representatives, but, outnumbered and unsupported, he could do little to moderate it. (Ben Wattenberg, a neoconservative who would go on to write books about the perils of fertility decline, went along as an alternate.)

The Mexico City conference was set to occur just days before the Republican presidential convention began, adding to the pressure on the administration to deliver a victory to its restive antiabortion supporters. These conferences were worldwide media events, and for the right wing they represented the intersection of two great evils: birth control and the United Nations. With antiabortion leaders paying close attention, here was a chance for Reagan to prove that he was on their side.

The *New York Times* reported, "With anti-abortion groups warning of political consequences if the White House backs off, one Reagan aide said, 'You don't want major questions raised about the position the U.S. is taking a week before the convention.'"[64]

By the time the conference started, the politics that had shaped Bucharest a decade earlier were completely inverted. The developing countries, wrote scholars Jason Finkle and Barbara Crane, "no longer spoke of international population assistance as racist, genocidal, or imperialistic, or accused Western nations of advocating population control as a substitute for foreign aid. More and more, the poor nations had come to realize that problems of rapid population growth, infant and child mortality, urbanization, and migration must be addressed, with or without major transformations in the world economy."[65] China's leaders had lurched from denying overpopulation to panicking about it, instituting the coercive one-child policy in 1979.

Meanwhile, the United States, once the champion of global family planning, adopted a mirror-image version of the old Marxist position, claiming that economic reform, not birth control, was the answer to demographic difficulties. "First and most important, population growth is, of itself, a neutral phenomenon," said the official U.S. policy statement. "It is not necessarily good or ill. It becomes an asset or a problem only in conjunction with other factors, such as economic policy, social constraints, need for manpower, and so forth." Government control of economies turned population growth from a potential asset into a liability; thus, the answer to overpopulation was laissez-faire capitalism.

Echoing Julian Simon, the U.S. statement also attributed concern for the environmental consequences of rapid population growth to a pessimistic "anti-intellectualism, which attacked science, technology, and the very concept of material progress." Environmentalism, in this view, while sometimes sincere and commendable, was "more a reflection of anxiety about unsettled times and an uncertain future. In its disregard of human experience and scientific sophistication, it was not unlike other waves of cultural anxiety that have swept through western civilization during times of social stress and scientific exploration."[66] America, on the world stage, was reducing environmentalism to a kind of neurosis.

The new U.S. position, dismissive of demographic issues, contemptuous of conservation, shocked technocrats, old-school Republicans, and liberals alike, and in the run-up to the conference it was widely lambasted. The lavishly credentialed Michael Teitelbaum—former staff director of the U.S. House Select Committee on Population and professor of demography at Princeton and Oxford—told Congress, "To put it bluntly, the paper would receive a failing grade in any undergraduate demography course in the country." Former Republican senator Robert Taft Jr. joined his Democratic colleague Joseph Tydings in a letter decrying the "adoption of a fundamentalist, know-nothing political philosophy with respect to population and development in the less-developed nations."[67] Retired general William Westmoreland wrote a personal note to White House chief of staff James Baker urging him "carefully to consider the long-range implications of a policy that will set back an important program that is beginning to show results in the interest of the countries involved and in our long-range interest."[68]

The new U.S. position also contradicted the CIA's findings. A then classified report issued early in 1984 warned, "Most Third World nations are overpopulated, and demographic pressures exacerbate economic and social problems, even if they do not yet present a direct threat to political stability."[69]

Yet this position, which once led members of the GOP establishment like vice president George H. W. Bush to champion population control, no longer had much of a constituency in an increasingly pious, populist Republican party. Debates over third world family planning would from then on be proxy skirmishes in the American abortion wars.

Abortion, of course, was the reason for the most significant U.S. policy shift announced at Mexico City, a new rule that the United States would not support organizations "which perform or actively promote abortion as a method of family planning," even if they did so with separate funding. Pro-choicers would come to call the policy the "global gag rule," since it prevented groups that were getting family planning money from USAID from referring their clients for safe abortions or from advocating for abortion law liberalization. "In dozens of aid-dependent countries around the world family planning providers, demographers and medical researchers are being forced to pretend that abortion does not exist," said a report from the Population Crisis Committee. "They are not permitted to talk about it or write about it or study it or try to make it safer."[70]

The most immediate victim of the new U.S. policy was the International Planned Parenthood Federation, which received more than $11 million a year, a quarter of its budget, from the United States.[71] But all kinds of smaller operations were affected as well. At the Kenyatta national hospital in Nairobi there was a ward devoted to septic abortions, which cared for between fifty and seventy patients a day. "Doctors were understandably appalled to hear that a 1988 professional management study of the hospital funded by AID would specifically exclude the septic abortion ward—one of hundreds of examples of the chilling effect of US policy debates," the Population Crisis Committee reported.[72] The United States was still the largest donor to international family planning programs, spending $290 million in the 1985 fiscal year.[73] Family planning organizations were faced with an unsolvable moral dilemma. To turn down American money would jeopardize their ability to help women who needed birth control, but to take it required ignoring desperate women with unplanned pregnancies.

In addition to damaging women's health care all over the world, the global gag rule would deform the political debate over abortion in several foreign legislatures. Because of the gag rule people working with women's health NGOs—precisely the people witnessing the staggering toll taken by unsafe abortion—couldn't participate in debates about liberalization without risking support for their other work. For American presidents since Reagan, either imposing or rescinding the Mexico City ban has become a kind of ritual to mark the arrival of a new political party in the White House. One of the first things Bill Clinton did was overturn it; on his first day in power, George W. Bush reinstated it. By the time this book is published, Barack Obama will almost certainly have repealed it once again.

The Mexico City statement also set a precedent by threatening to freeze contributions to the UNFPA if it was found to be engaged in "abortion or coercive family planning programs." Two years later Reagan did just that, claiming that the UNFPA was supporting forced abortions in China, a recurring right-wing allegation. Again, the policy was upheld by the first president Bush, reversed by Clinton, and reinstituted by Bush number two.

If the charge has stuck, it was partly because there was a grain of truth at the center. Despite important shifts in thinking, the Malthusian ethos remained ingrained in the major population organizations throughout the 1980s, and many were thrilled that the world's most populous country had become a convert. China conceived and carried out the one-child policy on its own, without anything like the kind of outside assistance India received. Even as it did so, though, the UNFPA—pressured by Japan, a major donor enormously concerned about population-related instability in Asia—gave China a $50 million grant for equipment and training in both demography and family planning.

The UNFPA did not support the one-child policy. It brought a famous American demographer to China to warn officials that the policy would eventually create a country where too few young people would be supporting too many elderly, precisely what is happening today. Nevertheless, as the historian Matthew Connelly argues, UNFPA funds helped pay for computers that were crucial in calculating birth quotas.[74] And, rather than speak out for the women being targeted by a campaign of reproductive totalitarianism, the organization was silent, or worse.

Indeed, in 1983, the UNFPA did something shocking both for its immorality and its political stupidity: It gave the first United Nations Population Awards, worth $12,500 each, to Qian Xinzhong, the architect of the one-child policy, and Indira Gandhi, who had since been reelected prime minister. In an official statement Bangladeshi ambassador Anwarul Karim Chowdhury, chairman of the award committee, said, "It is a matter of great honor and satisfaction for me and the members of the Committee, as well as for the United Nations, that the very first Population Award is being given to these very distinguished leaders of the two most populous countries in the world."

Theodore W. Shultz, a Nobel Prize–winning economist who served as an adviser to the awards committee, was appalled, and demanded that his name not be attached to the honor. In a letter to UNFPA head Rafael Salas, he argued that lauding Gandhi and Qian greatly damaged the agency's cause. "The harm was done by awarding the prize to a public official in China where public policy is responsible for the appallingly high rate of female infanticide and a prize to the head of state of India despite her cruel mandated sterilization," he wrote.[75]

He was right. By condoning coercion the UNFPA seemed to prove the most vehement critics of international family planning correct. The charges against the agency would continue to stick decades later, even after it had thoroughly reformed itself, providing a pretext for antiabortion forces in the administration of George W. Bush to strip its funding once again.

Malthusian ideas had been drummed out of the American mainstream from two directions. The world's population continued its swift growth, but at least in the United States talk of overpopulation was becoming taboo on both the feminist left and the conservative right. The old moderate establishment that led centrists of both parties to support family planning out of national self-interest had been seriously weakened. What remained were proponents of reproductive rights on one side and champions of religious traditionalism on the other. And, of course, the women all around the world whose health care—and sometimes very lives—were at stake.

The infrastructure the population movement had built still existed, but it would increasingly be run by people who shared Dunlop and Germain's ideas. The International Women's Health Coalition, once a radical outsider, would be at the forefront, organizing women around the world in governments and at the grass roots. Within a few decades an international alliance of women would spur massive changes, not just in population programs but in international law and human rights practice. All would begin to affirm the importance of reproductive rights, including, emphatically, abortion rights. There would be a kind of revolution, though the stultifying, banal patois of the development bureaucracy often served to obscure its import.

The next time there was a big UN Population Conference, in Cairo in 1994, members of the international women's movement would be the ones writing the platform. Adrienne Germain would be on the U.S. government delegation; Sandra Kabir would be part of the team representing Bangladesh. By 2004, Human Rights Watch would add reproductive rights to its portfolio; Amnesty International would follow three years later. Women who had been denied therapeutic abortions would eventually start taking their cases before international bodies, including the United Nations Human Rights Committee, the European Court of Human Rights, and the Inter-American Commission on Human Rights.

If the public at large didn't notice these changes, a number of religious conservatives certainly did. As the global women's movement fought to make reproductive rights universal, conservatives from around the world joined hands across theological divides in opposition to what seemed the ultimate in aggressive cosmopolitanism. United Nations meetings and conferences would become forums for seemingly obscure but often intense and consequential struggles between universal rights and religious and cultural tradition, between the liberties due each individual and the power of groups—nations, villages, families—to regulate their members.

"My best description of this whole period—which was very exciting, very anxiety provoking—is that I was just making it up as I was going along," Dunlop said of the early days of the coalition. "Literally making it up. We knew what our values were, but we didn't have any idea where we were really going in the long run. We just kept holding tight to those values and to those alliances.... We didn't realize going into it that such latent political opposition was lurking in the shadows."[76]

CHAPTER 4: **CAIRO AND BEIJING**

*The future war is between the religious and the
materialists.... Collaboration between religious governments in support of outlawing abortion is a fine beginning
for the conception of collaboration in other fields.*

—Iranian deputy foreign minister Mohammad Akbar Hashemi
Rafsanjani on his 1994 talks with the Vatican[1]

Cairo was tense as the 1994 UN International Conference on Population
and Development convened in a hall across the street from the scene
of President Anwar el-Sadat's assassination. There were threats from Islamic
terrorists and, correspondingly, thousands of extra policemen on the streets.
Right-wing Christians too were in an uproar, and outside the meeting, protesters held huge placards showing dismembered fetuses. There had been
enormous press attention in the run-up, and over three thousand journalists
had registered to cover the event, a watershed that would for the first time
enshrine reproductive rights as an international consensus.

On the first day Gro Harlem Brundtland, the prime minister of Norway,
took the stage. Eschewing diplomatic politesse, she electrified the room by
lambasting the Vatican. Morality, she said, "cannot only be a question of controlling sexuality and protecting unborn life. Morality is also a question of giving individuals the opportunity of choice, of suppressing coercion of all kinds
and abolishing the criminalization of individual tragedy. Morality becomes

hypocrisy if it means accepting mothers' suffering or dying in connection with unwanted pregnancies and illegal abortions, and unwanted children living in misery." The crowd applauded. She continued, "None of us can disregard that abortions occur, and that where they are illegal, or heavily restricted, the life and health of the woman is often at risk. Decriminalizing abortions should therefore be a minimal response to this reality, and a necessary means of protecting the life and health of women." Applause turned to cheers.

Vice President Al Gore, hobbling on crutches after a recent operation, followed with a generally conciliatory speech ("[W]hat is truly remarkable about this conference," he said, "is not only the unprecedented degree of consensus about the nature of the problem, but also the degree of consensus about the nature of the solution.") After him was Pakistani leader Benazir Bhutto, who, under pressure from conservatives in her own country, surprised many with a speech staking out a position on the right. "Our document should seek to promote the objective of planned parenthood, of population control," she said. "This conference must not be viewed by the teeming masses of the world as a universal social charter seeking to impose adultery, abortion, sex education, and other such matters on individuals, societies, and religions which have their own social ethos." She affirmed the importance of women's empowerment, but continued, "Regrettably, the conference's document contains serious flaws in striking at the heart of a great many cultural values, in the North and in the South, in the mosque and in the church." A few days later Mother Teresa faxed a statement to the conference calling abortion "the greatest destroyer of peace in the world today."[2]

At Cairo the culture wars went global as never before. Some of the most powerful people in the world faced off in an existential battle over how women's lives should be valued. Which is supreme—their rights as individuals or their roles as mothers? When culture and human rights collide, which should prevail, and who gets to decide?

In a way this was a fight over modernity itself, and it created some surprising bedfellows. The conference and all its surrounding drama marked the emergence of an odd but clarifying alliance between conservative Muslims and Christians, who formed a united front against the dread forces of feminism, secularism, and liberalism. This international ecumenical right endures to this day, continuing to influence global policy on women's issues.

At bottom, the alliance was based on a shared rejection of women's autonomy, and of secular values more broadly, at a time when the spread of such values appeared inexorable. In the 1990s, Westerners—especially Western elites—still envisioned a world where religious authority would become increasingly private and irrelevant to public affairs. In a way, the global regime of human rights was trying to move into the role the great world religions once occupied.

It was a time of giant, news-making conferences—among them the Rio Earth Summit in 1992, Cairo in 1994, and, a year later, the Beijing Women's Summit—that took place in an atmosphere of real optimism about global-ization. The knitting together of the world's markets and the hybridization of its cultures seemed to make Marshall McLuhan's vision of a "global vil-lage" an imminent reality. Globalization's critics, be they economic leftists or religious conservatives, were marginalized in mainstream political discussion. Conservative thinker Francis Fukuyama became a star with his book *The End of History and the Last Man,* which proclaimed the final triumph of liberal modernity and the emergence of "something like a true global culture, center-ing around technologically driven economic growth and the capitalist social relations necessary to produce and sustain it."[3]

Gathering in world capitals amid flurries of media attention and a cacoph-ony of activists, representatives from all the nations of the planet tried to hash out new norms for human relations to match a newly interconnected world. And at each of these meetings women were, for the first time, at the center of the agenda. "By the early 1990s, the Cold War was over, the Thatcher-Reagan tendency was replaced by kinder, gentler policies, the notion of 'human secu-rity' was being pushed by the [United Nations Development Program] and the World Bank, and the facts about the failure to close the gender gap were becoming ever clearer," wrote the historian Paul Kennedy. "The World Bank's chief economist at that time, Larry Summers, went on record as saying that the single best measure to improve conditions in the developing world would be to increase the access of girls and young women to education—a sweep-ing claim, but one entirely convincing to those who worked and observed in that field."[4] Women's rights seemed not only crucial but achievable, if only the energy of the cold war could be redirected toward social progress. This irenic vision, married to a lawyerly faith in the power of language, captured the imagination of newly networked activists worldwide.

Frances Kissling, the former president of Catholics for a Free Choice and a major presence in the international women's movement, described the big global conference declarations as "sub-rosa cultural statements about the nature of the universe, the nature of the world. They present a cosmology." They represented, she said, "the intellectual, conceptual attempt to move the paradigm of human relationships forward." This, of course, was profoundly threatening to many conservative religious leaders, who believed the basic patterns of human relationships were divinely determined and eternal, and who claimed the power to pronounce on them for themselves.

It's not surprising that women's bodies should be the battleground for such a titanic philosophical clash. Sex differences—and sex hierarchies—have always been at the very heart of social organization. As Margaret Mead wrote, "The differences between the two sexes is one of the important conditions upon which we have built the many varieties of human culture that give human beings dignity and stature.... Upon the contrast in bodily form and function, men have built analogies between sun and moon, night and day, goodness and evil, strength and tenderness, steadfastness and fickleness, endurance and vulnerability."[5]

Technological advancement, increased education, urbanization, and secularization almost inevitably undermine dichotomies between men and women, creating increased egalitarianism. Physical strength becomes less economically important, removing one justification for male dominance. Women have fewer children, and make greater investments in them, meaning girls are more likely to go to school and, eventually, into the workforce. As the political scientists Pippa Norris and Ronald Inglehart wrote in their 2003 book *Rising Tide: Gender Equality and Cultural Change Around the World*, "Modernization brings systematic, *predictable* changes in gender roles."[6] For those invested in older ways of understanding the world, this process is profoundly disruptive, even terrifying and enraging. Trying to trap women entirely within their wifely, maternal role is one way of fighting against it.

C onservatives, of course, are not the only ones with antediluvian tendencies. When Dunlop and Germain first started organizing for Cairo, it was partly to head off a far-left feminist faction that had gained prominence at the Earth Summit, a 1992 environmental conference in Rio de Janeiro. The late Bella Abzug, the Bronx-born former congresswoman famous for her progressive pugnacity (and her collection of ostentatious hats), had turned her attention to the international scene in the late 1980s. Her group, the Women's Environment and Development Organization (WEDO), organized a large feminist presence at the Earth Summit. The women who showed up attacked environmentalists who were concerned about overpopulation as complicit in reproductive coercion. Going further, a number of feminist attendees denounced most modern contraception as dangerous products of the sinister pharmaceutical industry. They regarded U.S.-funded birth control programs as imperialistic at best, genocidal at worst. "Don't say 'population control' around here," began a *Washington Post* story about the event. " 'Control' bespeaks coercion, forced sterilization and supposed First World fears of a dark-skinned planet. Don't even say 'population' too much—it's the word that never got credentials at the official Earth Summit."[7]

This feminist attack on contraception appeared to take Abzug by surprise. "She didn't understand the politics of this movement," said Dunlop. "She couldn't figure out what was going on—why they were so vigorously opposed [to family planning]."

The radical feminists had plenty of reasons for their suspicions. "At that point in time, there was a serious critique about the way reproductive technology has developed, in terms of not taking into account women's needs, side effects," said Sonia Corrêa, a leading Brazilian feminist. "And that critique was not incorrect at that point in time—the quality of the technology was really bad. Hormonal contraceptive methods have improved since then, [partly] because of the critique."

Nevertheless, when stridently articulated, that critique played right into the hands of religious conservatives. Coming out of Rio, it almost seemed as if radical feminists and the Catholic Church were allied against family planning, an impression that troubled a number of Germain and Dunlop's allies, women who'd long fought for reproductive rights in their own countries. In the aftermath Dunlop got calls from colleagues in Brazil, Chile, India, Nigeria, and elsewhere. "Dissembling on the left was going to make the Right's job easier," Dunlop said. "My colleagues were basically saying that to me. . . . They could see it. And so they said, 'We'd better get ready for Cairo. This is going to get much worse in Cairo.' "[8]

Alarmed, Dunlop and Germain contacted their network of women's rights activists from all over the world, offering to fly them to London for an immediate meeting. Around twenty came, including Sandra Kabir, Corrêa, and Gita Sen, an Indian economist who had cofounded Development Alternatives with

Women for a New Era, or DAWN, a group seeking to integrate the economic concerns of women in poor countries into development schemes and international feminist activism. Seeing a need to stake out a position distinct from the population lobby, the ultraleft feminists, and the church, they crafted a statement titled "Women's Declaration on Population Policies." A few months later they called a bigger meeting back in Rio de Janeiro. There, in an agonizing nine-hour session chaired by Sen, over two hundred women from around the world agreed on an edited version. Among their demands were a call for the elimination of demographic targets, access to all forms of contraceptives, economic equality and property rights, gender parity in the staffing of reproductive health agencies, and an end to female genital mutilation.

"What we wanted to do was, rather, simply throw the baby out with the bathwater; we wanted to redirect the money," said Dunlop. "We knew there were huge streams of money going into contraceptive development, and we wanted that money to go in a different direction." Out of that meeting came the Cairo lobby—a core group of activists who would work both to shape the positions of their own governments and to corral a fractious global feminist movement behind a common agenda.

With Bill Clinton, a stalwart supporter of reproductive rights, in the White House, they had an unprecedented opportunity to shape the American position. The administration invited Dunlop to be part of the official delegation, but she suggested that Germain go instead. Germain could be cold and cutting—"Nobody would feel good after she destroyed every argument within sight," Dunlop said[9]—but no one was better prepared for the agonizing semantic warfare that such conferences entail. "The thing about Adrienne is that she knows more than anybody else," said Tim Wirth, the former U.S. senator from Colorado who headed the American team. "I always thought that Adrienne was my best tutor. You know, 'Where's my lesson plan today?' I still say that to her when I see her."

UN summits like Cairo end with a declaration and a detailed plan of action, largely agreed upon in advance and then signed by most world governments. Even before the conference begins, then, there's a bureaucratic gauntlet of preparatory committees (prepcoms, in UN jargon) in which country delegations wrangle over the wording of the final document. Whenever one of the preliminary meetings took place, the International Women's Health Coalition raised money to bring their colleagues from other countries to lobby their own delegations, so they had a presence both inside and outside the official negotiations. (By the end of the conference they'd spent a million dollars in donor funds.) "Sometimes we were not allowed in the meeting room," recalled Kabir. "Then we'd try to get in and then get caught and thrown out. This was great, great fun, I must say."[10] If they had to, the women would corner government representatives in coffee shops, hallways, even in the bathrooms.

From the beginning Germain made sure that the United States joined with the Dutch and the Scandinavians in pushing for a declaration very different from the dry demographic arguments of old. In this she would find a crucial ally in Nafis Sadik, the head of UNFPA and the secretary-general of the Cairo conference.

A Pakistani doctor who was the first woman to lead the UN population agency, Sadik had strong convictions about women's rights that had been nurtured in her years working in family planning in her home country, where wives were often treated as chattel. Once, a patient's husband dismissed Sadik's concerns about his wife's health by announcing how much he'd paid for her. "So, I lose my wife," he said. "Well, if I can't use her sexually, then what use [is she] to me?"[11] Experiences like these taught Sadik that no technocratic approach to reproductive health would mean anything without a guarantee of political rights, and she was determined to tackle potentially incendiary issues like abortion and adolescent sexuality. Her agency was full of people who thought in old-fashioned population control terms, so she went outside it for help in crafting the Cairo declaration.

Wanting to assist her, the Rockefeller Foundation paid for Sharon Camp, a feminist-minded veteran of the population field, to help her write the statement from scratch. Other liberal foundations helped with research and, after three grueling weeks, Sadik had a remarkably progressive document.

"What I did in the plan of action was to write into it my own personal belief, which is that if you provided real reproductive choice to women, you didn't need to worry, to that same degree, about demographic targets," said Camp.[12] Among other things, the draft called for international action to address unsafe abortion, a major cause of maternal mortality worldwide, and for reproductive health services for adolescents. "It was very much an argument for making abortion safe," Camp added.[13] The language would get watered down in negotiations and rewrites, but the thrust of it would survive.

Seeing all this, the Vatican was profoundly alarmed. "Now, it seemed as if an alliance was being forged by the world's only superpower, UN agencies, some European governments, and a well-funded group of powerful nongovernment organizations in order to enshrine [their] defective notion of freedom in international law, in the name of 'reproductive rights,' " wrote papal hagiographer George Weigel. "This was a battle that had to be joined."[14]

The church has always considered abortion wicked, but even within the context of Catholicism, John Paul II was extraordinarily concerned with contraception and fetal life. In his fawning, nearly thousand-page biography of the late pope, Weigel wrote of how seriously the Vatican took Cairo. "This was not another public policy disagreement between the Holy See and a national government," he wrote. "It was the crucial human rights issue of the 1990s, and it was being played out on a global stage. In every cultural history, a great, defining question emerges.... For John Paul II, the abortion issue was not one issue, but *the* issue for the emerging world culture that would sustain, or corrupt, the free societies of the future."[15]

One of his opening salvos was the making of a saint. That April, for the first time in history, Pope John Paul II beatified a married woman with a living husband. Gianna Beretta Molla was an Italian pediatrician and a mother of three when, thirty-nine and pregnant with her fourth child, a tumor was discovered in her uterus. An ardently committed Catholic, Molla refused an operation that would save her life but kill her fetus. Before giving birth she told her doctor, "If you have to choose, there should be no doubt. Choose—I demand it—the life of the baby." A week after her daughter was born, Molla died. Her last moments, according to the Vatican, were full of "unspeakable pain." By honoring this martyr to motherhood the pope clearly was rebuking a feminist movement that sought to free women from the tyranny of biology. Molla, Weigel wrote approvingly, was "a woman whose life and death stood in sharpest contrast to the Cairo draft document's image of marriage and the family."[16]

In his fight against Cairo, though, the pope would use much more than religious symbolism. In addition to being the seat of Catholicism, the Vatican is also a sovereign state, so it is alone among religious entities in claiming official representation at the UN. Since 1964 the Holy See—the government of the Vatican—has had permanent observer status at the world body, the same status Switzerland had at the time, meaning that while it can't vote in the General Assembly, it can participate in UN conferences and debates much like any other state. Because the language of conference declarations is typically adopted by consensus rather than majority vote, a single holdout can essentially shut down the process. Thus, a country with just over a thousand citizens, most of them celibate men, plays an enormously important role in UN deliberations, especially on social issues. Its representatives are seasoned diplomats and approach topics like abortion with a single-minded fervor often unmatched by the delegations of liberal nations.

A few months before the conference, 140 papal nuncios—the church's diplomatic representatives—were summoned to Rome. "John Paul II had decided to declare his own state of war against the United Nations," Carl Bernstein and Marco Politi wrote in their biography of the pope, *His Holiness*. "He was furious. His closest friend in the Vatican, Cardinal Deskur, had never seen the pope in such a rage."[17] The entire diplomatic machinery of the church was mobilized to pressure sympathetic countries to join the Holy See in opposing the Cairo document. In Bolivia, for example, the church maneuvered to get a liberal women's rights activist removed from her country delegation; only the intervention of Niek Biegman, the Dutch ambassador to the UN who served as the Cairo conference's cochair, got her back in. Such behind-the-scenes wrangling happened all over the world, and both Sadik and Biegman continuously circumnavigated the globe to shore up support against the Holy See's attacks.

There was even an unusually rancorous confrontation between Sadik and the pope himself when she visited him the March before the conference. "He was quite angry about the approach we were taking," said Sadik. "Why had we taken this new approach to individual rights? And I said, 'What other kinds of rights are there?'"

"There are couples' rights," said the pope.

Sadik responded that in societies like her own, women lack equal status in marriage and aren't even consulted in family decisions. She started talking about unwanted pregnancies caused by rape, including rape within marriage.

"I was trying to paint him a picture of women in the developing world," she said. He listened, and then, she recalled, he said, "Some of the irresponsible behavior of men was perhaps caused by women." Sadik was stunned.

The conversation lasted less than an hour. Bernstein and Politi note that after Sadik's visit, "[t]he photographer who routinely took pictures of papal audiences was strangely absent. Evidently, Vatican protocol dictated that Nafis Sadik wasn't worthy of a photograph."[18]

In its crusade against the UNFPA the Vatican reached beyond Catholicism to seek an alliance with conservative Muslims. Before the Cairo conference Vatican officials met with representatives of the World Muslim League, the Organization of the Islamic Conference, and the World Muslim Congress, emerging with a statement criticizing the UN for undermining family values. "An aggressive and extreme individualism is ultimately destructive of society and can lead to a situation of moral decadence, promiscuity and breakdown of values," it said. Later that summer the papal envoy in Tehran, Monsignor Romeo Panciroli, met with representatives of the Iranian government; shortly after, a senior Iranian official announced that the Vatican had Iran's "full endorsement" on opposition to reproductive rights language in the Cairo document.[19] In August the official Libyan press agency reported that Vatican diplomats were supporting Libya's attempts to resolve its differences with Western governments, which shunned the country since the 1988 bombing of Pan Am Flight 103 over Lockerbie, Scotland. "The press agency linked this supposed Vatican assistance to Libya's condemnation of the Cairo document," reported the *International Herald Tribune*.[20] Soon Cairo's Al-Azhar University, a major center of Islamic learning, joined the opposition to the draft conference statement.

"The Vatican sent emissaries to every Muslim country asking them not to attend the conference, or not to send anyone important," said Sadik. "They mounted a huge démarche. I also then called the U.S., the UK and all the Muslim countries myself, and suggested they should start a démarche also. I myself called many leaders whom I knew very well, including Benazir Bhutto in Pakistan. The climate in the countries was a little bit tense, because they were worried about the religious leaders. Benazir was being advised by the minister of foreign affairs that maybe it was something she should just skip. But she was bold enough—she came." Two other female Muslim leaders—

Prime Ministers Tansu Çiller of Turkey and Khaleda Zia of Bangladesh—got cold feet. Iraq, Saudi Arabia, the Sudan, and Lebanon boycotted entirely.

The Vatican-Muslim alliance was never really about birth control or abortion, since most interpretations of Islam don't share the church's absolutist stance on either. To be sure, abortion is highly restricted under Islam, but not the way it is in Catholic teachings. Islamic jurisprudence differs as to when, after conception, a fetus is "created"—some scholars say 40 days, some 90 days, some 120 days. "If the mother is endangered by the pregnancy, all schools bow to medical opinion and permit a therapeutic abortion," Donna Lee Bowen wrote in the *International Journal of Middle East Studies*.[21] Health-mandated abortion is allowed in both Saudi Arabia and Iran.

Conservative Muslims tend to differ even more with Catholics on contraception. Concerned over population pressures, Iran's Islamic government has at times been a keen advocate for family planning and a major provider of contraceptives and voluntary sterilizations; their use was sanctioned by a fatwa from Ayatollah Khomeini.[22] (Not that that made the American Life Lobby's charges that Richard Benedick had cooperated with the shah on a campaign against the Islamic family any less inflammatory.) No Muslim country bans birth control.

For the Vatican and its Muslim allies, what was at stake went far beyond family planning. Throughout the 1990s international law was changing in crucial ways that increasingly put the rights of individual women above the rights of groups to preserve their traditional customs and hierarchies. In 1993 the Vienna World Conference on Human Rights declared, "The human rights of women and of the girl-child are an inalienable, integral and indivisible part of universal human rights. The full and equal participation of women in political, civil, economic, social and cultural life, at the national, regional and international levels, and the eradication of all forms of discrimination on grounds of sex are priority objectives of the international community." Cairo intended to take this new international commitment even further, and the Beijing women's conference in 1995 would carry it further still. An amorphous architecture of soft power was evolving, with NGOs helping to shape international declarations that were then used by various bodies to interpret international law.

Of course, all this could appear terribly ephemeral. These UN documents are unenforceable and more often ignored than implemented. Sometimes the elevated rhetoric of international law appears grotesque when juxtaposed to sordid reality. While diplomats spoke loftily of human rights in Vienna, a few hundred miles away ethnic cleansing made a hell of Bosnia and a mockery of international ideals. Women's rights were enshrined in international law while, once again, mass rape was deployed as a weapon of war.

Yet if the terrible ways the international system falls short overshadow whatever progress it makes, that doesn't mean the progress is insignificant. In fact the victories women won at these various conferences had much more than merely rhetorical impact. Armed with these agreements, women around the world have succeeded in pressuring their own governments to live up to them, and have sometimes been able to appeal to international human rights courts when they don't. The idea that women's rights could trump even so inviolate a principle as national sovereignty was something new in the world.

The importance of these UN declarations can be hard to see from the United States because they carry no weight here: An American lawyer, judge, or politician who challenged a domestic law on the ground that it violated a global agreement would be either ignored or reviled. (When Supreme Court justice Anthony Kennedy cited international norms in the Court's ruling that the execution of minors is unconstitutional, prominent conservatives howled for his impeachment.) In Europe and many developing countries, though, the dynamics are different, and it's not uncommon for judges to invoke international agreements, or for national laws to be brought into accordance with them.

This is easiest to see when it comes to treaties like the United Nations Convention on the Elimination of All Forms of Discrimination Against Women (CEDAW), which has been ratified by every nation in the world save the United States, Sudan, Somalia, Iran, Qatar, and a handful of Pacific Islands states. The United States originally played a strong role in drafting the treaty, which was adopted by the UN General Assembly in 1979. Among other things, CEDAW calls for countries to establish the legal equality of women and men; to eliminate discrimination in education and employment; and to "modify the social and cultural patterns of conduct of men and women, with a view to achieving the elimination of prejudices and customary and all other practices which are based on the idea of the inferiority or the superiority of either of the sexes or on stereotyped roles for men and women."

Prejudices against women obviously remain very much intact in most of the world. Nevertheless, CEDAW matters. In Tanzania a court cited the treaty when overturning a law that prohibited women from inheriting clan land from their fathers. In Colombia the treaty was used to secure constitutional protections against domestic violence, which had previously been seen as a private matter outside the penal code. In an Indian legal case stemming from the gang rape of a woman by men she worked with, a court found "that by ratifying CEDAW and by making official commitments at the 1995 Beijing world conference on women, India had endorsed the international standard of women's human rights," and thus had to protect women from sexual abuse and harassment.[23]

As a treaty, CEDAW is more binding than the declarations that come out of global conferences like Cairo and Beijing. But they work in synergy: As the India decision shows, international declarations can determine how legal treaties like CEDAW are interpreted. The statements that emerged from the meetings in the 1990s also had a kind of persuasive power. The Cairo program of action contained—for the first time ever—an explicit call for countries to eliminate female circumcision. Soon after a number of African nations, including Senegal, Burkina Faso, Ghana, Tanzania, and Togo, outlawed the practice.[24]

The outcome of Cairo would determine how a great many international aid organizations operated in the field. "Since Cairo, UNFPA, UNHCR, the Red Cross, and a host of international NGOs have joined to provide reproductive health services to women in emergency situations," Sadik pointed out in a 1999 speech. "The latest such effort is in response to the Kosovo crisis, where an estimated dozen or so children were born daily just in Albania's camps."

Finally, the notion that reproductive rights are human rights would transform the major human rights organizations. In 2003, Human Rights Watch undertook an analysis of international law pertaining to reproductive rights. "We came to the conclusion that not [just] in our opinion, but in the opinion of those authorized to interpret international human rights law and to state where it is right now, women have a right to decide over their bodies, including in matters related to abortion," said Marianne Møllmann, the advocacy director of the women's rights division at Human Rights Watch. As a result, in 2004 Human Rights Watch adopted the position that the denial of reproductive choice is a denial of human rights, and it now documents violations—including forced sterilization and employer-mandated pregnancy tests—all over the world. Amnesty International followed suit in 2007, calling for the right to abortion in cases of rape, incest, and threats to the life and health of the pregnant woman, and for the decriminalization of abortion worldwide.

All these epochal issues swirled around Cairo, rendering every word of every official sentence enormously fraught. Despite all the public drama, as in most international conferences much of what mattered happened out of sight. Hammering out the final document was a painstaking, often miserable process, with delegates sitting in small, windowless rooms and negotiating until 3:00 or 4:00 A.M. It took tremendous stamina to keep up the fight since, while great existential divides underlie much of the debate, the process itself was often concerned with the pettiest linguistic minutia, seemingly irrelevant but potentially packed with hidden meanings.

The absurd parsing hit its apotheosis at a late-night session toward the end of the conference when, a Dutch diplomat recalled, a delegate from Iran said, "Mr. Chairman, I propose to delete the words 'fertility regulation.' Mr. Chairman, I want to delete it from the text." Then he added, "And I want to replace it with the words 'regulation of fertility.' "

The head of the Swedish delegation, one of the most ardent supporters of reproductive rights, was immediately suspicious. What was behind this maneuver? "Let's ask for a time-out!" he said to his Dutch colleague. Taking a break, they conferred outside. It turned out that the Iranians objected to the phrase "fertility regulation" because according to the World Health Organization definition it could include "interrupting unwanted pregnancies." By using slightly different wording the Iranian representative could assure his government that he had not acceded to the right to abortion.

"It was torture," said the Dutch diplomat. Yet all this painfully precise wrangling also opened up fissures between the Vatican and some of the Muslim countries. The alliance was always shaky, both because of mutual distrust and because the Muslim nations wouldn't stand firm with the pope against birth control. Catholic and Muslim differences about family planning could be glossed over in the run-up to Cairo, when newspapers were full of stories about their "unholy alliance." But in the excruciating technical negotiations of the conference itself, Muslim states were willing to make deals on reproductive issues, because their bigger concern was promiscuity and homosexuality, which they saw encompassed in the words "sexual rights." By agreeing to drop that phrase Germain got the Iranian representative to agree to language on "adolescents' sexual and reproductive health and rights," something the church never would have done.

Meanwhile, Egypt, as the host of the conference, was heavily invested in making it a success. Bitterness was mounting as the Holy See's delegation blocked a compromise statement on abortion. The draft said that in countries where abortion is legal it should be safe. The Vatican found this unacceptable. Seeking to both mollify the church and to criticize the Soviet practice of relying on abortion as a primary form of birth control, Biegman added the sentence: "In no case should abortion be promoted as a method of family planning." But the Holy See rejected that, too. Breaking protocol, frustrated delegates yelled and booed. Maher Mahran, Egyptian minister of state for population and family affairs, joined in the criticism. "Does the Vatican rule the world?" he asked. "We respect the Vatican, we respect the pope, but we don't accept anyone to impose his ideas. If they are not going to negotiate, why did they come?"[25]

Distraught at the mounting anger, the Vatican softened its stance. Without assenting to the language on abortion, it allowed the negotiations to advance. Eventually, after ten agonizing days, a remarkable final document emerged. "Advancing gender equality and equity and the empowerment of women, and the elimination of all kinds of violence against women, and ensuring women's ability to control their own fertility, are cornerstones of population and development-related programmes," it said. The statement declared reproductive rights to be universal and called on all the nations of the world to put women's empowerment at the center of the agenda. All governments and relevant NGOs, it said, need "to deal with the health impact of unsafe abortion as a major public health concern." Adolescents, it said, should be given comprehensive sex education and reproductive health services. Female circumcision should be banned. Demographic targets and quotas should be jettisoned. The agenda of the International Women's Health Coalition, once dismissed as quixotic and radical, would henceforth have a global imprimatur.

Not wanting to be isolated, eventually the Holy See joined the consensus, though it rejected the sections dealing with reproductive rights and abortion, and reiterated its objection to the use of condoms in HIV-prevention programs. (On contentious UN agreements such an à la carte approach by member countries is not uncommon.) "Some interpreted the final Vatican stand—to partially endorse the document—as an effort by the church to start rebuilding bridges within the diplomatic community," said the *National Catholic Reporter*.[26]

Later, Weigel even tried to give the pope credit for the triumph of humanism over demographic utilitarianism. "By appealing to the better angels of a universal human nature through the power of the word," he wrote, "John Paul had forced the moral core of the population argument onto the center of the world stage, changed the nature of the public debate, and helped shift the framework of discussion from 'controlling' population to empowering women."[27]

At Cairo, though, there was no question who the real winners were. When the gavel went down to close the meeting, the women's rights activists erupted in gleeful triumph, dancing down the aisles of the conference center. The dancing continued that night at a party on a barge sailing down the Nile. "It was a moment I never would've thought of in the years of my professional work leading up to Cairo," said Germain. "It was just such a victory for and by women. It was a pushback to the Holy See big time. It was a pushback even to the Islamic group, because of the commitments on adolescents. It was really a big deal."[28]

The Irish writer and politician Conor Cruise O'Brien called it "the greatest diplomatic defeat the Vatican has sustained in the 20th century."[29]

Going into the 1995 international women's conference in Beijing, the global feminist movement seemed to have the wind at its back, but there were reasons to fear disaster. Politically, China was as perverse a location as Bucharest had been for the 1974 population conference. One UN official defended the decision to hold the conference there by arguing that it could help speed reform, saying, "[C]ountries can be shamed into changing."[30] Despite such hopes, the Chinese government had no intention of allowing the kind of raucous activism that had prevailed in Cairo. At its behest NGOs representing Taiwanese and Tibetan women were denied UN accreditation. The NGO forum itself, which drew more than thirty thousand women, was exiled to a muddy, unfinished compound an hour from the conference site, making it impossible for activists to lobby their country's delegates as they had in Cairo. Human Rights Watch published a pamphlet designed to aid attendees detained by the police.[31]

Meanwhile, just months before the start of the conference, Harry Wu, a Chinese-born dissident who spent nineteen years in prison camps before emigrating to America, was arrested as he tried to enter China and charged with spying and stealing state secrets. There was outrage in the United States. Democratic congresswoman Nancy Pelosi urged Hillary Clinton to skip the conference in protest, writing, "[T]he presence of the First Lady in Beijing would be a boost to the repressive Chinese regime and a setback for those brave dissidents who speak out for freedom."[32]

Equally appalled by Chinese atrocities and by feminism, Republicans attacked the entire event. "American interests would be best served if the Administration politely withdrew from a conference that is shaping up as an unsanctioned festival of anti-family, anti-American sentiment," said Texas senator Phil Gramm.[33] New Jersey congressman Chris Smith tried to cut off funding for the U.S. delegation. America's evangelical Christian right, largely absent at Cairo, bestirred itself, mounting what the *Washington Post* called "[a]n unprecedented campaign to assert their agenda internationally by making their voices heard at the Beijing meeting." James Dobson, the influential leader of Focus on the Family, sent out two million copies of a letter describing the event as "the most radical, atheistic and anti-family crusade in the history of the world."[34]

In the end Harry Wu was deported to the United States just days before the conference began, clearing the way for Hillary Clinton to attend. The speech she gave turned out to be one of the high points of her tenure as first lady. It was both a ringing endorsement of the goals of the international women's movement and, as the *New York Times* reported,[35] the most forceful denunciation of China's human rights abuses ever delivered by an American official on Chinese soil.

> It is a violation of human rights when babies are denied food, or drowned, or suffocated, or their spines broken, simply because they are born girls. It is a violation of human rights when women and girls are sold into the slavery of prostitution....It is a violation of human rights when a leading cause of death worldwide among women ages fourteen to forty-four is the violence they are subjected to in their own homes by their own relatives....It is a violation of human rights when women are denied the right to plan their own families, and that includes being forced to have abortions or being sterilized against their will. If there is one message that echoes forth from this conference, let it be that human rights are women's rights....And women's rights are human rights, once and for all.

Her speech lasted twenty-one minutes. When she finished there was a brief pause as the translations concluded. Then, wrote Carl Bernstein, "suddenly there was something approaching pandemonium as hundreds in the hall leaped to their feet and began a long-standing ovation for the first lady.... Her speech became front-page news around the world, noted (in countries where its message was consistent with cultural and governmental principles) for its power and eloquence."[36] It "may have been her finest moment in public life," said the *New York Times*.[37] China's *People's Daily* was less enthusiastic. It accorded her a mere one line, buried on page two: "The American Mrs. Hillary Clinton also spoke at the conference."[38]

Feminists around the world were feeling victorious. By the end of Beijing, wrote Sonia Corrêa, "[w]e were exhausted but exhilarated. The achievements had been outstanding. So outstanding that, looking back, I dare say that most of us went back home in a sort of Platonic dream mood in which perfection of form and language is mistaken for reality."[39]

Reality, disappointing and complex, would soon reassert itself. The language of the UN, while attempting to create new norms, glossed over deep, roiling controversies in many member states. Country leaders may have signed on to CEDAW, Cairo, and Beijing, but on the ground vast numbers of people rejected the very notion of women's equality. UN documents spoke both of ensuring equal rights for men and women and of respecting traditional cultures, never acknowledging that those two goals could be in direct conflict.

Charges of cultural imperialism were bound to arise, and not just from the expected quarters. Once again arguments against outside interference would bend the left and right edges of the political spectrum toward each other, as camps on both sides challenged the universal assumptions of global feminism.

For the moment, though, global feminism was triumphant, and the consequences for both national laws and individual lives would be real and lasting. If you looked hard enough you could trace a line between the high-level negotiations at Cairo and Beijing and a young Masai girl spared circumcision and early marriage and kept in school in Kenya. There would be backlashes and setbacks, but also glimpses of the better world that's possible when girls and women are able to slip the fetters that bind them.

CHAPTER 5: RIGHTS VERSUS RITES

On February 6, 2007, two women, both of whom had been circumcised in Africa, met in the conference room of a small foundation on Fifth Avenue in New York City for a highly unusual debate. It was the fourth annual Day of Zero Tolerance Against Female Genital Mutilation/Cutting, an occasion for events across the globe dedicated to abolishing the practice. Put together by the Bronx-based Sauti Yetu Center for African Women, the New York gathering was much smaller than those taking place in Washington, D.C., London, and other capitals. It drew about thirty women, half of them African immigrants from countries including Senegal, Sudan, and Kenya, where female circumcision is common. Several of them were shocked to realize that, unlike parallel events in other cities, this one wasn't so much a discussion about how female circumcision can be eradicated as about whether it *should* be.

The custom of cutting off all or part of girls' external genitalia—deeply ingrained in large swaths of Africa and parts of Asia and the Middle East—obviously has its defenders, as evidenced by how tenaciously it has endured in the face of a global campaign to eliminate it. Indeed, as the anthropologist Richard Shweder argued in a much discussed 2003 paper, "it is a noteworthy fact that in at least seven African nations 80–90% of the popular vote would probably vote against any policy or law that criminalizes the practice of genital modification for either boys or girls."[1] Yet apologists for female circumcision don't interact much with the global women's movement, which is generally no more inclined to debate the merits of the practice than it is to ponder the upside of rape or wife beating.

That's what made the Sauti Yetu event so unique, and so charged. At first glance the two speakers seemed to symbolize the dichotomy between modernity and tradition, cosmopolitanism and cultural authenticity. Fuambai Ahmadu, the American-born daughter of a Sierra Leonean family, wore knee-high leather boots under a stylish rust-colored skirt, and her long hair was pulled back in a sleek, low ponytail. A postdoctoral fellow at the University of Chicago with a Ph.D. from the London School of Economics, she looked younger than her forty years. Beside her was Grace Mose, regal in a red African tunic, matching skirt, and head wrap. Her perfect English was deeply accented by her native Kenya, where she had grown up in an Abagusii village in the country's southwest. It was easy to imagine her as a champion of the line of midwives who've made their living cutting girls since the beginning of recorded history, women who are now being jailed in some countries for practicing a trade that once brought them money and pride.

But it wasn't that simple. Ahmadu, not Mose, is the high-profile defender of female circumcision and the role it can play in inducting African girls into their societies. "My sitting here is a perfect example that female initiation can have a place in a global society," she insisted. "I don't see that initiation is somehow an impediment to girls' development." Circumcision and all that it represents in her culture, she said, "is an important source of my social identity. It's what links me with my mother, my grandmothers, my aunts, my female ancestors. It celebrates our history, our connection." As she spoke, Mose, a fervent campaigner against the practice, glared at her, outraged. Unruffled, Ahmadu continued, arguing that in Sierra Leone, "female circumcision is empowering."

Toward the end a Senegalese woman, incensed by Ahmadu, stood up and said, "I really feel very frustrated seeing an African sister defending female genital mutilation." A few people applauded. She herself, she said, had not been cut, and saw the practice as indefensible. "There is one thing we have to clarify. We have used here the term 'female circumcision,' which is a term that I do not like at all. Because it puts together two things that are totally different. We [should] talk about female *mutilation*. Why? When we circumcise a boy, that is *skin* that is cut off. Now when a female is, I'll say, excised, that is the whole part that is taken out. That is completely different!" As she spoke, Mose passed around a book titled *Female Genital Mutilation,* open to a photo of a circumcised woman with a huge demoid cyst protruding from her vagina like the crown of a baby's head.

Ahmadu had been calm and poised all evening, but there was an under-current of controlled anger in her voice as she responded. "I am glad that you referred to me as sister. I believe that we are both sisters," she said. "In Senegal, in Gambia, in my country, Sierra Leone, there are words that we can use, as circumcised women, against uncircumcised women that are *very* insulting and very nasty and very offensive." Comparing these slurs to the word "mutilation," she continued, "I may be different from you and I am excised, but I am *not mutilated.* Just like I will not accept anybody calling me by the 'N' word to define my racial identity, I will not have anybody call me by the 'M' word to define my social identity, my gender identity."

A hmadu sees herself as speaking for African women who value female genital cutting but are shut out of the rarified realms of international civil society. "The anti-FGM activists have access to the media, and they have enormous resources, so they're able to influence the media in such a way that most of the women who support the practice cannot," she told me later that evening. "Even if they did, a lot of them are illiterate, so they can't even speak the necessary language, and they cannot respond to charges of backwardness and barbarity."

A global sophisticate, Ahmadu is an unlikely tribune for their voices, but she's also a symbol of the issue's complexity. Female genital cutting doesn't just pit traditionalists against modernists. It highlights a conflict between the Enlightenment universalism enshrined in so many United Nations documents and the positions held by *both* cultural conservatives and postmodern relativists. Recondite as this may seem, it's a conflict of far more than academic interest, because it gets to the heart of questions underlying the global battle for reproductive rights.

Like international debates over family planning and women's empowerment, the controversy over genital cutting is about who has the right to intervene in the sexual practices of others, about absolute standards and the prerogatives of culture. In the campaign to eradicate female circumcision, a powerful alliance of rich country donors and poor country activists are telling traditional societies that they must change for the sake of their girls. They are trying to eliminate a practice that causes many women incalculable agony but that millions value deeply, in part for its role in warding off sexual chaos. International institutions are pressuring national governments to supersede the child-rearing decisions of families, and thus protect girls from harmful traditions. The power of global norms to shape individual destiny is being tested on a massive scale.

Because the terms—female genital mutilation, or cutting, or circumcision—are so contested, it's best to be as clear as possible about what's at stake. The World Health Organization classifies four primary types of what it calls female genital mutilation (FGM), although they tend to overlap. Type I, which in its very mildest forms can be analogous to male circumcision, involves everything from the cutting of the prepuce of the clitoris to a full clitoridectomy. Type II, common in Egypt and central Africa, is the excision of the clitoris and the inner labia. Type III, infibulation, is the removal of most or all of the external genitalia, and the stitching or suturing together of the cut flesh over the vaginal opening, with a small aperture—sometimes a mere pinhole— for urination and menstruation. A woman must be literally ripped open by her husband, an excruciating process that often takes several attempts. It is practiced almost exclusively by Muslims and is performed in Sudan, Somalia, northeastern Kenya, Eritrea, parts of Mali, and in a small section of northern Nigeria.[2] Type IV includes a miscellany of less common practices, including stretching the labia or clitoris or putting caustic substances into the vagina in order to tighten or narrow it.[3]

All these procedures tend to be performed in unsanitary conditions, without anesthesia, using knives, razors, or scissors. In some places, particularly Egypt, there have been efforts to medicalize the practice and have doctors or nurses, rather than midwives or barbers, perform it, which makes it safer but also, many feminists fear, even more entrenched. According to the World Health Organization between 100 million and 140 million women around the globe have undergone genital cutting. Each year around 3 million African girls are cut, almost half of them in Egypt and Ethiopia.[4] Immigration has brought female circumcision to Western countries. According to the U.S. Department of Health and Human Services, as of 1990, 168,000 girls and women in the United States had either undergone circumcision or were at risk of being subjected to it, and it's safe to assume that number has only grown in the ensuing years.[5]

Not surprisingly, the health consequences of genital cutting can be dire.

According to the World Health Organization, immediate dangers include severe pain, shock, excessive bleeding, difficulty urinating, infection, psychological trauma, and even death. "Long-term consequences that have been documented include chronic pain, infections, cysts and abscesses, decreased sexual enjoyment, infertility, posttraumatic stress disorder, and dangers in childbirth," WHO says. Those last dangers can be significant; in an extensive study they found that "deliveries to women who have undergone FGM are significantly more likely to be complicated by caesarean section, postpartum haemorrhage, episiotomy, extended maternal hospital stay, resuscitation of the infant, and inpatient perinatal death than deliveries to women who have not had FGM."[6] Female genital cutting, the study reported, was responsible for an additional one to two infant deaths per one hundred deliveries.[7]

The WHO's statistical analysis has been challenged by opponents of the anticircumcision movement. In a dialogue on a *New York Times* science blog, the anthropologist Shweder, well known as a defender of cultural relativism, wrote, "[T]he harmful practice claim has been highly exaggerated and…many of the representations in the advocacy literature and the popular press are nearly as fanciful as they are nightmarish." A close, critical reading of the WHO study, he wrote, "suggests to me that again there is not very much to write home about."[8]

For many doctors who treat African women, though, there's little question about the negative effects of female circumcision—especially Type III, infibulation. "It is painful and destructive," said Nawal Nour, a Boston gynecologist and one of the United States' leading medical experts on female circumcision. A graduate of Harvard Medical School, Nour is the founder of the African Women's Health Practice, the country's first gynecological clinic devoted to African immigrants. She treats hundreds of infibulated women, mostly from Sudan and Somalia, although she has patients from other parts of the continent as well.

Like some defenders of the practice, she avoids the term "female genital mutilation" because, she said, "most of the women I treat don't consider themselves mutilated." Many consider infibulation beautiful. When they first realize American women are almost all uncircumcised, they tend to react with pity and disgust, not envy.

"Part of what I do here in the United States is to bring down that sensationalistic perspective—oh my god, these are barbaric individuals, how horrific, how can parents do this to their daughters," said Nour. "When you truly understand the issues of female circumcision, it's a tradition, it's a rite of passage, it's something that is celebrated in a lot of these places." She understands why people like Shweder oppose blanket condemnation. "But they go a step too far, because I see the women who do have long-term complications. These long-term complications can go from minor, chronic vaginal infections to inability to penetrate, to have intercourse, to infertility, to very painful intercourse, to inability to deliver a baby," she said. "You can't tell me that they don't have chronic issues."

No one knows exactly when, why, or how infibulation began, but in Africa the practice has been tied up with globalization for hundreds of years. The political scientist Gerry Mackie has speculated that it derives from an area in what is now northern Sudan, and that it spread into other parts of Africa via the slave trade, becoming less severe as it diffused. (Interestingly, infibulation is often referred to as "pharonic" circumcision in countries that practice it, but it's called "Sudanese" circumcision in Egypt.) "The geographic distribution of FGM suggests that it originated on the western coast of the Red Sea, where infibulation is most intense, diminishing to clitoridectomy in westward and southward radiation," he wrote in an influential 1996 article. "Whatever the earliest origins of FGM, there is certainly an association between infibulation and slavery."[9]

According to Mackie's hypothesis, the demand for concubines among imperial Muslim rulers

> induced an eastward flow of female slaves through the mainly polygynous Sudanic Belt into infibulating slave centers in Sudan and a westward flow of Islamization and FGM. Arabized pastoralists raided northeastern Africa for slaves and, because Islam forbade the enslavement of Moslems, ventured further as closer sources converted. The Sudanic slaves were shipped down Nile Valley routes or through the Red Sea to Egyptian or Arabian markets.... The further radiation of clitoridectomy follows the channel of raiding and trading west to the Atlantic and southeast to Kenya.[10]

Mackie cited Joao Dos Santos, a seventeenth-century missionary, who wrote of a group in Somalia who had "a custome to sew up their Females, specially their slaves being young to make them unable for conception, which makes these Slaves sell dearer, both for their chastitie, and for better confidence which their Masters put in them."[11]

Even in the twentieth century the practice spread in the Sudan as Arabs from the country's north moved into indigenous areas in the south and west. "As unschooled Islamic people who erroneously believe female circumcision to be part of their religion spread into these indigenous areas, they bring with them their customs which are eventually adopted by the less socially and economically advantaged indigenous population in order to make their daughters more marriageable," wrote Hanny Lightfoot-Klein in her 1989 book, *Prisoners of Ritual: An Odyssey into Female Genital Circumcision in Africa,* which was pathbreaking for its comprehensive, on-the-ground research. She continued, "The spread of the practice is so complete that I found that in the city of Nyala in the west of Sudan, where the pharonic was completely unknown 50 years ago, it now saturates the area completely. The same is true of the somewhat more remote town of Nyertete where it was first introduced 20 years ago and where all of the population now practice it."[12]

The relationship between female circumcision and Islam is complex, if undeniable. The practice predates Islam, and isn't sanctioned by many orthodox interpretations of the religion; it is mentioned nowhere in the Koran and is virtually unknown in Saudi Arabia, for example, where it is widely considered barbaric. Nor is it practiced exclusively by Muslims in Africa—indeed, in Tanzania the highest circumcision rates are in predominantly Christian areas.[13] Nevertheless, in large parts of Africa, Islam and female circumcision—especially infibulation—have been deeply intertwined. Closely tied to the conservative Muslim obsession with female virginity and chastity, it's meant to attenuate women's sexual desire and provide a physical barrier against premarital sex.*

---

* Despite the connection between Islam and female circumcision, it's important to mention that not long ago clitoridectomy was also occasionally practiced in another chastity-obsessed society, Victorian England. Famed obstetrician Isaac Baker Brown, elected president of the Medical Society of London in 1865, claimed he could cure insanity, epilepsy, and hysteria through the excision of the clitoris. (See Elizabeth Sheehan, "Victorian Clitoridectomy: Isaac Baker Brown and His Harmless Operative Procedure," *Medical Anthropology Newsletter,* vol. 12, no. 4 [August 1981], pp. 9–15.) In the United States, Dr. John Harvey Kellogg, of cornflakes fame, advocated the same operation—as well as the "application of blisters and other irritants to the sensitive parts of the sexual organs"—as a cure for nymphomania. (See John Harvey Kellogg, *Ladies Guide in Health and Disease* [New York: Modern Medicine Publishing Company, 1902], pp. 550–51.)

A host of related beliefs surround female circumcision in the communities that perform it. "The belief that uncircumcised women cannot help but exhibit an unbridled and voracious appetite for promiscuous sex is prevalent in all societies that practice female circumcision," wrote Lightfoot-Klein.[14] In addition, some cultures believe that left alone a woman's clitoris will grow to grotesque, penislike proportions, or that it is poisonous and will kill a man who comes into contact with it, or that it impedes fertility.[15] Nawal Nour recalled, "I had a woman who said to me, 'I really feel it's important that my granddaughter be circumcised, because at this stage if I hadn't had my clitoris removed it would be touching the ground!'"

Christian missionaries who encountered female circumcision were generally appalled and tried their best to stop it, though some, finding that their opposition hindered their attempts at conversion, condoned and even embraced it. When sixteenth-century missionaries in Ethiopia attempted to put an end to the practice, men refused to marry uncircumcised girls. "Circumcision was eventually allowed again on the urgent advice of Rome, so that the ground gained by the missionaries would not be lost as the converts failed to marry and reproduce," wrote Lightfoot-Klein.[16]

British colonialists took a similar tack. They tended to see female genital cutting as a hideous, heathen custom to be eradicated by their civilizing mission, but they could also promote it in the service of other priorities. "As early as 1906, Church of Scotland (Presbyterian) missionaries at Kikuyu preached against excision together with its attendant celebrations, dances, and teachings as 'barbaric' and 'indecent,'" wrote historian Lynn M. Thomas in her book *Politics of the Womb: Women, Reproduction, and the State in Kenya*. "Missionaries soon realized that female initiation posed a direct challenge to their education efforts, as girl students routinely left mission schools when their time for initiation approached. In an effort to stem the losses, missionaries experimented with holding female initiations on mission grounds.... [They] were carried out by the 'usual Kikuyu woman circumciser.'"[17]

Throughout the ensuing decades the British made various attempts to ban female circumcision in Kenya, often eliciting furious opposition. In the late 1920s, Thomas wrote, thousands of young people gathered at schools or mission stations to perform *Muthirigu,* a form of dance-song mocking anticircumcision campaigns. "Elder of the Church, your uncircumcised daughter is pregnant and she will give birth to dogs," was one lyric. *Muthirigu* was banned as seditious in 1930, but by then, wrote Thomas, "young men and women had already made their point. The vigor and scale of their performances had demonstrated to colonial officials the depth of local commitment to female excision."[18]

Interestingly, in one region of Kenya the colonial government actually *enforced* circumcision, and at an earlier age, because officials felt it prevented an even greater ill: abortion. The Central Kenyan Meru people condoned sexual play among uninitiated, unmarried adolescents but considered children born to uncircumcised girls to be cursed, a view shared by some neighboring groups, including the Masai. Among the Meru, Thomas wrote, such pregnancies were dealt with by abortions, which were performed by men called *muriti wa mauu,* or "remover of the womb."[19] The colonial district commissioner considered rampant abortion "the principal social problem of the Meru people" and helped institute a policy of forced mass circumcisions in order to combat it. "He argued that apart from saving the Meru from 'tribal death,' it would reduce the age of marriage, compel men to shoulder the responsibilities of wife and family at a younger age, encourage them to farm, and, by shifting agricultural control from women to men, facilitate the development of cash crops."[20]

Meru was an exception; in most of Kenya colonial opposition to female circumcision was fairly consistent and had the effect of imbuing the practice with anticolonial authenticity. In his 1938 book, *Facing Mount Kenya,* Jomo Kenyatta, the founding father of independent Kenya, described female circumcision as "the very essence of an institution which has enormous educational, social, moral, and religious implications, quite apart from the operation itself. . . . [L]ike Jewish circumcision, [it] . . . is regarded as the conditio sine qua non of the whole teaching of tribal law, religion, and morality."[21] In the 1950s, defiance of the British ban on circumcision was associated with support for the anticolonial Mau Mau rebellion.

This legacy is often used to tar efforts to eradicate the practice as a kind of neocolonialism or secular missionary work. "[T]hese days at least two things have changed since the 1920s and 1930s in Africa: anesthesia is more available, and the 'civilizing' missionary efforts of militant Protestants have been supplemented and even supported by the evangelical interventions of global feminists and human rights activists," wrote Shweder.[22]

Yet many African feminists bristle at the idea that opposition to excision and infibulation has been imposed on them by Westerners. Circumcision, insisted Grace Mose, is meant to instill humility and submission in women, and to prepare them for a life of pain. In the modern world, she insisted, women should have options besides stoic forbearance. "Why don't we learn ways in which we can overcome hardships instead of enduring them?" she asked during her debate with Ahmadu. "We are not opposing it because we are following what the West is telling us. It's because of our own personal experience. There is no Western woman who came to tell me, 'This practice is painful.' No. That is an experience that I went through, and I understood how painful it was....No woman should have to deal with that."

Throughout the late 1970s and 1980s anti-FGM activism was the preserve of a disparate group of women working in small numbers in their own countries. The most well-known American opponent was Fran Hosken, a flamboyant Vienna-born polymath whose obituary described her as a "journalist, photographer, painter, author, urban planner, furniture and jewelry designer, entrepreneur, social activist, and world traveler."[23] For many years her self-published reports were a singular source of Western information about the practice, though even allies could find her overheated rhetoric counterproductive.

"The problem was, she was so emphatic and so strident that she didn't appreciate that her attitude and her language was, I would say, insulting to the Africans," recalled Joan Dunlop. "It was as though they didn't understand what this problem was, and they needed to be told what to do about this problem....I felt Fran Hosken did more damage than she did good, frankly."

At around the same time in England Efua Dorkenoo was waging her solitary crusade. A nurse and midwife from Ghana, Dorkenoo was moved to action after seeing the effects of circumcision on the African immigrants she treated. A founder of FORWARD, one of the world's premier anti-FGM organizations, her activism eventually led Britain in 1985 to pass a law criminalizing female circumcision, though the law was initially poorly enforced and she continually faced resistance from white liberals cowed by multiculturalism. "She did monumental work," said Taina Bien-Aimé, the executive director of Equality Now, an international NGO that fights human rights abuses against women.

Meanwhile, a small, brave group of African women soldiered forward in their own countries. "You had tiny, tiny groups that sometimes consisted of one person who was really risking her life out there to talk about the issue," said Bien-Aimé. "The way they did it was really breaking the taboo, because very often it was part of a secret society, and the girls didn't even know they were going to get cut until the knife was between their legs."

Such activism is dangerous now, and it was even more so then, when the women trying to change things lacked international allies. They were threatened with violence, the rape of their daughters, and the burning of their buildings. No one was enlisting the media or human rights movement on their behalf. "This is pre-Internet, preglobalization of information," said Bien-Aimé.

Since then the creation of the international women's movement has vastly amplified the voices and influence of such dissidents. More than any other region in the world, in Africa the politics of sex and gender are bound up with the institutions of global governance, which are themselves under pressure from the women's movement to intervene against discrimination. Humanitarian activist and Harvard fellow Alex de Waal has described how African activists, unable to access or influence their own governments, have been able to work through international NGOs to impact local policy. "Africa's new democracies are characterized by the diffusion of power and influence throughout international institutions and the increased permeability of these institutions to activism by elite civil society," he wrote.[24] He was talking about AIDS activists, but his analysis is equally true for feminists: "Blocked from direct routes of access, African activists meet with their Western counterparts, who have access to policy makers in Washington and Brussels, who in turn squeeze African governments."[25]

Until the 1990s few in the West were willing to pressure African governments to do anything about female circumcision. When Patricia Schroeder, a pioneering Democratic congresswoman, first got involved with the issue, "You couldn't get Amnesty International, you couldn't get anybody interested," she said. "It was interesting, because if you were doing something to people because of their religion or their race, everybody went off with a twelve-alarm fire, but if it was done to women it was cultural, and you should leave it alone." She pushed the State Department to try and influence countries where the United States was providing foreign aid, and to include female circumcision in its human rights assessment, but she had no luck until the election of Bill Clinton.

The Clinton administration took women's human rights far more seriously than any previous White House, but that wasn't the only reason that female circumcision suddenly became a part of American foreign policy. Starting around the time Clinton was elected, a series of high-profile events catapulted the previously obscure, taboo issue onto both the American and international stage like never before.

First, in 1992, Pulitzer Prize–winning author Alice Walker published *Possessing the Secret of Joy*, a novel about an African woman named Tashi who, spared circumcision as a child, later chose to undergo it as a gesture of anti-colonial authenticity, a mistake that plunges her into agony and madness, her sexuality destroyed and her soul nearly annihilated.

When the novel came out, said Bien-Aimé, people suddenly started talking about female circumcision in their living rooms, although both journalists and human rights campaigners still shied away. (Equality Now was formed the same year to address the sexual abuses that big human rights organizations refused to touch—female circumcision as well as rape, honor killing, and sex trafficking.) In 1993, Walker collaborated with the British documentarian Pratibha Parmar on a nonfiction book and hourlong documentary about female genital mutilation, both titled *Warrior Marks*.

The next year millions of people, including many world leaders, would tune in to CNN and see a horrifying clitoridectomy performed by a barber in a Cairo slum. The UN population conference had just begun and the world's attention was on Egypt when the CNN broadcast aired. It began by introducing Nagla, a smiling ten-year-old in a flowered skirt. "She's excited to be the center of attention, fearful of what might happen next," said a voiceover by Gayle Young, CNN's Cairo bureau chief. "This morning she'll be circumcised." The tape cut to the barber polishing what looked like a razor or a small scissors, and Young explained that he circumcised thousands of girls each year. "He doesn't bother to wash his hands," she said.

Nagla leaned against her father, her legs spread wide, as her family looked on. A female relative ululated. The barber bent in and cut her quickly and, as he did, she started shaking and wailing. "Shame on you, it's finished, so you can get up and go play," he told her. She kept screaming, shocked by the pain: "Daddy, daddy, there is a sin upon all of you!"

Afterward the barber explained his trade to the camera. "It's a tradition, a cleansing," he said. "Some girls come to me with a big clitoris, which creates friction, so that that girl gets hot and excited, she's boiling."

It ended with Nagla in bed, looking ill and agonized. "I want you to know, Dad, that I didn't want to be circumcised and you did it to me," she said. "Don't be a brat," her grandmother retorted.

The CNN piece shook the conference. "My memory of it was that the Americans were stunned, they had no idea," said Joan Dunlop. "I'm talking now about people on the U.S. delegation who were not close to these topics. It opened the eyes of the West." A group of American officials met with Egyptian president Hosni Mubarak, and Congresswoman Constance A. Morella, a Maryland Republican, confronted him about female circumcision. "I said that [the law] must be enforced, . . . that I'd seen the CNN film," she told the *Washington Post*. "[Mubarak] said it's hard to get rid of the practice, but he said he didn't think it was happening anymore in Egypt."[26]

Mubarak was either dishonest or woefully misinformed: Female circumcision was and remains almost universal in his country, practiced by Muslims and Coptic Christians alike. Regardless, the government was deeply embarrassed. Police detained the freelance producer who had arranged the filming "under a law making it a crime to disseminate information damaging Egypt's image," the Associated Press reported, and arrested the girl's father, the barber who performed the circumcision, a plumber who assisted him, and a florist who introduced the CNN producer to the family.[27]

The uproar set off a wave of defensive nationalism in Egypt. A radio journalist called the broadcast "a crime against Egypt at a time when the whole world was looking toward Cairo," and a publicity-loving Egyptian lawyer filed a lawsuit against the network, claiming it had defamed the nation by showing its citizens as "backward, barbaric people."[28] A prominent Islamic cleric, Sheikh Gad el-Haqq, issued a fatwa calling on all families to circumcise their girls.[29]

"Swept up in the international uproar but still immersed in a national culture that generally supported [female genital cutting], the Egyptian government floundered," wrote political scientist Elizabeth Heger Boyle.[30] Unable to pass a ban through Parliament, Mubarak tried to do it administratively, forbidding female circumcision in public hospitals. But Sheikh Gad el-Haqq's outrage over the restriction led to an absurd compromise in which circumcision would only be performed in hospitals one day a week, a limitation that in the end was mostly ignored.[31]

Two months after the Cairo conference a seventeen-year-old girl from Togo arrived at Newark airport, told a customs officer that her passport was fake, and asked for asylum, saying that if she was sent back to Togo she'd be forced to undergo genital mutilation. Fauziya Kassindja was the fifth daughter of a prosperous, liberal-minded Muslim man who opposed his tribe's practice of excision. When he died, under tribal law, control of both his property and his children passed to his siblings instead of to his wife. Her father's sister moved into her house, evicting her mother, and her father's brother became her legal guardian. The two of them arranged her marriage to a man who was almost three decades older and who had three wives already, and her fiancé insisted that she be excised.

"I was terrified because I had known girls who had died from having it done," Kassindja wrote later. "My mother's own sister had died from it, and I'd heard my parents speak of the event with horror."[32] So, with the help of her mother and oldest sister, Kassindja ran away, first to Germany, and then, with the help of a Nigerian she met there, to the United States. "I'd seen a lot of news reports at school about how America was always helping the needy, feeding hungry children, sending aid to refugees," she wrote. "My teachers at school had said it was a great country. They said people believed in justice in America. If I went there and I told them what had happened to me, surely they'd sympathize."[33]

Instead, she was imprisoned—for a time in maximum security—for over a year. She was shackled, held in isolation, subjected to arbitrary strip searches, and even teargassed. Not until the *New York Times* wrote about her, leading to a barrage of publicity, did embarrassed officials release her, pending resolution of her case. It came soon after. On June 13, 1996, in a precedent-setting ruling, the Board of Immigration Appeals granted her asylum. It was the first time that female genital mutilation was recognized as a form of persecution.

As the atmosphere around the issue shifted, Democrats were able to move forward with anti–female circumcision legislation. Schroeder succeeded in getting a ban on female circumcision passed in the United States, over the objections, oddly enough, of both Orthodox Jews and left-wing feminists. "Some of the Orthodox Jewish community really got all over us and didn't want us pursuing the issue, because they were afraid it would go into male circumcision," she recalled. "I had a lot of rabbis and others hollering, 'Please just be quiet about this.' Then we had some very progressive women's groups saying, You should stay out of this, this is their culture, we're being cultural imperialists. For which my response was 'This is plain child abuse. You've got to be kidding me.'"

Working with Democratic senator Harry Reid, Schroeder also spearheaded a law mandating that countries work to eliminate the practice or face cuts in foreign aid.[34] At around the same time USAID started funding groups like the Population Council to work on eradication efforts abroad.

Some African leaders were enraged by the interference. In a 1999 speech marking the end of Ramadan, Gambian president Yahya Jammeh accused the West of spending millions to undermine African culture and Islamic values. "FGM is part of our culture, and we should not allow anyone to dictate to us how we should conduct ourselves," he said. Then he issued a veiled threat to anti-FGM campaigners, saying, "There is no guarantee that after delivering their speeches they will return to their homes."[35]

Nevertheless, most African countries did move against female circumcision, either through laws or bureaucratic directives.[36] The pressure came from both inside and outside, as African feminists leveraged international institutions to force their own countries to act.

I n July 2003 the heads of government of the African Union countries approved one of the world's most progressive treaties on women's rights, the Protocol to the African Charter on Human and People's Rights on the Rights of Women in Africa, often referred to as the Maputo Protocol, after the city in Mozambique where it was negotiated. Though little noticed in the United States (or among the vast majority of African women), the Maputo Protocol was a major achievement for African feminists, who were the driving force behind it. It essentially amended the African Charter, a human rights treaty that because of its stress on protecting traditional cultures had sometimes been interpreted to condone customary and religious laws that discriminate against women. According to the African Charter, "The promotion and protection of morals and traditional values recognized by the community shall be the duty of the State," which arguably could be read as a defense of practices like female circumcision.[37]

In contrast, the Maputo Protocol puts the individual rights of women first. It obliges states to "ensure that the right to health of women, including sexual and reproductive health, is respected and promoted," and it requires the prohibition, "through legislative measures backed by sanctions, of all forms of female genital mutilation." Child marriage and forced marriage must also be outlawed. And the protocol called for governments to legalize abortion in cases of rape, incest, and threats to the life and health of the mother, making it the first international treaty that affirms abortion rights.

The protocol went into effect in 2005, after Togo became the fifteenth country to ratify it. "On FGM, it's as progressive as one can get. It condemns the practice. It is not ambiguous," said Charles Ngwena, a constitutional law professor at the University of the Free State in South Africa. "The expectation is that states are going to do everything that they should do in order to eradicate the practice." Officially, at least, female circumcision is now recognized as a human rights violation at the highest level of African law, even as it remains a cherished rite among many African people.

Gambia, which had initially registered reservations to the protocol, ratified it fully in April 2006. "Now that we know the serious consequences of our practice, it would amount not only to sheer folly and indifference to refuse to change, it may also amount to a high degree of callousness to allow adults to continue to inflict on helpless innocent babies and children such dreadful pains instead of the love, affection, and protection they ask for," Gambia's secretary of state argued at the National Assembly. "The cultural beliefs of the past may not be good anymore, because we now know that they are not too good for our health and well-being."[38]

Fuambai Ahmadu watched the emergence of the elite anti-FGM consensus with anger and incredulity. "Alice Walker is one of my favorite writers, so I was very excited to read *Possessing the Secret of Joy*," she recalled. She expected to identify with it, since there are, at least on the surface, powerful parallels between the novel's story and her own. After all, Tashi, Walker's narrator, seemed to be seeking what Ahmadu says she found by undergoing excision. "The operation she'd had done to herself joined her, she felt, to these women, whom she envisioned as strong, invincible," Walker wrote. "Completely woman. Completely African."[39]

Instead, Ahmadu was shocked by the dissonance between Walker's brutal tale and memories of her own circumcision. "I remember I was on a flight from Washington to London, and I read it and I just couldn't believe it," she said. Indeed, her reaction to the book did much to inspire her current career. "This is what sparked my interest in learning more about the meanings of [circumcision], because I had read *Possessing the Secret of Joy* and *Warrior Marks*, and I saw that [they] conflicted in every way possible with what I had experienced and what I had seen," said Ahmadu.

Most glaringly, Ahmadu felt that Walker and other anticircumcision activists distorted the impact of circumcision on women's sexuality. One of her key arguments is that circumcised women can still enjoy sex—her own excision, she said, hasn't affected her ability to orgasm at all. Some excised women, she suggested, have internalized the West's message about female genital cutting, and thus blame their lack of a clitoris for frustrations and ailments that may have other causes. Indeed, she posited that anti-FGM campaigns, rather than circumcision itself, was causing some African women to feel that they'd been damaged irrevocably.

Growing up in Washington, D.C., Ahmadu wrote in a 2007 essay, her Sierra Leonean aunts, cousins, and friends "seemed as obsessed with dating, boyfriends and sex as many 'normal,' 'liberated' American women of the same age group." She recalled going to nightclubs with her cousins and hearing tales of their sexual adventures. Excision never came up in these conversations, "most likely because circumcision was not seen as relevant to enjoyment (or lack of enjoyment) of sex." She continued, "Should I now doubt the experiences of these circumcised Sierra Leoneans, now that I 'know' all about the 'harmfulness' of excision and the supposed diminishment of women's sexual enjoyment?"[40]

Fortunately, wrote Ahmadu, "my Sierra Leonean agemates and I came of age at the tail end of an epoch of general ignorance about these African traditional practices in the West—a pre–*Warrior Marks* era that was about to witness the worldwide 'outing' of 'FGM' in Africa." Since then, she wrote, "[t]here has been no shortage of anti-FGM campaign materials, magazine articles, news specials, talk shows, hospital centers, social welfare offices and so on seeking to edify circumcised African women and girls regarding the harsh but necessary 'truth' that we are sexually 'mutilated.' Once celebrated and feared in their traditional African communities as the custodians of 'matriarchal' power, female circumcisers have been shamed, tried, imprisoned, and forced to accept and apologize for their supposed collusion in 'patriarchal' crimes against their own gender."[41]

Ahmadu's family comes from the Kono ethnic group, which lives in northeastern Sierra Leone. For the Kono, circumcision is at the center of girls' initiation into Bondo, a powerful female secret society (initiation into the male counterpart, Poro, also involves circumcision). "Bondo promulgates feminine interests: peace (through marriage alliances), sexual conduct, fertility and reproduction," Ahmadu wrote in a fascinating essay, "Rites and Wrongs: An Insider/Outsider Reflects on Power and Excision," which is part anthropological scholarship, part memoir.[42] Politically, wrote Ahmadu, "the separate male and female leaders of Bondo and Poro, called *soko* and *pamansu,* respectively, are all powerful."[43] Their power transcends the village level to shape national politics. "There is nobody who can dream of sitting in office in Freetown that does not have the approval of the Bondo hierarchy," she told me.

Many Kono women see anti-FGM campaigns as a threat to their power. During the 1996 election campaign, the *New York Times* reported, Bondo women pledged to support the president in return for his promise to check anti-FGM lobbying, and his wife sponsored mass circumcisions to garner votes.[44] After he won, the person he nominated for minister of gender and children's affairs was held up in parliament because she was thought to be uncircumcised and thus unfamiliar "with our adored customs," in the words of one MP. Educated women who haven't been cut will sometimes submit to the practice if they want to enter politics, and outside attempts to curb it are met with passionate protests.[45] In March 2008, Agence France-Presse reported, hundreds of Bondo women staged a procircumcision demonstration in the town of Kailahun. Calling the rally a "show of strength," one Bondo leader said, "Any organisation that has accepted funds from overseas donors to wage war against FGM is fighting a losing battle. Let donors keep their money; we will keep our culture."[46]

As a teenager, Ahmadu didn't know precisely what Bondo rites involved—initiates aren't supposed to tell the uninitiated. When she finally asked her cousins outright, they broke the code of silence to explain, though they didn't know enough about their own anatomy to be very accurate. One told her, "Oh yeah, they cut you, but I think mine grew back." So Ahmadu had a vague sense that Bondo involved some kind of genital cut, but mostly she just associated it with female strength.

There had never really been any question that she'd be initiated. "Among the Kono, Bondo is part of life, it's part of the culture," she said. "There's an expectation that all girls are going to go through Bondo. So in a sense it's your right. It is your privilege. And if you don't, then you are being denied your right. For me, it was something I was very excited to belong to. It's always talked about. I cannot go a day among my relatives and not hear somebody make a reference to Bondo. So for me it was a question of when, not if."

Ahmadu's initiation was postponed because her family wanted her to go through it with an aunt around her own age, but her aunt lacked a green card and thus couldn't leave the United States. By the time her aunt's papers were in order, she'd decided she didn't want to be circumcised, so her aunt stayed home while the family flew Ahmadu, then a twenty-two-year-old senior at George Washington University, and her eight-year-old sister to Sierra Leone to join Bondo during the Christmas break.

It was a discombobulating, sometimes thrilling and physically agonizing experience. There were days of feasting, dancing, and celebration as they visited their family's ancestral villages. The initiation itself took place in Koidu, the capital of Kono, where her mother's sisters lived. Ahmadu knew what was going to happen, but she couldn't bring herself to tell her little sister, because she didn't want to frighten her. She wasn't a virgin, and she started to worry that she'd never enjoy sex again, but her cousins assured her that she would. "I reasoned that whatever it was I was going to endure, it would be worth the experience, the excitement of watching and being involved in the drama around me," she wrote.[47]

The initiates were served a bitter, tasteless ceremonial meal said to contain important medicines. They were bathed in a river and smeared in pale mud, then sprinkled with perfumed talcum powder. Their hair was braided ceremonially. In a video taken by one of Ahmadu's uncles, the girls appear ghostly but smiling. "Drums were beaten as money was tossed from the crowd to the braiders," she wrote. "Mock battles took place between what I later understood were members representing my father's lineage, *fa den moe*, and those standing in for my mother's line, or *bain den moe*." A woman painted in white clay kept yanking Ahmadu and her sister off the ground, metaphorically kidnapping them, only to release them when representatives of her father's family offered her "a substantial amount of money."[48]

Later that evening a nurse who was a close friend of her mother's broke protocol by explaining to Ahmadu how the circumcision was going to unfold. She said she was going to give her an anesthetic injection—itself somewhat controversial, because stoically bearing the pain is part of the point—as well as oral painkillers and antibiotics. She explained that there were nearby clinics in case of emergencies. "I was suddenly struck by the full extent of what I had allowed myself to get into," wrote Ahmadu.[49]

They were secluded in a house and given more medicinal leaves. None of them were allowed to sleep. Celebrations went on all night outside. The next day they were taken to a sacred grove—the Bondo bush. "I was hoisted up by four or five of these stocky women," she wrote. "I looked down: a large leaf had been laid on the ground directly underneath my buttocks.... Terror finally overcame me as the women's faces, now dozens, now hundreds, moved in closer all around my near naked body suspended in mid-air. They grabbed my legs and arms apart. The women's screams, the sound of drums, and then a sharp blade cut deep into my flesh on one side and then on the other. As I cried out in unimaginable agony, I felt warm blood ooze down between my thighs. Perhaps for the first time since I was an infant, I vomited."[50]

Afterward, Ahmadu begged her mother to take her home, and her mother felt guilty and apologized. But in time she came to place a profound value on her initiation into Bondo—especially once she realized that it wasn't going to impede her sex life. "For the majority of Sierra Leonean women, Bondo is an institution of women's empowerment," she said. "It's about women's traditional power and their links with ancestors. Because it's mainly women in the rural areas that are part of Bondo, I think it's an important way that women who are educated, who are working in urban areas, or out of the country, can connect with women at the grassroots." Ahmadu has a son; were she to have a daughter, she said, she hopes her girl would choose to join Bondo as well.

To talk to Ahmadu is to begin to understand why a practice that causes so much pain nevertheless remains so entrenched and so zealously defended by its ostensible victims. Female circumcision has no more eloquent advocate. She reminds us that what public health officials call "harmful traditional practices" are in fact the very texture of life for many people, the rituals and norms that imbue existence with order and purpose.

All the same, for Ahmadu circumcision was a choice, one she made as an adult. For the overwhelming majority of girls who undergo it that is not the case. Most have such options only when a cluster of deeply rooted values, beliefs, and hierarchies begin to deteriorate, a process that causes anguish and panic for some and offers the promise of liberation to others. The fact remains that, in general, the more alternatives girls have and the more exposure to the outside world, the less likely they are to opt for these old ways. And when they don't, the anticircumcision movement is sometimes the only powerful social force on their side.

Nowhere in the world is that more clear than at Kenya's Tasaru Ntomonok Girls Rescue Center, a shelter that houses dozens of Masai girls who have fled their villages in their desperation to remain intact. Located on the edge of Narok, a dusty market town in Kenya's fabled Rift Valley, Tasaru is testament to the lengths to which some girls will go to escape painful traditions once they glean the merest hint of a way out.

Foreigners visiting Africa adore the Masai, the seminomadic herdsmen who live in Kenya and Tanzania, because in an increasingly homogenized world, they cling tightly to their traditions. A Nilotic people who emigrated from Sudan and southern Ethiopia a thousand years ago, they live in some of East Africa's richest game areas, and tourists on safari love to take pictures of statuesque Masai men in their red *kikoi* robes, walking sticks, and stretched earlobes, and of Masai women adorned with elaborate beaded jewelry. Traditional Masai dancing entertains visitors at fancy lodges.

Narok itself is culturally mixed, though it became less so after 2007's disputed presidential election, when Masai mobs drove out the Kikuyu, long the country's dominant ethnic group.[51] Resentment toward the Kikuyu—and the political order they represent—runs deep among a tribe that saw little benefit from Kenya's development. "The Masai have struggled more than most other tribes to come to terms with the modern world," Jonathan Clayton wrote in the *Times* (London) in 2004. "They have taken badly to farming, land enclosures and the Western values propagated through state education." This, wrote Clayton, has led them to cling more tightly to traditions like circumcision, and to force their daughters into early marriages in order "to protect their daughters from Western influences and fend off economic hardship."[52]

Agnes Pareyio, the founder of Tasaru Ntomonok, has dedicated her life to fighting such customs. A Masai woman in her early fifties with an open, friendly face and a comforting, imposing maternal bulk, Pareyio has a gap where her two bottom middle teeth should be, a traditional Masai body modification. Besides that, when I first met her the only outward sign of her ethnic heritage was the beaded bracelet she wears. Her hair was braided and coiled in a bun. When she goes into the surrounding villages she sometimes shocks other Masai by wearing trousers, though on special occasions she dons the colorful robes and elaborate jewelry for which the Masai are famous.

Pareyio grew up in an ordinary Masai village, though she didn't have an entirely ordinary childhood. Her father had been forced by the colonial government to attend school, an experience that convinced him of the importance of education. He sent Pareyio to boarding school, where she had a friend from a community that didn't circumcise their daughters and was horrified to hear about the practice. For Pareyio's mother and grandmother, excision was a natural and unquestioned part of life—it was unthinkable that a woman could be married until her clitoris and labia had been cut off. But Pareyio's friend planted doubts in her mind.

During the December holiday when she was fourteen, Pareyio returned home from school to find her family preparing a great feast. She asked her mother what was going on, and she replied, "All these people are here because there's a ritual that is going to be performed." Pareyio realized what they were planning and told her mother that she refused to let it happen. Her mother enlisted Pareyio's father for support, but he backed his daughter. Upset, her mother told Pareyio's grandmother, who came screaming, "Who is that that is saying she will not be cut? What are we going to call her? Are we going to call her a child? Or a woman? What will we call her?"

Within the village everyone was talking about it, calling Pareyio a coward. Eventually, the pressure became too much for her, and she agreed to go through with it. Her legs were pried open and her genitals slashed off. Afterward, an old woman felt the wound to make sure nothing was left. The pain was horrible, and it came back twice as badly every time she urinated. She has regretted it her entire life.

Luckily, she was sent back to school, and her parents didn't marry her off until she was eighteen. Soon after her marriage, Pareyio got involved in Maendeleo ya Wanawake, a nationwide women's organization, where she became a local leader and, before long, a campaigner against female circumcision. To demonstrate the consequences of the practice, she commissioned a model of the female reproductive tract with detachable parts from a local woodworker, then walked with it from village to village, talking to any group who would listen. She spoke about shock, pain, and hemorrhaging, and explained how circumcision complicated delivery. "After excision, what is left is a scar," she said. "During birth, the body cannot expand as it is supposed to," leading to prolonged labor and even brain damage in babies. Furthermore, she argued, women "must have their right to enjoy sex." The only point of circumcision, she said, "is just to tame a woman, depriving them of their sexual rights." She compared herself to a car without a key to start the engine.[53]

Pareyio quickly became an infamous figure. "When I started showing this model, my husband thought I was crazy," she said. People mocked him—and threatened her. Embarrassed, he took another wife, and she took her four children and went to live on her own.

Then, in 1999, a girl who had heard Pareyio speak in her church ran away from home. She was twelve years old, and on the eve of her circumcision she made her way to Narok from a village forty kilometers (about twenty-five miles) away. According to Pareyio, the girl came across a local teacher and told her, "I'm looking for a woman by the name Agnes who visited us. She said to us that it's not good to be cut, that it's wrong to be cut, and that there was a need for us to go to school. I want to go to school. I don't want to be cut." But instead of taking the girl to Pareyio, the teacher, herself a Masai, brought her back to her parents' home. The girl was excised the following day.

Pareyio was shocked when she learned what had happened. She tracked down the girl and arranged to enroll her in boarding school, but knew that wasn't enough. In the future, if girls ran away there needed to be a place for them to go. Soon enough, more did. Rebellion, it seemed, was a contagion that could spread. Pareyio found housing for the girls among some of her local supporters while she looked for something more permanent.

Then, in 2000, Pareyio had a serendipitous meeting with Eve Ensler, of *Vagina Monologues* fame. A playwright-turned-global-activist, Ensler's great cause is violence against women, and her V-Day campaign raises money for grassroots women's groups worldwide. On a trip to Kenya she saw Pareyio in the field, doing a presentation in a village with her wooden model. Enormously impressed, Ensler bought Pareyio a jeep—V-Day is written across the top—so that she could cover more ground, and started fund-raising for a shelter. In 2002, Tasaru Ntomonok—which means "rescue the women" in the Masai language—was born, and the girls started coming, on foot and by bus, from dozens and even hundreds of kilometers away. Sometimes Pareyio will get a tip that a girl is about to be cut or forced into a marriage, and she'll drive out to get her. Once, with the help of local police, she saved a nine-year-old girl who, in the words of the UNFPA, "was being frog-marched to her husband's home to become his fourth wife."[54]

The phenomenon of the runaway girls was bigger than just Tasaru. In February 2003 the BBC reported that at least one hundred girls from Kenya's southwest region had sought shelter in churches after fleeing home to escape circumcision. "No one helped them run away," said a local women's rights

activist. "They know we have been teaching against the dangers of FGM."[55]
Dozens of others have fled to the Centre for Human Rights and Democracy in
the Rift Valley town of Eldoret, not far from the Ugandan border.[56]

The Tasaru Ntomonok Girls Rescue Center consists of three low brick
buildings with orange trim on Narok's outskirts. One of them has "V
Day Safe House For The Girls" emblazoned across the front, and inside a war-
ren of small, basic but immaculate rooms are painted a cheerful blue, each
with two sets of bunk beds. Most girls stay there only when they first run
away and during holidays; as soon as she can, Agnes uses funding from Ensler
and UNFPA to enroll them in nearby boarding schools. (It costs around one
thousand dollars per girl, per year.) During the summer of 2007, Tasaru was
caring for sixty-eight girls. More than one thousand have passed through, and
almost seven hundred have stayed long term. Three of the first runaways have
just started college.

There's something magical about these girls' bravery, about the way they
left their whole worlds behind them rather than submit to a fate that once
seemed immutable. Anne K., a moon-faced fourteen-year-old with the big
sloe eyes and tiny nose of an anime character, was only eleven when she left
home after her father ordered her circumcised against her mother's wishes. She
spoke softly, almost whispering, as she explained how her mother helped her
sneak away at 4:00 A.M., how she walked forty kilometers through the bush
on an empty stomach; how she encountered many wild animals, including
elephants, though luckily, "they didn't beat me."

She knew of Tasaru because Pareyio had visited her village, and other girls
had run away before her. "At Tasaru, I was welcomed," she said. "At the time I
came to Tasaru I didn't know many things, such as the importance of education." Her mother had had eight children, but Anne was the only girl, and as
such her domestic burden was heavy. "When I was at home, I wake up in the
morning, I prepare breakfast for my brothers. After that I go to school. After
school I start working again," gathering firewood and washing clothes. She
was tired all the time. Tasaru introduced her to a life where her happiness was
valued. "At Tasaru we have leisure time, we play, we sing together," she said.
"Agnes, she has helped us. She has saved our lives." Sitting in a classroom at

the Narok boarding school where she's in grade six, she said, smiling shyly, that she hopes to become a pilot someday. Her teacher mentioned that she's first in her class.

Anne's parents have never visited her. If her mother tried, Anne said, she'd be beaten. Pareyio tries to reconcile girls with their mothers and fathers, but it can be a long, difficult process. In 2004, Equality Now publicized a hideous case of forced mutilation following one Tasaru girl's reunion with her family. After running away in 2001, sixteen-year-old Santeyian Keiwua returned home when her mother promised to leave her and her fourteen-year-old sister, Dorcas, intact. Her mother kept her word, but one day when she was away, the girls' brother and a group of neighbors beat them, held them down, and had them cut. When their mother returned home she rushed them to the hospital, where they stayed for nine days. "The way this thing was done does not fit any description. It was done in a very malicious manner," the examining doctor told a Kenyan newspaper.[57] With police after him the girls' brother fled, and they returned to Tasaru, terrified that if they went home, they'd be forcibly married as well.[58]

Some mothers come to see their daughters while they're living at Tasaru, but their fathers rarely do. Especially in its early days there was considerable rage toward Pareyio. "They were very much against Tasaru. They say you are going against the tradition of the people," said Hellen Kamaamia, a local teacher who serves as Tasaru's treasurer. Besides, men typically pay for their wives with cattle, the Masais' traditional source of wealth; fathers who can't give their daughters in marriage are literally poorer for it. Furious men—fathers or would-be husbands—would sometimes show up outside Tasaru's door with swords, demanding their girls back, and Pareyio would have to face them down. "Agnes is bold," Kamaamia said with obvious admiration.

It helps to have the law on her side. In 2001, Kenya passed the Children's Act, which bans circumcision for girls under eighteen, as well as forced marriage. As we've seen, some question what is accomplished by national laws against female genital cutting, given how unpopular and poorly enforced they are. There is even evidence that such laws are leading some Masai to cut their girls at ever younger ages, before they can protest or escape.[59] But it was the Children's Act that allowed Pareyio to save the nine-year-old bride and that lets her call the police when fathers come threatening. Activists sheltering other runaways also say the law made it possible for them to protect girls from their families.[60]

Despite her stalwart rejection of harmful traditions, the last thing Pareyio wants is for the girls at Tasaru to end up alienated from Masai culture. Instead, she wants Masai culture to change to embrace strong, educated girls. Female circumcision is the way girls have traditionally been initiated into Masai womanhood. Pareyio sees much of value in the initiation process, and she's trying to keep it alive without the cut.

Each August groups of girls come to Tasaru for an alternative rite of passage ceremony. Many of them are girls who ran away, but some are brought by parents who have themselves been convinced to eschew circumcision. For five days the girls go into seclusion, where Pareyio teaches them about sexual and reproductive health, HIV prevention, and the harms of cutting. She invites old women from the community to give them all the instructions about maintaining a home and a family that usually accompany circumcision. On the last day, amid songs, feasting, and gifts, the girls are declared adults.

Slowly, Pareyio's community has started to see her as a leader rather than a threat. Through UNFPA Tasaru bought a maize-grinding mill that former circumcisers can use to replace their lost income; some of them have become Pareyio's most important allies.[61] In 2004, frustrated that the law against female genital cutting wasn't being enforced strongly enough, Pareyio ran for deputy mayor of Narok district—and won. "There is a lot of respect now, because people have seen that I take their girls to school," she said. "I don't mess up their daughters."

No outsider could ever create the kind of change Pareyio has, but Pareyio couldn't have had such a profound impact without outside help. That, ultimately, is what the anti-FGM movement—and the global reproductive rights movement more broadly—is about. To support people like Pareyio—as well as those fighting to implement the Maputo Protocol or struggling against draconian abortion bans or the terrible iniquities of sharia law—is to reject relativism. It is to believe that other cultures, like our own, can change in necessary ways without being destroyed.

For those understandably skeptical of Western interventions in the poor world, that might look like imperialism. Liberals have many reasons to sympathize with people struggling to hold on to their ways of life in the face of the hegemonic steamroller of globalization. But they have even more reason to sympathize with people who are fighting for individual rights in societies that demand subsuming such rights to tradition and myths about sexual purity. After all, even if relativists like Shweder truss them up in fashionable third-worldism, such demands are the very essence of reactionary conservatism. That's true whether they are made by the Vatican, an imam, or a tribal hierarchy. When some people are willing to risk their lives to escape tradition, it's hard to see the difference between culture and tyranny.

Save for a few corners of Scandinavia, there is no society on earth that does not discriminate against women, and no place where such discrimination is not ardently defended *by* some women, who usually see it as a respectful, safeguarding recognition of difference. Women's rights, then, will always, at one time or another, conflict with culture. The loss of the status quo, of ancient ways of doing things, is genuinely painful for some. One can see that and still see that solidarity means taking sides.

CHAPTER 6: **THE GLOBALIZATION OF THE CULTURE WARS**

As NATO bombs fell on Kosovo in 1999, around 850,000 people, the vast majority of them ethnic Albanians, fled into Albania and Macedonia. Serb soldiers were on the rampage, and Kosovar Albanian women were being raped systematically, some for days on end. Such rapes, wrote Human Rights Watch, "were not rare and isolated acts committed by individual Serbian or Yugoslav forces, but rather were used deliberately as an instrument to terrorize the civilian population, extort money from families, and push people to flee their homes. Rape furthered the goal of forcing ethnic Albanians from Kosovo."[1]

When people are driven from their homes, their most immediate needs are, obviously, food, shelter, and emergency medical care. As Merle Goldberg and Harvey Karman always knew, though, reproductive health needs can be acute, especially when sexual violence is prevalent and people are displaced for many months. One of the UNFPA's mandates is providing for the reproductive health—including safe childbirth—of refugee populations. So after the war the UNFPA sent several experts to review the situation and see what needed to be done.

One of them, Manuel Carballo, the coordinator of the International Centre for Migration and Health, reported back on the need to make plans for dealing with pregnant refugees. "Ensuring healthy pregnancies and safe deliveries among women in camps and 'on the road' is already a major challenge and supplies and equipment in this domain are already called for," he wrote.[2] Another UNFPA consultant, a psychologist specializing in sexual violence and trauma, investigated the particular needs of rape victims. Among her conclusions: "It is assumed that many women who have become pregnant as a result of sexual violence will seek to terminate their pregnancy. Abortion is legal in Federal Republic of Yugoslavia and in Albania, where it is legal up to 12 weeks, and up to 22 weeks in cases of pregnancy as a result of rape. As per the Programme of Action of the International Conference on Population and Development, any provision of abortion should be safe and post abortion counseling should be offered promptly." Emergency contraception was legal in Albania and, she wrote, it "should be a part of any medical response to women who have been victims of sexual violence, as an option for these women."[3]

Thus, the UNFPA provided safe delivery kits—including soap, razor blades, and plastic sheeting—as well as emergency contraceptives, manual vacuum aspirators, condoms, underwear, and sanitary pads. Manual vacuum aspirators can, of course, be used to perform abortions, but they're also necessary for treating incomplete miscarriages and complications from unsafe abortions. What the UNFPA was doing was standard practice and would have gotten little notice had the antiabortion activist Austin Ruse not shown up.

During the late summer of 1999 the Population Research Institute, a right-wing Catholic group dedicated to fighting international family planning, sent Ruse on an eight-day fact-finding tour of Albania. "The concern was that the refugee women were being coerced into sterilizations and even abortions," he wrote in an article titled "UN Pro-life Lobbying: Full Contact Sport," published in the antiabortion journal *Human Life Review*.[4] Ruse admitted he didn't find what he was looking for. "In the eight days I was there, I discovered only one case that could be considered an abuse," he wrote. "A peasant woman in Vlora had been given an abortion at the government's regional hospital and not been told of the negative medical consequences to her. As to bribes with food and medicine, I saw none."[5] Nevertheless, with no evidence at all, he asserted that the UNFPA was working with Milošević to ethnically cleanse the Kosovars. "UNFPA was only too happy to assist the Serbs with the demography question," Ruse wrote. "UNFPA had long been charged with cutting human-rights corners in cozying up to oppressive regimes like China's and Peru's. And here it was clearly aiding Milošević in his desire for fewer Kosovars."[6]

Ruse spread this slander among the Kosovars he encountered and among sympathetic right-wing pundits at home. At the time Niek Biegman was Holland's NATO representative, and he learned what Ruse was doing while visiting Dutch troops in the field. Such rumormongering, he said, was "criminally irresponsible." Had the traumatized Kosovars believed that the UNFPA had been complicit in Milošević's genocide, Biegman said, "they might have killed the UNFPA people."[7]

Back in the United States Ruse got the conservative media to pick up the story. "Now that NATO troops have ended ethnic cleansing in Kosovo, there's reason to fear that the United Nations Population Fund will do what the Serbs failed to: pacify the region by reducing the Albanian population," columnist Rod Dreher wrote in the *New York Post*. His sources were Ruse and Steven Mosher, head of the Population Research Institute.[8] The story made the rounds of the Catholic press, forcing the UNFPA to defend itself, even though doing so kept the invented "controversy" alive.

Ruse was part of an aggressive new kind of global right-wing movement. As the 1990s progressed, religious conservatives were learning from the success of the international women's movement and, in many ways, imitating it. Like Goldberg and Karman in Bangladesh, they started taking direct action on the ground. Like Germain and Dunlop, they organized coalitions of sympathetic groups worldwide that could work at the grassroots, national, and international levels. They formed NGOs, had international conferences, and made their way onto country delegations for United Nations meetings. They eventually would find unprecedented influence in the administration of George W. Bush, which shared Ruse's cavalier attitude toward the truth.

American-style culture wars became ever more globalized. The American right had long demonized groups working toward social progress—whether on race, poverty, women's equality, or gay rights—as deracinated elites out to destroy the values of the salt-of-the-earth majority. Now a group of conservatives, mostly based in the United States, sought to take this critique international and to mobilize traditionalists throughout the world against global feminism. They presented themselves as opponents of cultural colonialism even when, after 2000, they were supported by the government of the world's only superpower.

When women's groups first started organizing within the United Nations, their primary opponents were governments like the Vatican and Iran. The American antiabortion movement had stayed on the sidelines, pressuring U.S. politicians but otherwise ignoring the mechanics of the UN process. That's not surprising: Right-wing religious movements in the United States, especially Protestant ones, have typically hated and feared the United Nations, often seeing it as the seat of a satanic plot against Christianity. (In the *Left Behind* books, Tim LaHaye's hugely popular series of evangelical end-times thrillers, the anti-Christ is the UN's abortion-promoting, peace-promising secretary-general. In the video-game version of the books, players form Christian militias to battle demonic global "peacekeepers" on the streets of New York City.)

Catholics don't generally share this eschatological aversion. Pope John Paul II may have loathed the reproductive rights agenda at the United Nations, but he was a passionate supporter of the UN itself, and saw international law as crucial to world peace. There is, though, a millenarian, conspiracy-minded strain in American Catholicism—particularly in the radical antiabortion movement—that has much in common with the broader Christian right. It imagines secret societies engaged in a plot to crush the faithful under the boot of a godless one-world government. As the 1990s ended and the new millennium began, this strain would be increasingly visible on the global stage.

In the wake of Cairo and Beijing, various American religious-right groups began to realize that whatever their feelings about the world body, by ignoring the UN they were ceding powerful political ground. Thus a number of zealous antiabortion activists began focusing on international institutions, learning the byways of a system they despised. Unlike the older, Vatican-led conservative coalition, they weren't content to play defense against feminist initiatives at the United Nations. They went on the offense, working wherever they could to try to roll back reproductive rights both nationally and internationally.

A crucial figure in this process was Father Paul Marx, a Catholic priest from the Midwest known for his anti-Semitic rhetoric. Marx was a longtime advocate of natural family planning, which he taught all over the world, founding the *International Review of Natural Family Planning* in 1976. Perhaps due to his international experience, his antiabortion activism always transcended U.S. borders. "Contraception-sterlization-abortion is a worldwide plague that has already engulfed more than two-thirds of mankind, and I am convinced it will spread through the rest," he wrote in a 1984 newsletter.[9]

In 1981, Marx founded Human Life International—the organization Rafael

Cabrera represents in Managua—in Washington, D.C. "From the hub of the political world I shall launch forth to devote two or three months a year to spreading the prolife/pro-family gospel, mostly in the underdeveloped areas that I know so well from having visited 51 countries," he wrote. "In Asia, Africa and Latin America, I shall introduce prolife/pro-family literature and audiovisual aids, planting or nourishing the natural family planning (NFP) movement."[10]

Marx claimed absolutely fealty to the pope, yet he routinely ignored papal injunctions against anti-Semitism, giving frequent vent to his obsession with the link between Jews and abortion. "A famous genetics professor in Paris told me that the leaders of the abortion movement in France were Jewish. I saw one, a Jewish female liar, do her thing on behalf of abortion at the World Population Conference in Bucharest," he wrote in 1977.[11] He sounded the same theme a decade later: "If you have read my book *The Death Peddlers*, notice how many Jews helped lead the infamous 1971 abortion-planning meeting in Los Angeles, which I exposed; some 40 percent of the speakers were Jewish. Also, note the large number of abortionists (consult the Yellow Pages) and pro-abortion medical professors who are Jewish."[12]

Muslims were reviled as well, although the threat they posed was of a different sort. Marx worried endlessly that they were outbreeding Christians, especially in Europe, a fear that's increasingly heard on the right today. "Dr. Emmanuel Tremblay, a French scientist, has calculated that if current trends hold, France will be largely a Moslem country by 2035 (thank you, contraception-sterilization-abortion)," he wrote.[13] (Tremblay is the leader of France's largest anti-abortion group, Laissez-les vivre.)

In the United States, Human Life International consistently has been intertwined with the most extreme elements of the American antiabortion movement. Its spokesman, Don Treshman, once praised the sniper-style shooting of a Vancouver abortion provider as a "superb tactic." Hours after Michael Griffin murdered a Florida gynecologist, Treshman started raising money for the killer's family.[14]

Human Life International's rhetorical radicalism made it hard for the group to work effectively on Capitol Hill or in global forums, so in the late 1990s the group created two spin-off organizations. The first was the Population Research Institute, a branch of HLI that became a separate outfit in 1996. The split, HLI explained in a press release, was "to enable [PRI] to operate more effectively in the secular world, out from under the mantle of a Catholic pro-life organization. As the parent organization, Human Life International has continued to provide the overwhelming majority of funding to the Population Research Institute.... To date, HLI has invested well over $1,000,000 in starting PRI."[15] As its name suggests, the Population Research Institute is mainly concerned with population policies and organizations, especially the UNFPA. Despite its attempt to pass as a legitimate research group, its scientific veneer is terribly thin: According to a fund-raising letter, its goal is to "drive the final nail into the coffin of U.N. Population Fund abortionists."

Ever since it became an independent organization the Population Research Institute has been run by Steven Mosher, a man whose history gave him good reason to abhor and distrust population programs. In the early 1980s, Mosher was an aspiring China scholar whose expulsion from his Stanford Ph.D. program made headlines. The controversy started when, while doing fieldwork in his then wife's village in southern China's Guangdong province, Mosher convinced officials to let him attend meetings where women with unapproved pregnancies were browbeaten into having abortions. "Mosher called the sessions 'classic brainwashing,' including appeals to patriotism and statements that the babies' lives could not be 'guaranteed' after birth," reported the *Washington Post*. "Some women forced to have abortions, he said, were in their eighth and ninth months of pregnancy, so determined were Chinese officials to limit the country's massive population growth."[16]

After leaving China, Mosher wrote an article about coerced abortion there for the *Sunday Times Chinese Weekly,* a Taiwanese magazine. The piece included a photo he'd taken of a woman being prepared for an abortion. (Her face was unconcealed, which could have left her vulnerable to government reprisals.)

Furious about Mosher's exposé, Chinese officials for a time banned all further field research in their country by American academics, and accused Mosher of bribing villagers and smuggling antique coins out of the country, among other offenses. The government was clearly trying to discredit a critic, but when Stanford started investigating they reportedly found damning evidence, some of it provided by the wife Mosher had recently divorced. She seconded the charges of bribery and accused her ex-husband of endangering her relatives in the village.[17] A university committee eventually accused Mosher of "illegal and seriously unethical conduct," and his department unanimously voted to expel him.

Both Mosher and the university refused to make public a forty-seven-page report on the school's findings. In the aftermath he claimed that by throwing him out Stanford was caving to Chinese pressure. Unsurprisingly, the ordeal left Mosher militantly opposed both to population programs and the Chinese government. (Among his books are *Hegemon: China's Plan to Dominate Asia and the World* and, with Republican California assemblyman Chuck DeVore, the political thriller *China Attacks*.) His outrage at China's one-child policy is justified, but it's left him intensely paranoid about the UNFPA and international family planning, which he argues is part of a "New World Order" conspiracy. "The assault on human dignity frees the proposed world government to selectively reduce the population of the world to a manageable number," he wrote.[18] Overpopulation, according to Mosher, is a myth. "In fact," he wrote, "the entire population of the world could live in the state of Texas, in single-family dwellings with front and back yards."[19]

In 2002 the Population Research Institute would play a major role in convincing the Bush administration to defund the UNFPA. Meanwhile, though, Human Life International realized that it needed another front to lobby inside the UN, which had denied Marx's own organization NGO accreditation due to the group's "attacks on Islam," its "aggressive language," and its general hostility to the "purposes of the United Nations."[20] Seeking another way in, Human Life International formed the Catholic Family and Human Rights Institute (C-FAM) in 1997, under the auspices of its Canada branch. In order to gain access to the UN, its connection to its parent organization was kept hidden. A confidential organizational chart had a dotted line down the center, with the names below it marked "visible." Those above the line were all employees of Human Life International–Canada.[21]

C-FAM's first director was Ann Noonan, but she was soon pushed aside by her aggressive, savvy deputy, a former journalist named Austin Ruse. At the UN, Ruse would act like a right-wing Joan Dunlop, organizing a disparate international coalition of fundamentalists. Behind the scenes C-FAM worked closely with the Vatican. According to an internal document, "Though not publicized, one of C-FAM's major mandates will be to act as a real resource and information office to the Holy See delegation."[22] But Ruse displayed far more hostility to the United Nations as an institution than the official church did, and he could play rougher.

The creation of C-FAM roughly coincided with the birth of a similar Mormon initiative, the World Family Policy Center, run out of Brigham Young University and headed by law professor Richard Wilkins. According to its Web site, the group was formed to counter pressure on the UN "to adopt legal norms that pose serious threats to family stability, parental rights and religious liberty," and it serves as a kind of think tank for international opposition to the feminist movement.

Wilkins soon teamed up with Dr. Allan Carlson, a conservative Lutheran who headed the Howard Center for Family, Religion & Society. Located in Rockford, Illinois, the Howard Center was a spin-off of the ultraright Rockford Institute, a nationalist, isolationist outfit known for its barely concealed anti-Semitism and white supremacism.[23] The Howard Center was an unlikely outpost for an emerging global interfaith network, but by the mid 1990s that's essentially what it had become.

A historian by training, Carlson's Ph.D. dissertation had been a damning examination of the work of Gunnar and Alva Myrdal, the social democratic progenitors of Sweden's ultraprogressive family policies. Most of his work in the ensuing years was focused on the United States, but the UN world conferences of the 1990s—as well as the demographic situation of the former Soviet republics—grabbed his attention, and in 1997 he organized a conference in Prague to bring together religious, antifeminist conservatives from all over the globe. It was called the "World Congress of Families." "We want to exert a counterforce to the devastation of the family that is being wrought by the forces of modernity," John Howard, the Rockford Center's founder and the conference's cochair, told a Utah newspaper.[24]

Wilkins was at the Prague gathering, and he and Carlson soon started collaborating. Together they organized the second World Congress of Families, held in 1999 at the UN's Palais des Nations in Geneva. It attracted over eight hundred, including a delegation of twenty-five or thirty people from Iran. C-FAM was a cosponsor.

High-profile speakers included Alfonso Cardinal López Trujillo, president of the Pontifical Council for the Family; Jehan el-Sadat, widow of Egyptian president Anwar el-Sadat; Max Padilla, Nicaragua's Opus Dei–affiliated minister for family affairs; and S. Shahid Husain, senior adviser to the Organization of the Islamic Conference mission to the United Nations. Margaret Ogola, a Kenyan pediatrician, prize-winning novelist, and Opus Dei supernumerary who runs an orphanage for HIV-positive children, donned traditional African dress to condemn the "worldwide dissemination of a culture of pleasure as the ultimate desirable good."[25] Her speech, said Carlson, was "Lincolnesque."

For many attendees this was exhilarating stuff. In the past it was liberals who had always claimed to speak for the downtrodden representatives of poor nations, but now Western conservatives were basking in anti-imperialist righteousness. "It is absolutely necessary for the South to join forces with religious groups around the world and global anti-abortion movements to bring pressure to bear on pro-abortionists and perpetrators of global population control through artificial methods," declared Cameroon's Maria Morfaw, who had led her country's NGO delegation to Beijing. Proclaimed Austin Ruse, "Our friends in the developing world have been coerced long enough. It is time for us to come to their defense on a very broad scale."

These newly organized cadres had their first confrontation with the women's movement in March 2000, at a United Nations meeting in New York held to review the progress that had been made since the Beijing conference. Reverend Jennifer Butler, who represented the liberal Presbyterian Church (USA) at the UN, recalled the scene. She was sitting in the balcony of a UN conference hall listening to a speech when "a crowd of men from Mormon and Catholic groups suddenly began streaming through the backdoors of the conference hall as if on cue.... They wore professional business suits like the ones bankers and lawyers prefer. Their hair was short and clean-cut. The few women among them wore power suits and perfectly coifed hair. All of them wore bright campaign buttons emblazoned with a single word: 'motherhood.' "[26]

Groups of robed monks, bearded and stern-faced, encircled women from feminist organizations and started praying for their souls.[27] Others "blocked the entrances to discussion rooms, booed statements they disagreed with and surrounded delegates they saw as proponents of the Pill and of abortion," reported Deutsche Presse-Agentur, the German press agency.[28]

All this was small scale, though, compared to what Human Life International's fronts could accomplish once they got George W. Bush onboard. "[T]he prospects for our movement at the UN rest chiefly on the outcome of the next US presidential election," Ruse wrote in 2000. "If the next US administration is pro-life, everything will change."[29]

One of the very first things that George W. Bush did upon taking office was to reinstate the global gag rule, resulting in clinic closures and contraceptive shortages worldwide. Still, early on it wasn't entirely clear just how much damage the new president would do to sexual health internationally. Colin Powell, the secretary of state, was a big supporter of the UNFPA, and, probably at his behest, Bush's first budget proposal asked for a $25 million appropriation to the agency, the same amount the United States had given the year before. In written testimony to the Senate Foreign Relations Committee, Powell said, "We recognize that UNFPA does invaluable work through its programs in maternal and child health care, voluntary family planning, screening for reproductive tract cancers, breast-feeding promotion and HIV/AIDS prevention.... We look forward to working with you and your colleagues to secure the funding necessary for UNFPA to continue these activities." Congress responded, exceeding the administration's request by appropriating $34 million for the fund.

Days later, though, Congressman Chris Smith joined with fifty-four other members of Congress to urge the president to freeze the money, citing the Population Research Institute's charges about UNFPA complicity in forced abortion in China.[30] Smith is easily the Population Research Institute's closest ally in Congress, and he made sure the organization had a voice in government debates. In October 2001 he convened a House panel to look at the group's allegations, calling Mosher and his colleagues to testify, and on January 31, 2002, he wrote to Bush imploring him not to fund the organization. The UNFPA, he wrote, "clearly supports a program of coercive abortion and involuntary sterilization." He cited evidence from an "an undercover fact finding team" sent to Sihui, one of thirty-two counties where the UNFPA operates in China. "The investigators were told that family planning is not voluntary in Sihui, and coercive family planning policies in Sihui include: age requirements for pregnancy; birth permits; mandatory use of IUDs; mandatory sterilization; crippling fines for non-compliance; imprisonment for non-compliance; destruction of homes and property for non-compliance; forced abortion and forced sterilization," he wrote. The UNFPA, Smith charged, was complicit in these outrages.

That was the big lie. Early on, the UNFPA had failed to loudly and consistently condemn China's population-control abuses, but as a range of investigators would soon find, it was now working hard on the ground to combat them. The UNFPA had changed under Sadik's leadership and the mandate of the Cairo conference, and was now the only group able to work inside China to try to push the Chinese *away* from the compulsions of the one-child policy. When Bush took office, the UNFPA was working on a project in thirty-two Chinese counties that was meant to demonstrate how the state could move from coercive to voluntary programs. Suspending work in China would have meant giving up whatever influence the UNFPA had.

In his letter to Bush, Congressman Smith neglected to mention that the "investigators" who ostensibly uncovered UNFPA misdeeds were a Population Research Institute team. Based on their findings, Smith urged Bush to exercise a prerogative given presidents in the Kemp-Kasten Amendment, a Reagan-era law that orders money to be withheld from any organization or program that "as determined by the President of the United States, supports or participates in the management of a program of coercive abortion or sterilization."

Bush decided to freeze the money temporarily, pending a State Department investigation. Even before that team left for China, a three-person British delegation, chaired by Edward Leigh, an antiabortion Tory MP, embarked on its own fact-finding mission. Upon returning, Leigh told the *Washington Times* that "there was evidence UNFPA is trying to persuade China away from the program of strict targets and assessments. My personal line is British or U.S. funds should not be used for coercive family planning, and I found no evidence of such practices in China."[31]

The State Department mission concluded exactly the same thing. "We find no evidence that UNFPA has knowingly supported or participated in the management of a program of coercive abortion or involuntary sterilization in the PRC," it said in a post-trip report. "We therefore recommend that [the] $34 million which has already been appropriated be released to UNFPA."[32]

All the evidence, then, showed that PRI's allegations were unfounded. Indeed, by supporting the UNFPA the United States could have helped work against China's terrible abuses of reproductive rights. But instead of acting on the State Department's report, the White House kept it under wraps for almost two months, finally releasing it on the same day that it announced its decision to permanently cut off UNFPA funding. Powell was forced to defend a decision that contradicted his own office's findings, as well as his own evident beliefs. "Regardless of the modest size of UNFPA's budget in China or any benefits its programs provide, UNFPA's support of, and involvement in, China's population-planning activities allows the Chinese government to implement more effectively its program of coercive abortion," he wrote. "Therefore, it is not permissible to continue funding UNFPA at this time."[33]

The American contribution represented more than 12 percent of the UNFPA's budget, and its loss was a harsh blow, one that would mean *more* unwanted pregnancies and abortions all over the world. By defunding the agency the administration established a pattern that would mark everything it did in the field of reproductive and sexual health. Henceforth, expert opinion and international consensus would be no match for right-wing shibboleths. Abstinence would be promoted as the only option for young people trying to avoid HIV. Groups getting American support to fight the AIDS epidemic had to pledge not to support prostitution, stymieing efforts to provide services to sex workers. (Brazil, which has been especially successful at curbing HIV, in part by working with prostitutes' rights groups, chose to turn down $40 million in American funding rather than cooperate with its restrictions. "We can't control [the disease] with principles that are Manichean, theological, fundamentalist and Shiite," said Pedro Chequer, director of Brazil's AIDS program.)[34] American delegations to United Nations conferences on women and children began to look like panels at the World Congress of Families, staffed with people like Janice Crouse, head of Concerned Women for America; Christian radio host Janet Parshall, narrator of the hagiographic documentary *George W. Bush: Faith in the White House*; and John Klink, a member of the Vatican's team at Cairo.

"The Bush administration decided, for whatever reasons, that that was one area where they could throw social conservatives a bone," said Carlson, the World Congress of Families organizer. "I hope it was out of principle, but I'll settle for expediency." Either way, he noted, "they were very consistent."

Ellen Sauerbrey, a right-wing activist with scant experience in international affairs, became the American ambassador to the UN Commission on the Status of Women. "I always feel when I'm being introduced as a representative of the United Nations that I have to say I'm a conservative; I'm not a feminist," she told the Mormon group United Families International. She went on to cite that great expert in international human rights, Fox News demagogue Sean Hannity: "Sean Hannity, this morning, talked about visions and the differences in visions. My perception is that this prevailing vision at the UN is one that is based on rights, but rights without responsibility. Family, whatever you want it to be. Sexual freedom, anything goes. Practically every resolution that goes before the U.N. . . . somebody tries to figure out a way to put in 'reproductive services.'" In 2006 she was promoted, via recess appointment, to become assistant secretary of state for population, refugees, and migration.[35]

It's important to note that throughout all this the United States remained the world's largest donor to global family planning. Funding for international reproductive health stayed stagnant during the Bush administration, in part because congressional family planning champions repeatedly thwarted administration attempts to make deep cuts. In the fiscal years 2006, 2007, and 2008, for example, the administration tried to slash more than $100 million a year from global reproductive health programs, representing almost a quarter of the total U.S. contribution. But Congress held the line, even increasing the budget slightly in 2008, from $435.6 million to $457.3 million.

Because of the global gag rule, though, none of this money could go to the two organizations, the International Planned Parenthood Federation and Marie Stopes International, that have the most extensive infrastructure in the developing world. America's antiabortion politics thus ended up undermining all kinds of women's health services worldwide. Both the IPPF and Marie Stopes provide abortions in countries where they are legal, but they also offer other kinds of care, including family planning, HIV counseling, STD treatment, prenatal care, management of delivery complications, and childhood immunizations. When they close, there are often no other facilities to replace them. Because of the global gag rule twelve countries—Cape Verde, Chad, Comoros, Gabon, the Gambia, Mauritius, Solomon Islands, Sri Lanka, Tonga, Vanuatu, West Samoa, and Yemen—lost access to USAID-supplied contraceptives altogether, because in each the local IPPF affiliate was the only outlet for them.[36]

In other countries the gag rule forced clinic closings and led to contraceptive shortages. Kenya saw the closing of six of fifteen clinics run by the Family Planning Association of Kenya, the local IPPF affiliate—and the country's leading provider of Pap smear tests for cervical cancer. Marie Stopes, which provides half of all family planning services in Kenya, lost two clinics, while others laid off staff and raised their prices. Ethiopia's largest family planning organization, the Family Guidance Association—also an IPPF affiliate—lost more than a third of its funding.[37]

Meanwhile, agencies that accepted U.S. funds couldn't direct their clients to providers of safe abortion, even in cases where such abortion was legal. Ethiopia, for example, liberalized its abortion law in 2005 to allow women to end their pregnancies in the case of rape, incest, and on broad health grounds. In his guidelines for implementing the new law, the health minister emphasized the severity of the problem of unsafe abortion. "[U]nsafe abortion is one of the top 10 causes of hospital admissions among women," he wrote. "Unsafe abortion accounts for nearly 60% of all gynecologic admissions.... Due to the clandestine nature of unsafe abortion services, however, these figures represent only the tip of the iceberg and not the full magnitude of the problem."[38] But because of the gag rule, employees of American-funded NGOs in Ethiopia couldn't tell women how or where to access abortion under the new law. The United States was undermining Ethiopia's life-saving reforms from within.

Diplomatically, the Bush administration moved to undo the progress that had been made under Clinton at Cairo and Beijing. In December 2002, at a UN conference held in Bangkok to discuss ways of implementing the Cairo program of action, the Bush administration shocked much of the world when it implied that it was withdrawing America's support for the historic agreement. The United States, declared Assistant Secretary of State Arthur E. Dewey, "supports the sanctity of life from conception to natural death.... [T]here has been a concerted effort to create a gulf by pushing the United States to violate its principles and accept language that promotes abortion. We have been asked to reaffirm the entirety of the ICPD [International Conference on Population and Development] principles and recommendations, even though we have repeatedly stated that to do so would constitute endorsement of abortion."

Arguing that terms like "reproductive rights and reproductive health" were code for abortion, the U.S. team tried to strong-arm other countries into jettisoning them, essentially amending Cairo. It also attempted to strike a reference to "consistent condom use" as an AIDS-fighting strategy.[39]

"Our Philippine delegation received extreme pressure from back home, as well as inside the negotiation room, to come to the side of the U.S. delegation," said Filipino activist Gladys Malayang.[40] But it didn't work. With discussions deadlocked, the United States forced a vote, a highly unusual move in the consensus-driven world of UN confabs. Except for two abstentions, every country present voted against America. It was a striking rebuke. "Given the way the U.S. participated during the negotiations, it was clear they were determined to influence us," said one South Asian delegate. "I don't think they expected to come up against this unified Asian position."[41]

Unable to make common cause with Asian countries to fight reproductive rights, the United States, like the Vatican before it, found support in the more repressive quarters of the Middle East and North Africa. Even as the United States purported to fight a war against radical Islamism—a war it sometimes justified by the abuses Muslim fundamentalists inflict on women—American delegates joined hands with their colleagues from Iran and Sudan to undermine international agreements on women's rights. The country that once led the Western world in Cairo became the most powerful member of the fundamentalist alliance at the UN.

The right-wing Christian-Muslim coalition suffered a severe setback on 9/11, with hostility on both sides making it ever harder to work together. Before the attacks Carlson and Wilkins had been planning simultaneous World Congress of Families conferences in Mexico City and Dubai, with funding, Carlson said, from major evangelical organizations. After 9/11, that all fell apart. There were still contacts, "just at a much more careful level," he said. "We continued working with the Organization of the Islamic Conference up until 9/11. After that we had to be much more informal."

Eventually, however, Wilkins succeeded in partnering with the government of Qatar to organize a conference in that country's capital. Held in November 2004, the Doha International Conference for the Family brought together American groups like C-FAM and the Family Research Council with Muslim speakers, including Dr. Mahathir Mohamad, former prime minister of Malaysia, and Sheikh Yusuf al-Qaradawi, dean of the College of Shariah and Islamic Studies in Qatar. Qaradawi had earlier caused an uproar during a visit to Britain because of his support for wife beating and the execution of sodomites, though his apologists pointed out that he believes men should beat their wives lightly, and only as a last resort.[42] Representing the Bush administration was Allan Carlson's close friend Wade Horn, then the assistant secretary for children and families in the Department of Health and Human Services.

The Doha gathering imitated the form and language of big UN meetings, replete with preparatory conferences, a declaration, and a call for action. There was an official conference report written in perfect UN bureaucratese: "The purpose of the Doha International Conference for the Family was to reaffirm international norms, and establish proposals for action, that can inform an agenda for cooperative research, discussion, and policy development related to family life for the next decade." Following the conference the government of Qatar put forward a resolution at the United Nations acknowledging the event and welcoming its findings, which was approved without a vote. Organizers then used this perfunctory UN approbation to claim, absurdly, that as a result "the Doha Declaration takes its place in the formal canon of legal documents comprising the growing body of international law."[43]

Wilkins has since moved to Qatar to build a pan-fundamentalist think tank, the Doha International Institute for Family Studies and Development. According to its Web site, part of its writ is to combat mass media–engendered "moral globalization" that has "adversely altered long-standing societal norms and encouraged the disintegration of the family."

Carlson, meanwhile, remains convinced that conservative Christians have more in common with conservative Muslims than they do with Western liberals. "They share a common foe, which is a radical secular individualism that has turned against a common value system resting on the Abrahamic traditions, which involves a recognition of marriage and family as parts of the created order, as expectations," he said.

Such views might be dismissed as marginal, at least in American politics, but when it came to international women's issues the Bush team appeared to share them. In June 2002 the *Washington Post* ran a story headlined "Islamic Bloc, Christian Right Team Up to Lobby U.N." "Conservative U.S. Christian organizations have joined forces with Islamic governments to halt the expansion of sexual and political protections and rights for gays, women and children at United Nations conferences," Colum Lynch reported. "The new alliance, which coalesced during the past year, has received a major boost from the Bush administration, which appointed antiabortion activists to key positions on U.S. delegations to U.N. conferences on global economic and social policy." Lynch described American and Iranian officials huddled together during coffee breaks at the UN Children's Summit that May, and quoted Austin Ruse saying, "We have realized that without countries like Sudan, abortion would have been recognized as a universal human right in a U.N. document."[44] (Since Sudan boycotted the Cairo conference it was unclear which document Ruse meant.)

The abdication of American leadership on reproductive rights served to rally some in Europe. Increasing budgets for international women's health programs became a way for countries to defy the world's ever more unpopular superpower. In July 2002 the European Union stepped in to replace the withdrawn U.S. funding for the UNFPA, filling what EU development commissioner Poul Nielson called "the decency gap." Meanwhile, in 2004 Britain increased funding of the International Planned Parenthood Federation by £1.5 million, in recognition, Parliament Undersecretary of State Gareth Thomas said, of "the difficulties that our friends in America have caused for those who operate in this area."[45] Two years later the British government became the founding donor of an IPPF fund to increase safe abortion services around the world, contributing £3 million.

In 2007 over eight hundred people gathered in London for a first-of-its-kind global conference on safe abortion, organized by Marie Stopes International and Ipas. There were village midwives and high-level diplomats, doctors, politicians, activists, and more than a few clandestine providers who risk jail daily in countries where abortion is illegal. Attendees came from every corner of the world: Mongolia, Nigeria, the Philippines, Pakistan, Nicaragua, Poland, Indonesia, Sweden, and dozens of other nations.

Bert Koenders, the dashing Dutch minister for development, gave the closing speech, using language that sounded shockingly brave to American ears accustomed to Republican sanctimony but utterly ordinary to Europeans. "Women's access to quality sexual and reproductive health care services is a universal issue," he said. "And a woman's right to choose is a universal right." He warned of the risk of a "conservative trend in the world," spoke of the harm wrought by the United States, and ended with an unapologetic call for safe abortion to be made available worldwide.

"Unsafe abortion is a major killer," he said. "An estimated 189 women die every day. We will not reduce maternal mortality until this crucial issue is addressed. Unsafe abortion in Africa is the most dangerous, so we need a full package of good quality health services that *must* include safe abortion services.... Legalizing abortion has proven to be one of the most effective ways of reducing maternal mortality rates when it's flanked by setting up good health care facilities."

African health officials largely acknowledged this, but politics, both local and international, made it hard to act on. In May 2004, Kenya's Ministry of Health released a high-profile report on unsafe abortion in the country. Completed with help from the Kenya Medical Association, the Kenyan chapter of the Federation of Women Lawyers, and Ipas, it claimed that 300,000 abortions were performed in Kenya each year, the vast majority of them illegal, resulting in 20,000 hospitalizations and 2,600 deaths.[46] It recommended that Kenya honor the commitments it had made at Cairo, and there was some evidence that the government might be prodded to do just that. At the press conference publicizing the report, Health minister Charity Ngilu announced plans to buy manual vacuum aspiration kits for public hospitals to deal with emergencies resulting from unsafe abortions.[47]

Less than three weeks later fifteen fetuses, several near term, were found in garbage bags tossed beside the polluted Ngong River on the outskirts of Nairobi, and the abortion debate exploded across Kenyan headlines. According to press reports, security guards at the International Christian Centre, a Pentecostal church, saw three people dumping the bags out of a pickup truck shortly before midnight.[48] "They were strewn on the road, their little, innocent faces twisted in death," reported one newspaper.[49] With them were documents— medical records and, ostensibly, abortion-related billing information—said to implicate a prominent gynecologist, Dr. John Nyamu, who ran two women's health clinics in the city.

The case quickly became a major scandal. Nyamu and two of his nurses, one of whom was twenty-eight weeks pregnant, were arrested. Rather than illegal abortion, they were charged with murder, a crime that carries the death penalty. There's no bail for murder suspects, so the three of them sat in prison awaiting their trial.

The Catholic Church helped keep emotions stoked. On June 3, a standing-room-only crowd of two thousand attended a two-hour requiem mass for the fetuses, arranged in fifteen white caskets, at Nairobi's Holy Family Basilica. "We are sacrificing innocent unborn babies at the altar of science and technology," said Kenyan archbishop Raphael S. Ndingi Mwana'a Nzeki, who went on to argue that countries that had legalized abortion were now facing the crisis of low birthrates and gay marriage.[50] After the service the caskets were interred in Lang'ata Cemetery, their graves marked by white crosses saying "Here lie the unborn infants killed in May 2004 thro' abortion."[51]

From the beginning pro-choice activists, along with some of Nyamu's colleagues, were suspicious. Many were convinced Nyamu had been framed. For one thing, the bodies found by the river were so developed that they looked more like stillbirths than abortions. And if the doctor was going to dump the remains of late-term abortions, why would he include so much identifying information, and why leave it all by a church? Nyamu "was not that dumb," said Joseph Karanja, a gynecologist at Nairobi's Kenyatta Hospital and a University of Nairobi professor.

Karanja saw the persecution of Nyamu as an attempt to strike out against obstetricians, gynecologists, and other health care providers who were agitating for abortion law reform. "It was obviously an orchestrated affair," he said. "Within minutes of the discovery of the bodies, all the media was there. A minister who was known for his anti-choice views was also there."

There was, it should be emphasized, no proof that abortion opponents had planted evidence. But it would also soon emerge that the case against Nyamu didn't remotely hold up. The entire episode would remain murky and mysterious. Only one thing was clear: After the fetuses were found, the environment in Kenya changed dramatically. "We thought the dissemination of this study [on unsafe abortion] was going to spur on new activism, and a new determination by the ministry, but they actually succeeded in dampening things down," said Ipas vice president Eunice Brookman-Amissah.

Nyamu's trial finally began in late November. It was marked by raucous protests, as supportive health workers, wearing white lab coats and stethoscopes, stood off against more numerous antiabortion activists, some of whom were also doctors. The case dragged on for months, with Nyamu and the nurses, Marion Wambui Kibathi and Mercy Kaimuri Mathai, still locked up. According to Kenya's *The Nation* newspaper, the evidence offered by the security guards at International Christian Centre was "laden with contradictions and inconsistencies."[52] (The presiding judge would later describe one of them as not an impartial witness but "a person who had some mission to achieve.")[53] In April 2005, nearly a year after the saga began, Nairobi's chief pathologist told the court that a postmortem showed that the fetuses had been stillborn, not aborted.[54] In June, after Nyamu, Kibathi, and Mathai had spent over a year in prison, a judge acquitted them. They walked out of the court—and were immediately rearrested, this time on abortion charges. Finally, a month later, the charges were dropped and Nyamu returned to his practice.

Elsewhere in Africa liberalization was moving forward. The Maputo Protocol, which went into effect in 2005, called on states to "take all appropriate measures to . . . protect the reproductive rights of women by authorizing medical abortion in cases of sexual assault, rape, incest, and where the continued pregnancy endangers the mental and physical health of the mother or the life of the mother or the foetus." In 2006, health ministers from across the continent met again in Mozambique and agreed to the Maputo plan of action, which proposed concrete steps to expand access to safe abortion.

Dr. Chisale Mhango, director of reproductive health at the Malawi Health Ministry, authored it. American representatives, said Mhango, "contacted our ambassadors to express concern that the Maputo plan of action is promoting wholesale abortion, and they are alarmed that abortion can be so openly discussed at a meeting as never before." The health ministers were not swayed. "Our women are dying from abortion, and we just have to act on it," he said.

In June 2007, Kenyan vice president Moody Awori, a Catholic personally opposed to abortion, announced that ratification of the Maputo protocol was "high on Kenya's agenda." Awori noted that in Kenya, ten thousand to fifteen thousand girls drop out of school each year after getting pregnant. "Without recourse to termination of the unplanned pregnancy, their personal development is usually curtailed and the nation loses their development potential," he said. "At worst they die at the hands of [an] unqualified abortionist. This needs to be remedied."[55]

Conservatives immediately blamed foreign feminists. "Maputo Protocol a Blatant Case of Neo-colonialism," ran an op-ed headline in the Kenyan newspaper the *Sunday Standard*. "Could Africa be the place where the global enforcement of sexual and reproductive rights is being engineered?" writer Mark Mzungu asked. He warned of the "danger" in the protocol's reliance on the "western secularist view of woman primarily as a citizen with 'equal rights' regardless of her 'marital status' and not as a loving, caring wife and mother."

This was much like the argument the Vatican had made. In his 2007 New Year's speech to the Holy See diplomatic corps, Pope Benedict asked, "How can we not be alarmed, moreover, by the continuous attacks on life, from conception to natural death? Such attacks do not even spare regions with a traditional culture of respecting life, such as Africa, where there is an attempt to trivialize abortion surreptitiously, both through the Maputo Protocol and through the Plan of Action adopted by the Health Ministers of the African Union—shortly to be submitted to the Summit of Heads of State and Heads of Government."[56] Human Life International bought the domain names MaputoProtocol.org and MaputoProtocol.com, where it put up a Web site claiming that the treaty is "part of a decades-long campaign by Western elites to reduce the number of black Africans."

This wasn't a fight, however, that pitted Africans against Westerners. It was a battle between a cosmopolitan alliance of reproductive rights activists and an equally cosmopolitan network of religious conservatives. The globalization of the culture wars was revealing something important about the significant fissures dividing the world. In the aftermath of September 11, American politics abounded with talk about an epic clash of civilizations between Christendom and Islam. Such religious rivalries, however, masked an equally important polarization, both inside of countries and among them, between secular, liberalizing cultures and traditional, patriarchal ones. One saw women as ends in themselves, human beings with dignity and autonomy. The other treated them as the means of group cohesion and identity whose primary value lay in their relation to men.

When it comes to issues of sex and reproduction, religious conservatives across the world often have more in common with each other than with feminists within their own societies. The conservative Catholic writer Dinesh D'Souza acknowledged this in his 2007 book, *The Enemy At Home: The Cultural Left and Its Responsibility for 9/11.* "Yes, I would rather go to a baseball game or have a drink with Michael Moore than with the grand mufti of Egypt," he wrote. "But when it comes to core beliefs, I'd have to confess that I'm closer to the dignified fellow in the long robe and prayer beads than to the slovenly fellow with the baseball cap."[57]

Women's rights activists, too, have common interests that transcend national and religious borders. Because decisions affecting so many women's lives are now made at the international level, feminists in different countries have a critical interest in each other's success. And women worldwide have an especial investment in the ability of American feminists to try to move their country's policies in a more humane direction.

Domestically, American feminism can sometimes seem tangled up in trivialities, as journalists hype fights between career women and stay-at-home moms and movies like *Sex and the City* tout empowerment as something that can be bought at Barneys. In fact, though, the degree to which American politics takes women's rights seriously has epochal reverberations all over the planet.

At the same time, controversies in other countries can challenge the categories of the American feminist movement, with its emphasis on individual choice and suspicion of government inducements to procreate. In the first decade of the twenty-first century new kinds of demographic concerns are surfacing internationally. Easy access to abortion in Asia is being used to systematically eliminate female fetuses, creating a generation with a dangerous surplus of men. Declining birthrates in Europe portend a shrinking, aging, weakening continent (which, among other things, threatens to undermine the influence of the very liberalism that made Europe a champion of international women's rights). The global antiabortion movement stands ready to take advantage of these issues. Concern about overpopulation led to the expansion of reproductive rights. Now, fears about gender imbalances and the graying of Europe may be used to restrict them.

CHAPTER 7: MISSING GIRLS

Fatehgarh Sahib, a district in the northern India state of Punjab, is rich in rupees and poor in girls. Called the breadbasket of India, Punjab's wealth is built on agriculture; flat fields of ripe, gold wheat stretch out from straight, smooth highways, plowed by giant tractors driven by turbaned Sikh farmers. Unlike in southern India, women have little role in agriculture here, which is one of several reasons that so many in Punjab see them as a useless investment, one better avoided altogether.

India, like other Asian countries, has long had a pronounced son preference, which has translated into a population with more males than females. Punjab is one of several Indian states with a history of female infanticide that shocked the British colonialists, who found entire villages without a single girl.[1] The British banned female infanticide in 1870—almost a hundred years after they discovered the practice—yet more subtle forms of discrimination and neglect continued to cull India's population of girls, who were, and still are, fed less than boys and given less medical care.

"The actual murder of little girls has in a great measure ceased, but it has been replaced in some tribes by a degree of carelessness hardly less criminal," one observer wrote toward the end of the 1800s. "It is found in some districts that, when fever is prevalent, girls' deaths, especially in the first three years of life, so largely exceed those of males that it is impossible not to believe that but small attempts are made to save the girls, and in many places deaths caused by disease of the lungs or malnutrition suggest the same conclusion."[2]

The care deficit has never been eliminated, but it seemed to have been improving throughout the twentieth century, and in India in the 1950s and 1960s there were almost as many female children as male.[3] Even Punjab saw a sustained increase in girls relative to boys. That's why the publication of India's 2001 census came as such a painful shock. Girls and women were living longer thanks to increased medical care, but the sex ratio had nonetheless gone seriously askew.* In seventy districts, the ratio of girls to boys had declined by more than 50 points in the previous decade.[4] With 798 female children for every thousand males, Punjab had the worst sex ratio in India, and Fatehgarh Sahib, with a sex ratio of 766, was the worst district in Punjab.

The decline was overwhelmingly due to the epidemic spread of sex-selective abortion, which most people in India refer to as "female feticide." Sex determination tests first appeared in India in the 1970s through the use of amniocentesis and chorionic villus sampling, both relatively invasive procedures that had to be done by a doctor. It wasn't until ultrasound, which spread throughout the country in the 1990s, that sex determination became easy and accessible. According to a 2006 study by *The Lancet*, a conservative estimate is that there are half a million sex-selective abortions in India each year.[5]

"Ultrasound really came as a WMD," said Puneet Bedi, a Delhi gynecologist who is one of the country's most vocal activists against sex selection. "Parts of India where there is no drinking water or flush toilets, you can find ultrasound. They have no electricity—they carry their own car batteries." Ultrasound can only detect sex at around four months, meaning sex-selective abortions are usually late-term abortions, a more complicated, dangerous procedure than early abortions. It doesn't matter: Some women go through them over and over again, sacrificing their bodies for a boy.

General Electric, which dominates India's ultrasound market in concert with the Indian company Wipro, provided cheap credit to help practitioners buy the machines. "The present marketing strategy of GE-WIPRO to target smaller towns is a matter of concern," wrote Sabu George, a leading anti–sex selection activist.

---

* Sex ratio can be defined in several different ways. Internationally, most use the number of boys per 100 or 1,000 girls, which means that discrimination results in high sex ratios. But Indians tend to use the number of girls per 1,000 boys, so that areas of discrimination against girls are said to have low sex ratios.

Once a private practitioner in a small town buys a machine then there is great pressure on other doctors to buy. Multiple machines where there is little demand for legitimate prenatal care increases competition, reduces scan rates and motivates abuses like fetal sex determination so that clinics can recover their investment.... At the global level, it is imperative that those concerned with human rights expose the transnational corporations involved in marketing ultrasound machines for these purposes.[6]

But the bitter problem of the missing girls cannot simply be laid at the door of even the most callous corporate behemoth. The sins of capitalism may exacerbate it, but behind it are fantastically complex hierarchies of the world's most multifarious country, where feudalism and technocapitalism, extreme superstition and hypermodernity, purdah and professional women all coexist. Even as it highlights the desperate need for women's empowerment, sex-selective abortion sometimes looks, in a bizarre way, like a symptom of it. For reproductive rights advocates the whole issue has a looking-glass quality to it. It is a moral labyrinth that leads everyone but absolutists to sometimes uncomfortable and contradictory positions.

"You're going to get multiple opinions on everything on this," said Ena Singh, UNFPA's assistant representative in India and a particularly impassioned combatant against sex-selective abortion. (The day I met her a major Punjabi pop star, Rabbi Shergill, surprised her in her office; she had convinced him to make sex selection the theme of a new music video, which was about to debut on Indian TV.)

You're going to get multiple opinions on terminology; you're going to get multiple opinions on policy; you're going to get multiple opinions about rights, choice, gender, the way the law should be framed, the way it should be implemented, who should be implementing it. Because this issue is so fundamental, it's so deep, it impacts everything. It's about men and women—about every aspect of that relationship. It's about existence; it's about marriage; it's about love; it's about sex; it's about children; it's about globalization; it's about economics; it's about rights; it's about norms; it's about the media; it's about crime; it's about medicine; it's about medical ethics; it's about dowry; it's about property; and a hundred other things. Tell me what this is not about!

According to Amarjit Singh, a thirty-one-year-old family planning field-worker from Fatehgarh Sahib, ultrasound exploded throughout his area in 1994. "Even remote villages knew about it," he said. Infamous advertisements went up across the region: "Spend 500 Rupees today and save 500,000 Rupees later." The numbers were a reference to the sometimes crushing cost of dowry, the main reason Indians give for the misery that commonly greets the birth of girls. Amarjit* remembers salesmen traveling to Punjabi villages touting the wonders of the new innovations. The same year India passed a law banning sex-determination tests for the purpose of sex-selective abortion, but it was widely ignored. "Everything was practiced very openly," said Amarjit.

A tall man with an easy smile and a shadow of a beard, Amarjit donates some of his time to the Voluntary Health Association of Punjab, the primary NGO addressing sex-selective abortion in that state. Like most of the district's residents he's a Sikh, though he long ago cut his hair and stopped wearing a turban except on special occasions. Sikhs have the worst sex ratio of all the groups in India, and the worst among the Sikhs are the Jat Sikhs, the land-owning caste that Amarjit belongs to.

He recalled an old chant he heard from relatives. Decades before he was born, when infanticide was committed openly, it was sung by those killing girl babies.

Eat the jaggery
Spin the cotton
You should not come
Send your brother

Today Amarjit is as active an opponent of sex selection as one is likely to find in Fatehgarh Sahib. He has allied himself with Manmohan Sharma, the founder of the Voluntary Health Association of Punjab, a frail, ardently committed social scientist who has dedicated the last fifteen years to combating his

---

* Because so many Sikh men have the last name "Singh," and Sikh women the last name "Kaur," when dealing with groups, I'm going to refer to people by their first names to avoid confusion.

state's inequities, particularly those arising from sex discrimination. Amarjit insists that the mind-set that values men over women must be wiped out. And yet, less than twenty minutes after we first met, he explained to me why, in certain cases, he supports "female feticide."

"Supposing somebody has three, four, five girl children. In that case I think it's right that they plan a female feticide," he said. "You cannot change the idea of that woman who has three daughters. She keeps producing children in hopes of producing a son. So I think in such a situation it is acceptable. Sometimes in hopes of a son they produce too many girl children. They have no proper nutrition, education, or security. In that situation, it is very painful. Girls will be maltreated. They will not get good husbands."

The problem of sex-selective abortion is not, of course, limited to India. Across Asia it is reshaping the population in unprecedented ways. In most populations around 105 boys are born for every 100 girls. Male infants are weaker and more susceptible to illness, leading ratios to even out over time. The arrival of sex-selection technology has profoundly disrupted this equilibrium. According to the UNFPA, in 2005 six Asian countries reported imbalances of more than 108 male children for every 100 females: India, South Korea, Georgia, Azerbaijan, China, and Armenia. In China and India the situation has clearly deteriorated since the 1980s. "The fact that the child sex ratio has unexpectedly increased is going to influence the entire population over the coming decades: the entire population will gradually grow increasingly more masculine in their make-up, as the new generations born after the 1980s grow older," demographer Christophe Z. Guilmoto wrote of Asia.[7]

Immigration, meanwhile, has brought sex selection to the United States, Britain, and Canada, where advertisements for sex determination have appeared in newspapers aimed at the Indian diaspora.[8] A 2008 article in the *Proceedings of the National Academy of Sciences* documented skewed sex ratios among the children of Chinese, Korean, and Indian parents in the United States. "Using the 2000 U.S. Census, we find that the sex ratio of the oldest child to be normal, but that of subsequent children to be heavily male if there was no previous son," it said.[9]

But the problem of the missing girls has been especially confounding in

India, one of the two countries in the world where it is most prevalent. In the other, China, widespread sex selection is happening in the context of government compulsion. That makes the solution easy enough to see: End the one-child policy. India's situation is more complicated. It would be comforting to think that sex-selective abortion there is the product of poverty-driven desperation, of a kind of backwardness that could be remedied by development and education. Comforting, but wrong. In fact, while sex-selective abortion is sometimes motivated by economic need, other times it's the product of a twisted kind of consumerism.

It is widely practiced by India's emerging middle class, those with enough money and education to skirt the law and take advantage of technology. They fully embrace the two-child ideal that India's government—with outside help—pushed for decades, but only on the condition that they have at least one son. In a modernizing but still rigidly patriarchal society, boys hold out the prospect of a lifetime of economic security for their parents, while girls, who will join the household of their in-laws, are widely seen as simply a drain on expenses.

Female education is a remedy for almost every form of discrimination against girls—except this one. Indeed, in much of India higher rates of female literacy are correlated with higher rates of sex-selective abortion. This contrasts with China, where urbanites and those with higher education have the most normal sex ratios—despite the fact that the one-child policy is enforced more strictly in the cities.[10]

The posh, leafy suburbs of South Delhi, full of gracious homes occupied by professional couples with multiple servants, have sex ratios well under 900 girls for every 1,000 boys.[11] Bedi, a specialist in fetal medicine—and the father of two girls—has his practice there, in an elite neighborhood called Haus Kauz. He is a bearish man with a gray mustache, a Sikh from a caste, ironically, famous for female infanticide. A copy of the Dalai Lama's poem "A Precious Human Life" hangs on the wall of his office. On his desktop is one of his anti–sex selection PowerPoint presentations, which begins with a quote from Malcolm X: "It isn't that time is running out—time has run out!"

"This whole myth of somehow the poor women being forced to undergo sex determination and abortion is the biggest bullshit," said Bedi. "Seventy percent of the women who come to me [asking for sex determination], their husbands or their families don't even know that they're coming. The first demand for female feticide comes from the mother herself."

Bedi's patients, of course, are hardly representative of Indian women. They represent the richest sliver of Indian society: As he himself says, no one else can afford him. If the problem of sex-selective abortion were confined to people like them, it would barely show up in censuses. Still, the fact that even such privileged women seek out sex selection says much about how entrenched the preference for sons is throughout Indian society.

Given that Bedi is a high-profile crusader against sex selection, it seems strange that any of his patients would ask him for help in finding out the sex of their fetuses. That they do is evidence of how much cynicism and corruption surrounds efforts to ban the practice. According to Bedi, most doctors who declaim against sex selection in public profit from it in private, a view I heard echoed by doctors in Punjab as well. He speaks about sex-selective abortion in the shrillest possible terms, calling it a genocide, a holocaust. Still, some women assume that he must not really mean it, that for the right price he'll help them avoid the burden of girls.

Bedi exudes a poignant mix of urgency and fatalism; he believes that everything possible must be done to stop sex-selective abortion, and that none of his activism is having any impact at all. In the last fifteen years, he said, he has talked two women out of aborting female fetuses, one of whom was pregnant after a long period of infertility. Both of them come to see him every year or two to castigate him for ruining their lives. They come, he said, to "remind me what a mistake they made because they listened to me, while everybody in their peer group has sons, [women] who were also my patients but had gone to better doctors later and got sons and abortions, while they had not."

These women are not cowering victims, he insisted. They "are women like you, like my wife and my sister. Empowered, with big cars, big houses, and the best possible college degrees."

There are several reasons for the counterintuitive connection between prosperity, education, and sex discrimination. Wealthier communities in India's northwest—precisely those who can most afford decent schools for their children—have always been the most averse to the birth of daughters.

Members of the urban middle class want smaller families than poor people in the countryside, leaving less room for girls. Those with at least some education are better able to navigate the medical system, especially now that sex-determination tests have become illegal.

Most of all, though, more prosperous families are rejecting daughters because of the toxic, exponential growth of dowries. Dowry has been illegal in India since 1961, but that law is hardly enforced. In theory, dowry is a gift parents give to a daughter to ensure her future security; because she won't inherit any of her parents' property, it represents her share of their wealth. As it's practiced, though, dowry is a kind of tribute paid to the family of the groom. In much of northern India it's not a one-time gift, either: A girl's parents are expected to offer a continuous flow of presents to her husband's family, and to be somewhat abject before them. "In the power relations between the bride's and groom's families, the former always have to give in and put up with any humiliation, indignity, and oblique or direct insults on the part of the latter," wrote Indian sociologist Tulsi Patel.[12]

In recent years, with India suddenly awash in consumerist bounty, dowry demands have exploded, turning the whole thing into a materialistic free-for-all. In the high-caste communities where dowry had long been established, demands became inflated. At the same time, the custom took hold in places where it had never existed before as the upwardly mobile tried to imitate those further up the caste and class hierarchy.[13]

Historically, female infanticide was practiced mostly by the upper castes in India's highly conservative, Pakistan-bordering northern and northwestern plains, which stretch from Gujarat to Punjab, and that is where the problem of sex-selective abortion is most acute. Dowry is out of control in the region. "We have a developing society, and so much consumerism," said Nirupama Dutt, editor of the Punjabi edition of the *Sunday Indian,* a national newsmagazine. "It's so important to have the modern gadgets, ostentatious weddings." Her cousin, she said, from "a slightly backward rural area," considers the minimum acceptable dowry to include a television, a motorcycle, a refrigerator, and a washing machine, as well as quantities of gold. "This is the done thing," said Dutt. "Newspapers advertise package deals. And among the landlords, the Jats, a car is a must."

Exorbitant demands have been spreading from the north to the rest of the country, and as they have, sex-selective abortion has made inroads in parts of India where female infanticide had been unknown. A slight female deficit even appeared among children in the southernmost state of Kerala, where matriarchal traditions and leftist government combined to create a relative idyll of gender equality, with a female literacy rate of almost 90 percent, compared to less than 50 percent in India as a whole.

When dowry demands continue after marriage, a woman can become a kind of hostage in her in-laws' home, tormented, beaten, and even killed if enough money isn't forthcoming. In a not atypical story from May 2008, the *Times of India* reported that twenty-four-year-old Astha Jain was found hanging in her South Delhi home on her one-year wedding anniversary, her suicide note saying she could no longer bear her husband's family's dowry harassment. The in-laws owned a steel factory; her parents owned a paper business. According to her parents, they had already spent a crore—10 million rupees, or a quarter million dollars—during her wedding, and had given a Mercedes to the groom, Amit Jain, and gold rings to every member of the wedding party. In order to placate Amit's parents, they had handed over another 35 lakh, or $86,500, a few months before Astha's death. Their "greed could not be satisfied," said one of her relatives.[14]

On a searingly hot spring day in 2008, Amarjit Singh took me to one of the Fatehgarh Sahib villages where he worked. The people who live there are far from the rarefied realm of the Jains or of Bedi's patients, but the upper-caste Sikhs' section of the village has nearly as many modern conveniences as an American suburb. The houses are two stories high, with satellite dishes and designer water tanks shaped like birds or soccer balls perched on top. Behind the gates are courtyards big enough to park cars and John Deere tractors. Here, said Amarjit, there aren't more than 400 girls for every 1,000 boys. "The numbers look better because of Muslims and migrants," he said, both groups that have higher birthrates and more females.

Harpreet Singh, a lean, attractive man in white kurta pajamas and an orange turban, shared his late father's house with his brother, Narpreet. Each of them had one son. Harpreet, whose boy was six years old, planned to stop while he was ahead. "The money that I earn is not enough to raise a girl child," he said. "I have already got one son, so I don't want any second child at all." Another boy would create his own problems, forcing Harpreet to split his share of his father's land in two. If dowries keep growing as they have been, meanwhile, he estimated he'd have to spend at least 15 lakh—1.5 million rupees, or $37,000—by the time any daughter of his would marry. With one boy he feels assured that his family line will continue and his wealth won't be dispersed.

"I know my district is famous for having the least number of girl children," he said. He worries, sometimes, about where his son will find a bride. But no one wanted to spend their own fortune providing wives for Punjab's boys: As the famous Punjabi saying goes, "Raising a daughter is like watering your neighbor's garden." If anything, Harpreet thought that increasing competition for women made it all the more imperative that he invest everything in his only boy. With so few girls, he said, "the time will come when the girls will be choosers in marriage. So in most cases the girls will choose the richer families to be married into. So those who are financially weaker, they will not get brides. That will be a very big crisis in our society."

Faced with such economic fears, he found official attempts to change attitudes wholly unconvincing. Like elsewhere in India, when people in the village have sons, they decorate their houses and hand out sweets. Usually, there is no celebration for a girl. Lately, people connected to the government and NGOs had been distributing sweets for daughters as well, which Harpreet saw as insincere "showing off." Deep down, he insisted, they're as desperate for boys as everyone else.

A short walk down a brick lane led us to the home of Balwant Singh, a milk seller and practitioner of ayurvedic medicine, and his wife, Gurjit Kaur. They had two daughters, twenty and twenty-two, and a five-year-old son. "I am very happy that I have two girls," Balwant insisted. "Clinton has only one daughter, but I have two daughters." Both girls were studying: The eldest, Ranbir, was working on a master's degree in commerce, and the younger, Satvir, was getting a BA in ayurvedic medicine, like her father.

In the curio case in the small sitting room, though, along with the birds made of seashells, the stuffed dog, and the yellow fabric flowers, there were no photos of Ranbir or Satvir. There were only pictures of little Inderbir, a boisterous boy who ran around the room soaking up attention as his sisters sat decorously to the side or went back and forth to the kitchen with drinks.

"Those people who have only girls in a family, the neighbors think that family is useless," said Gurjit, forty-four. "I'm thankful to God that I have a son."

Balwant's sister, Charanjit, and her husband, Harpreet, a young policeman in a light blue turban, were visiting that day with their only son. They were silent as their relatives and I talked about sex selection until, suddenly, Harpreet's indignation boiled over. He burst out, speaking Punjabi, "Take a look at Muslim families in other states—they have got nine children, twelve children. Take a look at the girls in this family. One is studying ayurveda, one is preparing for her MBA. These are smaller families, and we are planning them rather well, we think. Whatever is being practiced here, take a look at how we have controlled the population growth."

Harpreet continued in a rapid soliloquy: "I am a Jat Sikh. I feel bad that people are always blaming us for killing our girl children. We love all our children—we love our boy children, and also we love our girl children. But through this thing, we have controlled our population in such a way that— take a look at our families—we don't have the kind of poverty that exists in other parts of the country, where they have five children, six children, seven children. They cannot even feed their children, forget about their education." His son, he said, is studying in the top school in the area. "If I had five children, I couldn't afford to keep him in the best school."

Harpreet's wife was sterilized, and as a government employee, he was rewarded for her operation. Policemen like him who have two children or fewer, and foreclose the possibility of having any more, get an extra five hundred rupees, or twelve dollars, every month. Thus, Harpreet was incensed that his community's highly successful mode of population control is now under attack.

"The government took such big trouble during Sanjay Gandhi's time to do all these things," Harpreet continued, exasperated. "But we are naturally doing it! We are not being coerced, we are not being forced. So what's the problem?"

For all his passion Harpreet spoke elliptically, avoiding any actual mention of sex-selective abortion, instead calling it "this thing." Only once, during a particularly heated moment, did he use the phrase *kudi maar,* which means girl killer.

India's government has spent the last half century trying to persuade, cajole, and sometimes coerce its population into having smaller families, and they have largely succeeded. In 2005 the country's total fertility rate averaged 2.9 children per woman, down more than 17 percent in just the last decade. Women in India's cities average only 2.1 children each. The decline has been felt even among poor people in remote areas. In rural Rajasthan, for example, the total fertility rate dropped from 4.7 in the mid 1990s to 4.0 ten years later.[15]

Son preference, though, has remained unchanged. "Since the desired family size has come down to two or three—two in many cases—they still want *at least* one if not more sons," said Saroj Pachauri, Asia region director of the Population Council. "That's where the distortions are occurring."

Population control, divorced from an appreciable increase in women's status, replaced one demographic problem with another. "Some things are so ironic when you look back," Pachauri said sadly, recalling her long history in India's population movement. "We did this with such good intentions, and it backfired on us."

A grandmotherly woman with a gentle face, bobbed hair, and a fashionably understated *salwar kameez,* Pachauri has been involved in the movement since the early 1970s; in many ways, its history is her own. She worked at the Ford Foundation's India office when Adrienne Germain was representing Ford in Bangladesh; like Germain she struggled to make population programs more responsive to women's rights. "I am absolutely convinced that unless you address the underlying gender problem, you will get nowhere," she said.

Yet India's population programs never did this before Cairo, when the focus was on reducing fertility at all costs. While the central government has become much more sensitive since then, some state governments continue to employ punitive targets and quotas, barring people with more than two children from local political office and denying them maternity benefits. Among India's elite there continues to be near unanimity about the necessity of population control. (As recently as 2003, India's Supreme Court characterized "the torrential increase in the population" as "more dangerous than a hydrogen bomb.")

It's impossible to say how much of India's fertility decline is due to state policy and how much to increasing wealth, urbanization, and decreasing agricultural plot sizes in the countryside. But the government has almost certainly played a partial role, suggesting that a colossal official mobilization can over time help change social norms. Had the campaign, with all its resources, focused on women's rights from the start, India's success in addressing overpopulation may not have come so much at girls' expense.

Despite the small recent decline in its child sex ratio, Kerala remains a model of what's possible. Until 1971, Kerala had the highest population growth rate in India, with an average of 4.1 children per woman. By 1992, enormous investments in women's education, freely available family planning, and comprehensive health care had led to India's lowest infant mortality rate, all helping to push fertility down to 1.8 children per woman without coercion or, at the time, a decrease in the proportion of girls to boys.[16] Kerala's women still both outlive and outnumber its men, although unless current trends are halted, their demographic superiority may not last.[17]

As early as the 1970s some predicted—approvingly—that sex selection could be a tool for limiting population. In May 1975, when amniocentesis was first being used for prenatal diagnoses in India, a group of Indian doctors published a report in the journal *Indian Pediatrics* that mentioned the potential of the new method for population control. "In India, cultural and economical factors make the parents desire a son, and in many instances the couple keeps on reproducing just to have a son," they wrote. "Prenatal determination of sex would put an end to this unnecessary fecundity. There is of course the tendency to abort the fetus if it is female. This may not be acceptable to persons in the West, but in our patients this plan of action was followed in seven of eight patients who had the test carried out primarily for the determination of sex of the fetus."[18]

After protests from women's groups, the government of India banned sex tests in public hospitals in 1976. Within a few years, though, private clinics offering sex determination appeared. In the mid 1980s a study commissioned by anti-sex-selection activists found that 84 percent of gynecologists in Bombay were performing amniocentesis for sex determination. "A majority of the doctors thought the sex-determination tests were a humane service for women who did not want any more daughters, and some even felt that they could be an important family planning device for our country," the activists wrote.[19] At one city hospital, of 8,000 abortions following amniocentesis, 7,999 were of female fetuses.[20]

Through the efforts of feminist organizers, the state of Maharashtra, where Bombay is located, outlawed sex-determination tests in 1988, and the central government followed suit in 1994. But sex-selective abortion was too popular to control. Most people are willing to leave their first child up to chance, but after one or two daughters they take matters into their own hands. "[I]t is with regards to later pregnancies among sonless couples that SRB [sex-ratio at birth] values tend to surge," wrote Guilmoto. "Parents want to avoid the 'worst-case' scenario—i.e., a family without a son."[21] Following the 2001 census the government made the anti-sex-selection law more stringent, and as a result prices went up, but other than that there was little evidence that people were being deterred.

Although feminists have taken a leading role in India's anti-sex-selection campaign, it's a supremely tricky issue for those who care deeply about abortion rights. Women's rights activists with experience in Western countries worry that the language of the campaign is shading into the idiom of the Western antiabortion movement. "Murder in the Womb" was the title of a six-part exposé aired on the national news channel *Sahara Samay*. Educational posters, produced by the government and by local NGOs, show swords and daggers pointed at fetuses. The almost universal use of the term "female feticide" or, in Hindi, *kanya bhronn hatya,* which literally means "the killing of young girls," begs the question of why feticide in general is OK.

Abortion up to twenty weeks was legalized in India in 1971 as part of the country's attempt to control population growth. It was never about women's rights. The Medical Termination of Pregnancy Act allows abortion for a wide range of reasons, including failure of contraception, but it is the doctor, not the woman, who has the right to decide whether an abortion is warranted. Unlike the legalization of abortion in the United States, the MTP Act wasn't associated with any sort of social upheaval or disruption in gender roles—

premarital sex remained as taboo as ever, and notions of wifely obedience as deeply engrained. That's likely why it passed without controversy, and why India has never had a serious antiabortion movement.

Yet while abortion is legal, unsafe abortion remains a major problem; in many places safe services either aren't available or aren't known, leading millions of women to seek abortions from traditional midwives and unqualified quacks. Research in the mid-1990s showed botched abortions were responsible for 13 percent of India's staggeringly high maternal mortality rate.[22]

Most abortions in India are for unwanted pregnancies, not sex selection.[23] Still, with the campaign against sex-selective abortion injecting the idea of fetal rights into the public conversation as never before, there was reason to fear that efforts to expand access to safe abortion would be hurt. "The biggest danger, which is the one we're dealing with right now, is that the anti-sex-selection campaigns not turn into antiabortion campaigns," said Gita Sen, the longtime women's rights activist and Cairo lobby veteran.

Dr. Sharad Iyengar and his wife, Dr. Kirti Iyengar, run an NGO called Action Research and Training for Health in the poor desert state of Rajasthan. They provide child immunizations, family planning, and prenatal care and safe delivery, running two friendly and basic but clean clinics that are open twenty-four hours a day for people in the surrounding villages. Thanks to a scheme meant to reduce India's maternal mortality, women are paid cash to have their babies in government hospitals, but some of the poor women ARTH serves would rather forgo that money and instead pay a nominal fee to ARTH to deliver at their centers, where they're treated with care and dignity.

Safe abortion is an important part of ARTH's work; health volunteers in the villages steer women away from the quacks, who are known as "Bengali doctors," and rotating gynecologists perform both manual vacuum aspiration and medical abortions at its clinics. These services are crucial. On a scorching April day in 2008 I visited a village where ARTH works, in a hilly, marble-mining area in Rajasthan's south. A small group of illiterate women, dressed brightly and wearing big, beaded nose rings and tarnished silver ankle bracelets, sat on the dusty ground around an ARTH employee using a specially designed picture book to teach them about reproductive and child health. One woman quickly volunteered that before ARTH local women used to seek abortions from a nearby practitioner "who gave some tablets and used some instruments." There was a lot of pain and bleeding, but they wouldn't tell anyone or go to the hospital. A young woman in a green sari—a teenager, or a little older—added that her mother died after taking some abortifacient plants given by a local *dai*, or midwife.

According to Sharad Iyengar, the campaign against sex-selective abortion has had a chilling effect on legitimate abortion providers in Rajasthan. "There is stigmatization of abortion. A lot of providers have become averse to providing abortion services," he said. "Some gynecologists are now against abortions. Those who do it, do it quietly—they're not ready to talk about it. The public health dimensions of unsafe abortion never were on the agenda.".

Elsewhere in India enterprising local officials tackled the problem of sex selection by targeting women who had had abortions. Krishan Kumar, deputy commissioner of the Nawanshahr district of Punjab, made national news for his success in combating sex-selective abortion. Partly, he did it through an impressive crackdown on illegal ultrasound operations and unscrupulous doctors. One gynecologist arrested during his reign, back at work after Kumar was transferred, told me with obvious self-pity that Kumar had been a "dictator." The gynecologist remained unapologetic: Anyone with a daughter should be allowed sex determination for her next pregnancy, he insisted, adding, "In no situation should there be a third child."

But Kumar also humiliated many women, organizing groups of volunteers to stage loud, public mourning ceremonies outside the homes of women thought to have had sex-selective abortions. "Two days ago when news came that an unborn girl had been murdered in her mother Manjit Kaur's womb, hundreds of villagers wearing white assembled outside Manjit Kaur's house and took out a 'funeral procession,'" reported the *Times of India*, noting that "sadness was writ large in the eyes of Manjit, who is already a mother of a three-year-old daughter."[24]

Feminists have been understandably alarmed. They've struggled against the phrase "female feticide," but it is used so widely that even the UNFPA sometimes employs it, prioritizing effective grassroots communication over global abortion politics. Worse, in local efforts, "female" is sometimes dropped. Official campaigns against "feticide" are especially problematic, given that many rural Indians are already unaware that abortion is legal.[25]

Some campaigners dismiss anxieties about abortion rights as a Western projection, noting that India has never had a real antiabortion movement. "Please understand, in this country there was no pro-life, pro-choice debate," said Bedi. "Nobody has ever fought for fetal rights. The medical profession has not. The ethicists have not. The temples and the gurudawaras have not. So to say that any voice against [sex-selective abortion] will give vent to the pro-lifers and hence restrict the reproductive choice of a woman is ridiculous."

Perhaps. But India *does* have pronatalist Hindu rightists, who have urged women to have more sons for the sake of communal demographic strength. The secretary of the Vishwa Hindu Parishad, a hard-line Hindu nationalist group, encouraged every Hindu woman to become an *Ashtaputra,* or mother of eight sons. The leader of the Rashtriya Swayamsevak Sangh, the VHP's parent organization, called on Hindu women to produce at least three sons each to ensure that Hindus do not become outnumbered by Muslims.[26]

With increasing efforts afoot to enlist religious figures in the fight against sex selection, some fear that they'll start attacking abortion rather than the preference for sons. "One of India's biggest pluses in being able to hold up women's reproductive rights around abortion has always been that the religious dimension has never been very strong," said Sen. "That doesn't mean that with the Hindu fundamentalists running riot all over the country, some crackpot doesn't pick that up."

Sex selection poses an additional challenge to women's rights activists, one that's philosophical rather than tactical. To confront the issue of sex-selective abortion as a feminist is to see the world in much the same way pro-lifers do, at least for a moment. It's to look in horror at a culture where potential life is tossed away in the quest for economic advancement and status, debasing all involved. It's to see some choices as illegitimate.

The American antiabortion movement has relished pointing out the contradiction. "It is perhaps obvious why sex-selective abortion is an embarrassment to feminism: while the preference for sons is deeply rooted in history, the other factors, such as reduced family size and cultural acceptance of abortion, are central pillars of feminist thought," wrote Douglas A. Sylva of the Catholic Family and Human Rights Institute in the *Weekly Standard.* "Since at least the 1995 Beijing Women's Conference, feminist champions have argued that international 'gender justice' could only be established if women possessed the reproductive rights necessary to reduce their family sizes, thereby liberating them for higher education and successful careers." It is never pleasant, he continued, "to admit that one's revolutionaries have begun to devour their own."[27]

There is indeed an inconsistency between believing in absolute reproductive choice and in wanting to outlaw abortions performed for the "wrong" reason. That's why American feminists tend to see domestic attempts to ban sex selection as threats to *Roe v. Wade.* Indian feminists, though, have never prioritized the concept of choice the way Westerners do, in part because whatever choices Indian women face are so constrained. Women's rights activists in India fight against the "choice" of families to pay dowry to marry their daughters off, and to both practice and glorify *sati,* in which living widows burn with their husbands on their funeral pyres.

"My own view is that the question of reproductive rights is much bigger than the question of just reproductive choice," said Sen. "The language of choice, while it's very useful in holding up individual rights, often misses that behind the way in which people make choices are a lot of social pressures, forces, relationships, and so on." A woman's choice to have a sex-selective abortion, said Sen, "may reflect the fact that she has very few rights."

This approach doesn't jibe with the debate about abortion in the United States, where rights and choice are seen as synonymous, and where feminists are constantly defending the right of women to make reproductive decisions unencumbered by others' beliefs about what is best for them or for society. But it is not, obviously, the job of Indian feminists to map their politics onto the ideological topography of the West. There may be no overarching philosophy that can reconcile the two stances, except perhaps for solidarity between groups of women working in vastly different contexts.

Distorted sex ratios pose a concrete threat to Indian women that goes beyond the disturbing demonstration of how little they are esteemed. Some have suggested, based on crude economic logic, that the deficit in women would raise their value. On the ground, this has not been the case. Already in northern India shortages of women have led to increases in sexual violence and trafficking for both marriage and prostitution. Though dowry has persisted unabated, men who can't find wives have begun importing poor women from the country's south and east, who then find themselves isolated in an alien culture where they don't even speak the language and may be treated as little more than chattel.

Parts of Haryana, which borders Punjab and has India's second-worst sex ratio, have witnessed a return of polyandry, in which one woman is shared among several brothers. In February 2006, Tripala Kurmari, an eighteen-year-old girl from one of India's minority tribes, was murdered there. "The tribal girl was brought to Haryana by an agent who promised to get her a job," wrote Gita Aravamudan, author of the book *Disappearing Daughters: The Tragedy of Female Foeticide*. "She was 'married' to Ajmer Singh who desperately wanted a male heir. However, soon after her marriage she found she was expected to sleep with all his brothers. When she refused, he killed her. The murder of Tripala Kumari gave a gruesome face to a form of sexual exploitation which has become increasingly popular in the women-starved states of Punjab and Haryana."[28] And this was before the hardest-hit generation in those states reached adulthood.

Sexual violence, meanwhile, reinforced some families' motives for rejecting daughters in the first place. The investment of family honor in girls' sexual purity, and the terror of losing it, long played a role in northern India's tradition of infanticide. As Amarjit Singh explained, "The Afghan plunderers on horseback used to come to Punjab to plunder and rob this area. They picked up beautiful women." People thought it was "better to kill the girls before they are picked up, raped, and taken away." In the twenty-first century there are no more invading hordes from the north and west, but the constant vigilance required to keep girls safe from violation is one reason people say they don't want them in the first place.

Declining sex ratios curtail female freedom in additional ways as well. Guilmoto speculated that the increased demand for women to serve as wives and mothers will cut off other opportunities. "The reduced number of women in these areas would have an interesting corollary, in that women's roles as wife, daughter-in-law or mother would become more essential to society," he wrote. "The enhancement of this traditional family role will, however, come at the expense of other life trajectories, such as remaining single or a career-oriented strategy. Indeed, if new incentives towards early marriage and childbearing are offered to women, this could lead to their temporary or permanent withdrawal from the workforce."[29] Evidence from societies with highly uneven sex ratios bear him out; in such places women have lower levels of literacy and labor force participation, and higher rates of suicide, than in countries where the numbers of men and women are more even.[30]

I t's not just women whose futures are imperiled. Countries with millions of alienated, unmarriageable men are likely to be both more internally insecure and externally belligerent. In their book *Bare Branches: The Security Implications of Asia's Surplus Male Population,* political scientists Valerie M. Hudson and Andrea M. den Boer show how historically, in areas where men have outnumbered women due to widespread female infanticide, superfluous single men have played a violently destabilizing role. To channel their aggression governments have sometimes embarked on campaigns of expansion, threatening nearby countries.

"The evidence suggests that high-sex-ratio societies, especially those with unequal resource distribution and generalized resource scarcity, breed chronic violence and persistent social disorder and corruption," they concluded. "Indeed, bare branches in high-sex-ratio societies contribute to this disruption on a larger scale than might be possible in societies with lower sex ratios."[31]

Hudson and den Boer adopt the term "bare branches" from nineteenth-century China, where surplus bachelors formed criminal gangs that eventually coalesced into rebel militias. Like India, China has a long history of female infanticide, practiced for many of the same reasons. Women's status, thought to be relatively high during the Shang and Zhou dynasties (1766–1122 B.C. and 1122–221 B.C.) fell during the Qin and Han eras (221–206 B.C. and 206 B.C.–A.D. 220) as arranged marriages, female seclusion, and the cult of chastity became institutionalized.[32] As in India, dowries portended financial ruin for parents of daughters, and a mania for virginity made the killing of girls seem less shameful than the threat of premarital sex. Hudson and den Boer quote a scholar from the time of the Song dynasty (960–1279) who claimed, "[T]o starve to death is a very minor matter, but to lose one's chastity is a major matter."[33]

In the first half of the nineteenth century, Hudson and den Boer write, the

Huai-pei region of northeast China had a series of natural disasters. The resulting poverty led to an increase in female infanticide and a sex ratio of around
129 men for every 100 women. Polygamy and concubinage, they write, further decreased the supply of wives. Thus, many poor men were unable to settle
down and achieve the status of respectable adults; instead, they built a kind
of antisocial subculture based on crime and martial arts. Eventually, the small
bands of bandits started to organize on a larger scale to try to and overthrow
the Qing dynasty in the Nien Rebellion.

"The Nien Rebellion," write Hudson and den Boer, "is an example of how
exaggerated offspring sex selection can threaten the stability of entire regions,
and even great empires."[34]

Beyond questions of demographics and geopolitics, India's epidemic of
sex-selective abortion—and, more generally, its pathological mania for
sons—victimizes individual women. It is way too simple to claim that all
women who abort female fetuses are forced into it, but despite the experiences
of Puneet Bedi and his elite patients, for some coercion is very real.

"In Gujarat, women do not decide whether they will have male children
or female children," said Ila Pathak, secretary of the Ahmedabad Women's
Action Group, a feminist organization based in Gajarat's largest city. "To be
frank, she is never consulted whether she will go to bed with the man. So there
is no freedom of decision."

Prosperous Gujarat, birthplace of Jawaharlal Nehru and cradle of India's
independence struggle, is famous in more recent years for right-wing Hindu
pogroms against Muslims. While Punjab has agriculture, Gujarat has trade
and industry; the Gujarati businessman is a national stereotype. Like elsewhere in India, its wealth is inverse to its tolerance for girls. The state's sex ratio
is 883 girls for every 1,000 boys. In Ahmedabad, it is 836. Pathak, a white-
haired, soft-spoken, retired English professor, has studied violence against
women in Gujarat extensively, spending several years combing through police
records to produce a systematic analysis of domestic violence cases and of the
circumstances surrounding women's deaths. "In Gujarat, so many women die
or commit suicide because they give birth to daughters," she said. "Husbands
torturing wives because of the birth of a daughter is not unique."

At around 8:00 P.M. one evening in May 2007, two confused, terrified women, Sunita Rajput and her cowife, Kajal, appeared with their daughters at the Kasturba Gandhi Memorial Trust, a shelter for abused women on the outskirts of Ahmedabad. They could barely walk and had to be helped from the gate. Both were covered with welts from beatings with a belt. Sunita needed a blood transfusion. They had just escaped from their husband, Rajesh Rajput, seller of ayurvedic remedies, a sadist who had forced the women to have eight abortions between them because they hadn't produced a boy.

When I met Sunita a year later she was in her late twenties. Her huge obsidian eyes, perfect almonds fringed by thick lashes, were still shadowed and often blank, and she often broke into tears as she spoke. She found it too painful to recount much of her past in detail, so Pratima Pandya, the shelter's director, told her story instead.

Sunita, who has a seventh-grade education, had married Rajesh ten years earlier, and after a year her first daughter, Anjali, was born. A year and a half later there was another girl, Kashish. It is the sperm that determines whether a baby will be male or female, but Rajesh blamed his wife, and, furious at his failure to have a son, he would beat Sunita terribly. His mother blamed Sunita as well, and after the first two daughters, she and Rajesh arranged for ultrasound tests followed by abortions for each of Sunita's next four pregnancies.

Each time she went, Sunita recalled with an angry little laugh, there was a sign outside announcing, as per the law, that the clinics did not perform sex-determination tests. "They should be stopped, they should not exist," she said. It should have been obvious to the doctors, she said, that she was there under duress: "Of course no mother wants to kill her baby. Of course Rajesh took me there forcibly."

The next two times Sunita was pregnant, Rajesh, assuming she was incapable of having sons, didn't even take her for ultrasound—he just brought her for abortions. Meanwhile, flouting Hindu law, he married another woman, Kajal, hoping that she could give him a son. At first he installed Kajal in his brother's house, not bringing her home until she was seven months pregnant. He treated her decently until she too gave birth to a girl. Rajesh didn't go to the hospital to see the newborn, and when Kajal brought her home, he held her up by one leg and started hitting her. Together, the two women rushed at him, fighting to save the girl's life. From then on he would torture the two of them together—beating them daily, driving nails into their fingers and ears, even forcing them to drink his urine. They weren't allowed any contact with the outside world. Kajal would eventually have two abortions as well. As Rajesh's persecution increased, Sunita stopped eating. They started to go mad.

The torments Sunita and Kajal faced, said Pandya, exceed anything she's seen in her many years at the shelter. It is not unusual, though, for abuse to escalate following the birth of a girl. "Almost for twenty years I have been working in this field," she said. "If a boy is born, [a woman's] position in the family becomes consolidated. If a girl is born, she has to face the usual torture."

Finally, when Sunita was pregnant for the ninth time, the two women made their escape together. Neither had any idea where to go—Kajal was an orphan and Sunita's family was too poor to help her. Fleeing their village, they got in a rickshaw and asked to go to the nearest town. They were sobbing, and the rickshaw driver asked what was wrong. They told him their story. Fortunately, he'd heard of the Kasturba Gandhi Trust, and he brought them there.

In addition to medical treatment, Pandya called the police and got the women legal representation. Rajesh was arrested and jailed, and two clinics where Sunita had undergone ultrasounds had their registrations suspended. Meanwhile, the story hit the local media. A young woman named Usha, who had been raped and branded with hot metal by cousins of the mentally retarded man she'd been married to, read about it in *Chitralekha,* a popular magazine. It inspired her to run away, too; today she shares a room with Sunita and her children at the shelter. At least one other woman also fled to Kasturba Gandhi after seeing Sunita's story.

Usha may have been moved by Sunita's strength, but Sunita feels anything but powerful. Several months after arriving at the shelter she gave birth, in a cosmic irony, to a boy, whom she named Dharmik. In jail Rajesh read about Dharmik in the paper and began sending letters to the shelter, demanding that Sunita and his son be returned to him and promising that he would no longer torture her now that she's succeeded in producing a male heir.

To Sunita's horror, Rajesh was released from jail pending the outcome of the trial, which, given India's glacial legal system, could take years. Hoping to pressure her, he beat up her father and brother. "Bring back Sunita to me," he told them. "I want my son back." As long as he's free she lives in terror that he will try to take Dharmik. Compounding her shock, Kajal, restless at the shelter, returned to Rajesh, assuming the more legitimate role of his only wife. (According to Pandya, a momentarily solicitous Rajesh, hoping to stop Kajal from testifying against him, promised to put the house, now partly in Sunita's name, in Kajal's instead.) "They are in that home," said Sunita, "and I am in an orphanage."

Sunita never leaves Kasturba Gandhi except for medical and legal appointments. She's learning handicrafts—embroidery and beading—but can't imagine how she'll ever support herself independently. The day we met she was sitting in one of the shelter's airy cement common rooms, which is half open to the leafy compound outside. Other residents were sifting wheat for chapatis. Eyes downcast, she rocked Dharmik in a rustic cradle; her lovely daughters, saucer-eyed and solemn, were perched protectively beside her.

She had only one wish: She wanted Rajesh back in jail. Please, she implored, wasn't there something I could do? "I don't want anything but that Rajesh should be punished." She started crying. "I don't have an identity!" she said, repeating it over and over, "I don't have an identity!" Her only hope was in the sleeping six-month-old. "When Dharmik grows up," she said, "I will have someone to cling to."

In the end, as long as women lack an identity without a husband or a son, sex-selective abortion will continue to deform India's—and Asia's—demographics. That's why what is happening in India is more complicated than modernization gone awry. Rather, social modernization has proven unable to catch up with technological progress. Indian society is reforming, slowly and incrementally. The very fact that Sunita escaped her hellish home, said Pandya, is evidence of a small shift. Twenty years ago, "she would have committed suicide," Pandya said. "That Sunita came here, it is a sign of seeking freedom." Gradually, she insisted, women are moving beyond utter dependence on men. Due to increased education, she said, "twenty, twenty-five percent of women who have faced such torture are trying their best to get out, the way Sunita or Usha did."

If you look hard you can see such faintly hopeful signs everywhere. Dutt, the editor of the *Sunday Indian*, comes from a family with an infanticidal history. Of her grandfather's sisters just one survived; an elderly female member of her great-grandfather's family put the others to sleep with overdoses of opium. Just two generations later she chose to remain single and to adopt a baby girl.

Some believe only a boy can light his parents' funeral pyres; indeed, that's said to be one of the many reasons Hindus are so desperate for sons. "Now girls are doing it," said Dutt. "I lit my mother's funeral pyre." Dutt, a large woman with a sweet smile, was wearing a royal blue *salwar kameez*; as she spoke, her teenage daughter, wearing jeans, did homework at the kitchen table. They seem more a remarkable exception than the edge of an emerging trend, but they are there nonetheless, in one of the most hostile parts of the country. There has been "slow change," said Dutt. "There has been a lot of change from the late nineteenth century until now. When I was born my mother distributed sweets. She was bored of having sons—I had six brothers. I opted to adopt a girl child. So there are exceptions like that, and slow change, but it is very, very rare."

The coming of sex-selection technology overtook this sluggish process, amplifying all the country's atavisms. Skewed gender ratios are the terrible result of one kind of progress. The ultimate solution will have to be progress of another kind. "Culture and tradition is not a monolith," said Bedi. "It is not permanent. It changes. For example, twenty years ago it was ridiculous to see a girl from a small town from [the state of] Utter Pradesh to come to Delhi, live on her own, and earn money, because the money she earned was a pittance. Now she works in a call center and earns ten times more than her father, and it is acceptable. Social acceptability follows economic compulsions." He is fulsomely cynical about the "awareness campaigns" and street plays put on by many NGOs. But, he said, "if people realize after two hundred years that those who have two daughters have a better quality of life than those who have two sons, then it will obviously change."

South Korea, the first Asian country to begin to reverse the trend of sex selection, offers a hopeful example that such change needn't take two hundred years. To be sure, South Koreans continue to have more boys than girls, but the ratio of male to female births has been declining since the 1990s.

Interestingly, it has been falling in tandem with the total fertility rate, the opposite of the usual pattern, in which the desire for fewer children leaves less space for daughters.[35]

"Until a few years ago, South Korea appeared to epitomize the pattern of rising sex ratios despite rapid development—with dramatic increases in levels of education, industrialization, and urbanization, as well as in women's education and participation in the formal labor force," researchers Woojin Chung and Monica Das Gupta wrote in a 2007 World Bank paper. "By the mid-1990s, South Korea was officially included as a member of the developed countries' club, the [Organization for Economic Co-operation and Development]. Yet sex ratios at birth rose steeply during this period."[36]

It was the same paradox now seen in India. As Chung and Das Gupta point out, "This flew in the face of over a century of social science theory," which had always posited that modernization lessened the pull of tradition and made status dependent on individual achievement rather than immutable identity. It also seemed to challenge the idea that increased education and female employment reduce gender inequalities within households.[37]

The operative word is "seemed." Chung and Das Gupta make an important distinction "between the *intensity* of son preference felt by people, and its actual *manifestation* on the ground in sex ratios," and they show that the two can actually move in opposite directions. When new technology makes sex selection accessible, sex ratios can get worse even as attitudes are getting more progressive. "Moreover," they write, "since educated women are typically better able to access and implement these new technologies, studies can even appear to suggest that gender outcomes for children are worsened by development, and even by improvements in the position of women."

This is a distortion, though, caused by a lag between social change and technological advancement. In fact, the number of South Korean women who said they "must have a son" fell slowly between 1985 and 1991, and then precipitously after that. Son preference, Chung and Das Gupta found, "declines with increasing socio-economic status, lower parental control, younger birth cohort, and older age at marriage." Less intense desire for boys is significantly correlated with living in cities, especially big ones.[38] It took a few years for behavior to catch up with beliefs, but eventually the new values snowballed through the population.

Interestingly, these changes took place despite the fact that until very recently South Korean government policy purposely worked to prop up patriarchy. (Abortion, in fact, is highly restricted in South Korea, though safe illegal terminations, performed by doctors, are widely available.) Thus, Chung and Das Gupta speculate that change could come to China and India even before they reach Korea's level of modernization. "It is notable that in China and India, public policies have sought to lead changes in social norms, whereas in South Korea public policies sought to *prevent* changes in social norms," they write. "Without these countervailing public policies, son preference may have declined in South Korea before it reached such high levels of development. This offers hope that in China and India, public policies will accelerate the process of change such that son preference may decline before they reach South Korea's levels of development."[39]

Despite such cause for optimism, though, to experts and activists in India the crisis is too acute to wait for an evolution in gender norms. Besides, as Sen pointed out, the Indian case is complicated by dowry. Had outsize dowry demands not proliferated across southern India, perhaps that region, more socially progressive than the north, might have seen something akin to the South Korean phenomenon, she said. As it is, though, sex selection can't be effectively tackled without taking on the system that turns women into financial liabilities—an epochal challenge, one that will require something close to a revolution in deeply rooted ideas about marriage and family. Dowry, said Sen, was a major issue for the women's movement in the 1980s, but it proved so implacable that dispiritedness set in. But no matter the difficulty, such efforts have to be revived, both for their own sake and for there to be any hope of righting the country's gender balance. "I think this is a nexus that has to be dealt with together," she said.

With masculinization out of control, almost everyone sees the need for more immediate intervention. "I think it's a struggle over the long haul, but some sort of tough and salutary short-term punishments for doctors who provide the service wouldn't hurt," said Sen. Some in the government clearly agree. In April 2008 the Health minister, responding to "shockingly low" conviction rates, called for tough new measures against sex determination practitioners, including longer jail terms, higher fines, and special public prosecutors to handle cases. "Launching the country's biggest ever campaign against the 'inhuman and uncivilised practise' of female feticide, Prime Minister Manmohan Singh...said no nation, society or community could hold its head high and claim to be part of a civilised world if it condoned the practice of discriminating against women," reported the *Times of India*.[40]

It remains to be seen whether this time the law will be enforced with more zeal than in the past. While most experts welcome such a move, few believe it will be nearly enough. Already technology is one step ahead. Though illegal, in vitro fertilization clinics offer sex selection without abortion to those who can afford it. Meanwhile, some Western companies are marketing at-home tests with names like Pink or Blue over the Internet for a few hundred dollars. Women using them send a drop of blood to the companies' laboratories, which claim they can tell the sex of the fetus a mere six or seven weeks after conception by analyzing fetal DNA in the mother's bloodstream. The Indian government has talked about blocking access to the companies' Web sites, an idea that only underscores how powerless it is to stem the adoption of new innovations by a free people hungry for them.[41]

There will be no easy answer. Once again India is faced with the specter of demographic catastrophe, and once again the only sustainable solution lies in making a massive commitment to women's rights. Doing what needs to be done would be controversial, socially disruptive, and extraordinarily difficult politically. As disparate as India's cultures are, most of them are bound up with female submission. Any threat to that order would arouse the rage of those who see the self-abnegation of women as the essence of virtue and the guarantee of group identity. Like any democracy, India will probably find it easier to slouch toward disaster than to infuriate the defenders of patriarchy. Ultimately, though, unless the country finds a way to break through the encrustations of centuries of misogyny, its democracy itself could be in danger from an unmanageable excess of men.

CHAPTER 8: **THE BIRTH STRIKE**

"Feminism is the new natalism."

—David Willetts, Tory MP

Warsaw's Palace of Science and Culture, built by the Soviets in the 1950s and originally named after Stalin, is the tallest building in Poland, and its tower dominates the city skyline. Inside, there's a domed amphitheater with chairs upholstered in a rich, bright red. In May 2007 thousands of conservatives from around the world convened there for World Congress of Families IV, subtitled "The Natural Family—Springtime for Europe and the World." The name was meant as a hopeful contrast to the ominous specter of "demographic winter," a right-wing term for the threat of first-world population decline that has, in recent years, come to obsess conservatives worldwide and worry a great many others as well.

A cosmopolitan gathering of anticosmopolitans, this World Congress of Families brought together speakers and participants from across the globe— delegates came from France, Japan, Venezuela, Lithuania, Pakistan, and Russia, among many other places—though Americans and Poles predominated. The Bush administration sent Ellen Sauerbrey, then assistant secretary of state for population and migration. Cardinal Alfonso López Trujillo, president of the Pontifical Council for the Family, was there from the Vatican. Many Polish government leaders attended, trading ideas with their American allies. (When it was over, Ewa Sowinska, the Polish official in charge of children's rights, asked psychologists to determine whether the children's TV program *Teletubbies* promoted homosexuality and should be taken off the air, an idea first espoused by the late Jerry Falwell.)

There were Mormons and Catholics, Eastern Orthodox and evangelicals, even a few Muslims and Jews. Despite the incompatibility of their faiths they had agreed, mostly, to put aside their theological disputes and to unite before a greater evil, one that seemed to threaten humanity itself: low birthrates, auguring shrinking societies in the developed world. "[T]he Natural Family faces a new time of crisis," announced meeting organizer Allan Carlson in his opening remarks. "Militant secularism would stamp out the religious and spiritual sentiments that animate the family home. Sexual radicals would twist and distort the procreative act, turning it away from the creation of new life. Neo-Malthusians would accelerate the disappearance of nations and the depopulation of the earth."

In this context, people at the World Congress of Families hailed Poland as a bulwark against the degenerate, self-indulgent, and dying cultures to the west. "If Europe goes much of the world will go with it," said a World Congress of Families statement. "Almost alone, Poland has maintained strong faith and strong families, though even Poland comes under severe pressure to change. Poland has saved Europe before. It is likely she will save Europe again."[1]

Conservative Polish president Lech Kaczyński, who served as the conference's honorary patron, sent a representative to give a speech celebrating his country "as a place of strong faith and strong families" on an aging continent, promising to promote "pro-family policy and pro-family mentality," and echoing Carlson's warnings about the "depopulation" of Europe.

Kaczyński, a former child actor turned Catholic nationalist, was elected in 2005. The next year his identical twin brother and former costar, Jaroslaw Kaczyński, became prime minister and brought the populist, ultraright League of Polish Families Party into his cabinet. For liberals this was deeply alarming: The League of Polish Families has some very unsavory associations. Its youth wing, All-Polish Youth, is named after an organization that conducted attacks on Jews in the 1930s, and in recent years members have hoisted Nazi placards at rallies.[2]

The League of Polish Families is deeply Catholic, militantly antiabortion, and antigay, but when I met with Krzysztof Bosak, a rising star in the party, he insisted that he's at least as concerned with "problems of demography" as with strictly moral or religious issues. The former president of All-Polish Youth, Bosak was elected to the Polish Parliament in 2005 when he was only twenty-three. Slight and sandy-haired, dressed in jeans and a blue sweatshirt, he looked even younger. Bosak noted that Poland, along with Ukraine, is hosting Euro 2012, a European football championship. "Who will build new stadiums?" he asked. "Now there is a discussion of inviting workers from China, from India, because our young people went to England, generally, and France. We have very serious problems."

Polish conservatives, said Bosak, are determined not to allow the kind of immigration that has reshaped populations elsewhere in Europe, making more Polish babies an imperative. "For example, when there were fights in Paris between young Muslims and police, everybody discussed them and said we don't want to have immigration here, we don't want to have such problems here," he said. "People get to understand that the state should support having children."

For the Polish right, the separation of sex from procreation leads, inevitably, to national collapse. "Europe is based on Greek culture, Roman law, and Christian values," Roman Giertych, head of the League of Polish Families, told the *International Herald Tribune*. "If Europe abandons these values and introduces such 'values' as abortion, marriage for homosexuals, adoption by homosexual partners, we are heading toward a catastrophe. Without religion, without the family, without people who protect those family values in Western Europe, we will be replaced by Muslims."[3]

Framing the issue this way, conservatives managed the neat trick of connecting sexual liberalism to the spread of Islam, and doing so at a time when liberals were worried about growing Muslim populations in part because of their extreme social conservatism. Gay people became the precursor to religious fundamentalism, rather than its victims.

One of the speakers at the World Congress of Families was the Latvian megachurch pastor Alexey Ledyaev, known for the elaborate eschatological rock operas that he writes, directs, and stars in. "One of the rock operas, which young Russian-speaking anti-gay activists promote on video-sharing websites, features a hero character wearing a tuxedo battling men in black tights armed with tiki torches," wrote Casey Sanchez of the Southern Poverty Law Center, a U.S. civil rights watchdog group. "Over heavy-metal guitar riffs, a military-like chorus sings of 'victory over the gays.'" The report quoted Ledyaev, "The first devastating wave of homosexuality makes a way for the second and more dangerous wave of islamization [*sic*]."[4]

At the World Congress of Families, the anti-Islam undertone to the rhetoric of demographic winter was not lost on the conference's smattering of Muslim participants. Farooq Hassan, Pakistan's former ambassador to the UN and a World Congress of Families regular, criticized some in the movement for focusing on the disparate birthrates between Christians and Muslims in Europe. After all, he noted, those really concerned with traditional gender roles should welcome the growth of Islam. "[C]learly in the current political-cum-social realities, this mantle of ambassadorial advocacy on behalf of the family has been carried by the Islamic peoples," he said in a speech to the gathering.

Nevertheless, despite Carlson's efforts to create an ecumenical fundamentalist brotherhood, these are not the kind of family values most Christian (or Jewish) conservatives had in mind. For many of them, the prospect of growing Muslim communities and declining birthrates among native Europeans has set off the kind of demographic panic not seen since Paul Ehrlich published *The Population Bomb* in 1968.

The debate has now come full circle. Once again politicians, religious leaders, and popular authors are sounding the alarm about a global crisis in birthrates. Fertility has fallen below replacement level in every developed country save the United States, where it hovers right on the edge. A new genre of declinist literature, ranging from anxious to apocalyptic, has appeared to warn of the coming population implosion and the loss of Europe to more fertile, faithful Muslims. There is Mark Steyn's *America Alone: The End of the World As We Know It*; Pat Buchanan's *The Death of the West: How Dying Populations and Immigrant Invasions Imperil Our Country and Civilization*; George Weigel's *The Cube and the Cathedral: Europe, America, and Politics Without God*; and Walter Laqueur's *The Last Days of Europe: Epitaph for an Old Continent*. A group called the Family First Foundation, which is close to the organizers of the World Congress of Families, released an hour-long documentary called *Demographic Winter: The Decline of the Human Family*. The right-wing *National Review* mockingly advertised a "Farewell to Europe Tour," including a visit to the "Islamic Republic of the Netherlands": "For this special two-day event, females traveling with our party will be allowed to disembark the plane *without a veil*!"[5]

The narrative of catastrophic population decline is a classically millenarian one, in which Europe, like Sodom and Gomorrah, is destroyed for its sins of secularism and feminism. "In short, the rise of feminism spells the death of the nation and the end of the West," declares Buchanan's best seller. News of Europe's imminent doom is often delivered with smirking schadenfreude. Predicting "the demise of European races too self-absorbed to breed," Steyn writes, "[i]n demographic terms, the salient feature of much of the 'progressive agenda'—abortion, gay marriage, endlessly deferred adulthood—is that, whatever the charms of any individual item, cumulatively it's a dead end. As fertility dries up, so do societies. Demography is the most obvious symptom of civilizational exhaustion, and the clearest indicator of where we're headed.... The design flaw of the radically secularist Eutopia is that it depends on a religious society birth rate."[6]

Republican Mitt Romney incorporated these ideas into the speech announcing the end of his quest for the 2008 Republican nomination. "Europe is facing a demographic disaster," he told the audience at the Conservative Political Action Conference, the premier gathering of the American right. "That is the inevitable product of weakened faith in the Creator, failed families, disrespect for the sanctity of human life, and eroded morality. Some reason that culture is merely an accessory to America's vitality; we know that it is the source of our strength. And we are not dissuaded by the snickers and knowing glances when we stand up for family values, and morality, and culture."

According to this view, secularism drains countries of their life force, leaving them vulnerable to conquest. "The Islamic presence in Europe is not the problem so much as the symptom of the problem," Carlson told me later. "The problem is that the Europeans have ceased to reproduce themselves, with a couple of exceptions, and have embraced a postmodern, postchild culture." Muslims, he said, "are coming in because there's a vacuum, and they're coming in because they're still growing, and a growing population next to a declining population, no matter what you put at the border, there is going to be a movement. That's been true throughout human history."

The decline of Europe, Carlson said, is "tragic, but it's also the inevitable consequence of the values revolution that cut through Europe in the nineteen sixties and seventies." All is not lost, however. "Some countries in Eastern Europe are reacting very positively, and trying to turn things around."

To hear all this one would think that pious countries like Poland are uniquely fertile oases on a barren continent, their multiparous women a pronatalist example to the world. That's what makes the right-wing argument about population decline so fantastically audacious. Poland does not have one of Europe's highest birthrates. It has one of its lowest—1.27 children per woman in 2006. That year the highest birthrate in continental Europe was in echt secular France, followed by the Scandinavian countries of Norway (1.9) and Sweden (1.85), both known for their liberal abortion laws, no-fault divorce, and national commitment to sexual equality.*

This is not a coincidence. In contemporary developed societies, birthrates are highest where support for working mothers is greatest, a fact conservatives simply ignore in their doomsday surveys of future European decrepitude. There is a tremendous irony in the way the antifeminist right has run with this issue, while the feminist left has ignored it. A great body of research, oddly unpublicized, shows that after a certain point of development liberalism doesn't cause population decline—conservatism does. Speaking of calls to restrict reproductive rights and reinstitute traditional gender roles in the service of population growth, Australian demographer Peter McDonald, incoming president of the International Union for the Scientific Study of Population, said simply, "If governments went in that direction, birthrates would fall even further."

The decline in fertility rates in the developed world is a real problem, one almost certain to lead to rapid population aging, slowing economies, exploding pension costs, and a need for more immigrants than can be comfortably assimilated. In order for a population with low child mortality to replace itself, each woman needs to have an average of 2.1 children. Demographers had always assumed that birthrates would stabilize around that number. Instead, after effective birth control became widely available in the 1960s, fertility

---

* The one conservative Catholic country with high fertility is Ireland, which averaged 1.93 children per woman in 2006. Ireland's total fertility rate fell quickly in the 1970s and 1980s—from 3.55 in 1975 to 1.87 in 1995—but never reached levels seen in continental Europe. Ultraegalitarian Iceland was also a demographic outlier, with 2.08 children per woman.

plunged below replacement in every developed country, although at various points it has recovered in the United States, France, Sweden, and Iceland.

According to leading demographers, countries can adapt without much trouble to fertility rates that are just a few tenths of a percent below replacement. Real problems start when they fall below 1.7, McDonald said. That's what has happened in developed countries where family and government institutions haven't evolved to fit modern women's ambitions. Italy, Japan, Poland, and Spain, for example, all have fertility rates of 1.3 or less.[7] Such numbers, wrote McDonald, "threaten the future existence of the peoples concerned." For example, if Italy's 1995 fertility rate remained constant, then without immigration, the country's population size a century hence would be a mere 14 percent of what it is today.[8]

With birthrates falling as longevity increases, the first world is about to get a lot older. "Today's developed countries stand on the threshold of a stunning demographic transformation," began a report from the U.S. Center for Strategic and International Studies.

> Throughout most of human history until well into the Industrial Revolution, the elderly only comprised a tiny fraction of the population—never more than 3 or 4 percent in any country. Today in the developed world, they comprise 16 percent. By 2030, the share is projected to rise to 23 percent and by 2050 to 26 percent. In some of the fast-aging countries of Western Europe, it will reach 35 percent by 2050—and in Japan it will approach 40 percent. By mid-century, at least half of Americans will be over age 40 and at least half of Europeans will be over age 50.[9]

There will be fewer young workers to support this expanding elderly population. To maintain pension systems, taxes will have to be raised or benefits cut, or both. An older population will put an increasing strain on health systems, which, again, will have fewer workers supporting them through taxes. Shrinking workforces will demand levels of immigration far greater than anything Europe has ever seen, which will likely spur nationalist backlashes. Militaries will lack for recruits. These are grave threats; Vladimir Putin has called Russia's low birthrates "the most acute problem facing our country today."[10]

S peakers at the World Congress of Families celebrated a vision of women saving their cultures by returning to their God-given vocation of homemaking. "A society that has no desire to continue in time, and has so low a birthrate as we have seen, is a society with little joy, and of course no future," said the Venezuelan countess Christine de Vollmer, president of the Latin American Alliance for the Family.

> [T]he great challenges for the modern woman are to remain women: to value and exercise the tremendous calling to be mothers and formers of the men and women who will lead the world in an awesome and promising future. And therefore to make the effort to subject her interests, her ambition, and her daily routine to teaching those little people that she will be contributing to the world.

This gets it completely backward. There is abundant evidence that if you want women in modern economies to have more babies, you need to help them reconcile work and childbearing, not encourage their subjection. In developing countries a lower status for women is associated with higher fertility, but once societies become highly industrialized and women taste a certain amount of liberation, the opposite is true. "Whereas previously the countries with the highest period fertility rates were those in which family-oriented cultural traditions were most pronounced and in which women's labor market participation was least, these relationships are now wholly reversed," wrote the political scientist Francis G. Castles.[11]

Yale political scientists Frances Rosenbluth, Matthew Light, and Claudia Schrag came to the same conclusion in a 2002 paper. "To put our thesis in the simplest terms, fertility is low where vested interests keep women out of the workforce, and higher where easy labor market accessibility and child care support make it easier for women to balance family and career," they wrote. (As we'll see, this holds true even for the United States, which at first glance seems like an exception to the rule.)[12]

In a similar vein, McDonald theorized that very low fertility is the result of a mismatch between women's modern lives and social institutions that still assume male breadwinners and female homemakers, forcing women to limit childbearing (or, in some Asian countries, marriage) so as not to be trapped in an unequal, antediluvian role. The first-world fertility crisis has been caused by women reacting to the constraints on their lives with a kind of birth strike. Further restricting their choices isn't just morally wrong—it's demographically counterproductive.

Some conservatives have realized this. In 2003, British MP David Willetts, then the Tory shadow secretary for work and pensions, published a report warning that both Europe's pension system and its economic strength as a whole are imperiled by low birthrates. "By 2050 Europe will have a shrinking population, a low underlying growth rate, and a falling share of world output," wrote Willetts. "By contrast the USA will have a strongly growing population, it will still be relatively youthful, and if anything its share of world output will be rising. There are many more important things in life, even in economics, than simply being big. However, the idea that Europe has a viable long-term option of becoming a cultural or economic alternative to America in these circumstances is pure fantasy. To understand the USA's future as the world's hyper-power you do not have to look far beyond these demographic facts."[13]

Europe, Willetts concluded, needs more babies. Several knees jerked in response. "It does seem extraordinary, the Conservative party urging people to have more sex," a spokeswoman for the Family Planning Association told *The Guardian*. "It is men who are delaying becoming parents too, and no amount of exhortation by the Conservative party will change these trends."[14]

But Willetts, a man once nicknamed "Two Brains" for his analytical brilliance, wasn't joining his conservative confreres abroad in urging women back to the realm of *Kinder, Kirche, Küche*. Quite the opposite. "The evidence from Italy, and indeed Spain, is that a traditional family structure now leads to very low birth rates," he concluded. In fact, he continued, "[a] brief tour of birth rates in four European countries helps demonstrate what modern family policy must be about. It has nothing to do with enforcing traditional roles on women. Feminism is the new natalism. In most of Europe women still aspire to having two children but in Italy and Germany it is very difficult to combine this with women's other aspirations."[15]

It is almost too elegant. The solution for overpopulation lay in giving women more control over their fertility and their lives. The solution to rapid population decline is exactly the same. To the extent that low birthrates are a threat to national identity and economic vitality, they constitute one of the best arguments yet for governments to finally take women's needs seriously.

Apparently, though, few governments will do that until they've exhausted every other option, no matter how farcical. The governor of the Russian province of Ulyanovsk responded to a national campaign to raise the fertility rate by giving couples a day off from work to have sex, with prizes, including refrigerators, washing machines, and a jeep, for those who gave birth exactly nine months later, on the country's independence day.[16] (One reporter found that as a result some women took labor-inducing drugs or had cesareans on the appointed day, overwhelming maternity wards and endangering their health.)[17]

In Singapore, where fertility rates have fallen below 1.3 children per woman, a branch of the government has set up an official matchmaking unit that runs dances, wine tastings, and cruises. Additionally, reported the *New York Times*, "the agency acts as a lonely hearts adviser, with an online counselor named Dr. Love and a menu of boy-meets-girl suggestions on its Web site, www.lovebyte .org.sg." Singapore's government-friendly *Straits Times* newspaper has done its part to encourage procreation, printing tips for having sex in the backseat of a car, including directions to secluded places to park.[18]

Less amusing has been the backlash against reproductive rights in countries like Poland. Abortion, freely available during communist times, was severely restricted in 1993. The influence of the Catholic Church, so important during Poland's struggle against the Soviet Union, was the main reason for the change. Still, demographic fears play an important part in the country's fierce antiabortion rhetoric. "Here in Poland this low birth rate is not discussed in a broader context. It is used as an argument against abortion," said Joanna Senyszyn, a pro-choice MP and vice chair of Poland's Democratic Left Alliance. Poles, she said, want to know "Who's going to work so we can have pensions?"

As a combination of religion and fear about national identity pushed Poland rightward, it inevitably collided with European institutions over issues of reproductive and gay rights. Not surprisingly, Polish conservatives were apoplectic in March 2007 when the European Court of Human Rights ruled in favor of Alicja Tysiąc, a Polish woman who sought redress after being denied an abortion she needed to save her eyesight. The state's treatment of Tysiąc, the court ruled, violated the Convention for the Protection of Human Rights and Fundamental Freedoms, a treaty that all members of the Council of Europe are party to, and it ordered the Polish government to pay her €25,000 (about $35,000).

Tysiąc, a mother of two, was already suffering severe myopia when she found herself pregnant for the third time in 2000. Her first two pregnancies had been difficult—both had been delivered by cesarean—and this time three separate ophthalmologists told her that if she brought a baby to term, she risked going blind.

She consulted a general practitioner, who issued a certificate saying that the pregnancy constituted a threat to her health. In addition to the danger to her eyesight, there was the risk, given her previous cesareans, of a rupture of the uterus. But when Tysiąc went to her local, state-run hospital, a gynecologist there, after examining her "visually and for a period of less than five minutes," according to the Court of Human Rights opinion, voided her certificate. At the end of the appointment, the Court said, the doctor "told the applicant that she could even have eight children if they were delivered by caesarean section."[19]

Such a response was not unusual. Under the 1993 law, abortion is supposed to be permitted in cases of rape, threats to the life or health of the mother, or severe fetal abnormalities. "In practice, however, it takes nearly a miracle for women to access legal abortion," wrote Wanda Nowicka, director of the Polish Federation for Women and Family Planning, the country's leading reproductive rights NGO. Only 150 legal abortions are performed every year.[20]

With an unemployed, "generally irresponsible" husband, Tysiąc said she couldn't have afforded an underground abortion, which would have cost five thousand zloty—more than two thousand dollars. So she went through with the pregnancy and, as predicted, lost almost all her vision. On September 13, 2001, an official disability panel found that Tysiąc now "needed constant care and assistance in her everyday life." She filed a criminal complaint against the gynecologist who had denied her an abortion, but despite her appeals it went nowhere. So, with the help of Polish human rights lawyers, she turned to Europe.

The European Court of Human Rights didn't rule in the Tysiąc case that countries must legalize abortion, but it did say a woman's rights are violated if she's denied access to an abortion that is legal under her country's own laws. The Polish system, said the court, "created for the applicant a situation of prolonged uncertainty. As a result, the applicant suffered severe distress and anguish when contemplating the possible negative consequences of her pregnancy and upcoming delivery for her health."[21]

Around the world reproductive rights advocates hailed the precedent, while in Warsaw, three thousand protesters waving the national flag gathered at a church near the Polish parliament. "A nation that kills its children won't survive!" read one banner. "Let the unborn see our Homeland," said another.[22] Poland appealed the ruling, but in September 2007, the court rejected the appeal. The right vowed to press forward with an attempt at a constitutional amendment banning abortion.

The same day the ruling was handed down, the European Parliament opened an inquiry into whether League of Polish Families head Giertych had violated EU antidiscrimination rules by proposing a law banning any mention of homosexuality in Poland's schools.[23] The polarization between Poland's right and Europe's mainstream led conservatives abroad to celebrate the country as a beacon of decency in a sea of decadence, and to project their own fantasies about Europe's demographic decline onto the standoff.

Restricting abortion, though, has done nothing to raise Poland's birthrate, which has been on a fairly sustained decline since the end of communism. With unemployment high and protections for working women poor, would-be mothers are understandably hesitant. The BBC quoted a thirty-four-year-old mother of twin baby boys who had postponed childbearing as long as she felt she could. She'd married late, waiting until she found a husband who would treat her as an equal. "I didn't want to be like my parents from the countryside," she said. "They work together in the fields and when they come back home my father just sits down and says, 'Wife, where's my dinner?' . . . I wanted my relationship to be based on partnership." Once wed, she was nervous about taking time off from work. "My friend came back from maternity leave and she was immediately sacked, allegedly because she hadn't instructed her replacement well enough before she took leave," she said. "I'll look for a job again when my children are old enough but I'm very pessimistic."[24]

I f conservatives have dominated the public discussion over population decline—despite the wrongness of their prescriptions—it may be because liberals and feminists have shied away from the issue.* Anxiety that European women aren't having enough babies seems objectionable, tainted by antifeminism, evoking fears of a brown planet. What could be more reactionary than the injunction to women to breed for the good of the nation? Pronatalism, after all, has at least as strong an association with eugenics as does population control, from Theodore Roosevelt's fulminations that the two-child family would lead to "race suicide" to Hitler's Aryan breeding schemes. (One of the many things that Nazi Germany and Stalinist Russia had in common was that both bestowed medals on mothers of large families.)

Attempts to raise birthrates have sometimes been brutally coercive. Obsessed with spurring population growth, Romanian autocrat Nicolae Ceaușescu instituted one of the most draconian pronatalist regimes in history in 1966, which he ramped up in the mid-1980s. Abortion was criminalized, miscarriages were investigated, steep taxes were levied on childless people, and girls and women were subjected to monthly gynecological exams to identify and monitor pregnancies. "[T]he fetus is the socialist property of the whole society," he said. "Giving birth is a patriotic duty.... Those who refuse to have children are deserters, escaping the law of natural continuity." By the time Ceaușescu was overthrown, Romania had the highest maternal mortality rate of any country in Europe, and 87 percent of its maternal deaths were caused by unsafe abortion. One of the first things the new government did was lift the country's ban on importing contraceptives. A few days later abortion was legalized.[25]

Given this history, fear of demographic decline can seem tied up with ugly

---

* One moderate Democrat who has taken it on is Philip Longman, a senior fellow at the New America Foundation and author of *The Empty Cradle: How Falling Birthrates Threaten World Prosperity and What to Do About It*. *The Empty Cradle* is an interesting book, but it either ignores or glosses over a great deal of scholarship about the link between female-friendly employment policies and higher fertility rates. Interestingly, in the acknowledgments of *The Empty Cradle*, Longman writes that he is "particularly indebted to the work of Allan C. Carlson, which, although not widely known, offers deep insights into the history of the family and its relationship to the growth of both big government and big business." Longman was both a speaker at the World Congress of Families in Warsaw and a talking head in *Demographic Winter*, in which he seemed to suggest that only a return to patriarchy can stave off the crisis of depopulation.

forms of nationalism. The world, after all, is not running out of people. According to UN estimates there will be more than nine billion human beings on the planet in 2050, an increase equivalent to the total size of the world population in 1950.[26] Most of these people will be born in less developed parts of the world—precisely those areas least able to absorb them. Liberals tend to recognize that as a problem. How, then, to speak simultaneously of overpopulation and underpopulation without lapsing into racism? As John Bongaarts, vice president of the Population Council, points out, European governments have invested heavily in family planning and population programs overseas. That makes it extremely awkward for them to worry publicly that their own birthrates are too low.

With fertility in the developing countries falling below replacement, one obvious answer to the disequilibrium is migration. In a better world than ours one could leave it at that. The truth is, though, that people and cultures are not interchangeable. There is a limit to how many foreigners any country can absorb without provoking a backlash from citizens who feel their own identities threatened. Ironically, as Willetts has argued, countries with stagnating population growth are precisely the ones that feel too threatened to let in lots of newcomers. "A country with a low birth rate is failing to produce sufficient people to carry its culture forward into the future," he wrote. "Consequently, many low-birth countries are resistant to migration for fear of the different cultures brought by immigrants. By contrast, countries with high birth rates are ones that have confidence about their future. For them migration is less of a threat. So countries with high birth rates might be those with high rates of migration as well."[27]

Besides, the number of immigrants needed to make up the shortfall in the birthrates of some European countries would be unfeasible in any society, no matter how confident. According to Willetts, "Germany would need to attract 188 million migrants, or 80 per cent of its total population by 2050, to maintain the current ratio between workers and pensioners."[28] Germany almost certainly will not do this and will thus grow both smaller and older, though how small and how old will depend on its success in turning fertility rates around.

Already throughout Europe, worries about low native birthrates are entwined with apprehension about growing blocs of unassimilated Muslims. In countries throughout the continent, Muslim immigrants live in isolated enclaves, alienated from the culture around them and its liberal values. In this respect the conservative analysis is not wrong, just exaggerated. Several European countries are indeed facing existential crises as they try to cope with expanding Muslim populations, while Islamic triumphalists predict demographic conquest. "We're the ones who will change you," Mullah Krekar, an Iraqi refugee who has lived in Norway since the early 1990s, told the Norwegian newspaper *Dagbladet*. "Just look at the development within Europe, where the number of Muslims is expanding like mosquitoes.... Every western woman in the EU is producing an average of 1.4 children. Every Muslim woman in the same countries [is] producing 3.5 children. By 2050, 30 percent of the population in Europe will be Muslim."[29] (Like right-wing Westerners warning of European doom, Krekar's numbers were, as we'll see shortly, exaggerated.)

Confrontations, sometimes murderous, between Muslim immigrants and their secular host countries have led to anguished debates about national identity and multiculturalism in many countries. There have been spectacular acts of violence: the terrorist atrocities in Madrid in 2004 and in London in 2005; the murder of Dutch filmmaker Theo van Gogh; the bizarrely disproportionate worldwide protests and embassy torchings in reaction to cartoons of the prophet Muhammad published by a Danish newspaper. After the 2005 riots that rocked France's immigrant suburbs, the cover of the British magazine *The Spectator* showed a red crescent superimposed over a map of Europe with the headline EURABIAN NIGHTMARE.

Beneath such newsmaking events there was the sense that cherished European values—including free speech, gay and women's rights, and secularism—were threatened. In the Netherlands, Pim Fortuyn nearly became prime minister by railing against the danger that immigrants posed to his country's famously tolerant culture. (He was assassinated in 2002, though, by an animal rights activist, not a jihadi.) Fortuyn was something unimaginable in the American context—a flamboyantly gay right-wing populist. His nationalism was intimately bound up with his homosexuality, his crusade against multiculturalism framed as a defense of liberalism. "I have no desire," he told one reporter, "to have to go through the emancipation of women and homosexuals all over again. There are many gay high school teachers who are afraid of revealing their identity because of Turkish and Moroccan boys in their classes. I find that scandalous."[30]

Such anxiety about multiculturalism, once taboo, has moved into the center of European political debate. A 2006 *New York Times* story began, "Europe appears to be crossing an invisible line regarding its Muslim minorities: more people in the political mainstream are arguing that Islam cannot be reconciled with European values." In France, reported Dan Bilefsky and Ian Fisher,

> a high school teacher went into hiding after receiving death threats for writing an article calling the Prophet Muhammad "a merciless warlord, a looter, a mass murderer of Jews and a polygamist." In Germany a Mozart opera with a scene of Muhammad's severed head was canceled because of security fears. With each incident, mainstream leaders are speaking more plainly. "Self-censorship does not help us against people who want to practice violence in the name of Islam," Chancellor Angela Merkel of Germany said in criticizing the opera's cancellation. "It makes no sense to retreat."[31]

It's a mistake to attribute these clashes entirely to demographics. Despite warnings of a coming Eurabia, Europe's Muslim population is not very large. It comprises about 4.6 percent of the continent's people, and that includes native European Muslims from Albania, Bulgaria, the Baltic states, and Cyprus. "[O]nly in France is the Muslim share of the population sufficiently large—currently 8 or 10 percent, and growing—to raise immediate concerns about the cultural hybridization of the society," wrote religion scholar Philip Jenkins.[32] Muslims make up about 4 percent of the population of Germany, 3 percent of the population of England and Sweden, and 2 percent of the population of Italy.[33]

Muslim immigrants in Europe and their descendants do have more babies than native Europeans, but their fertility is falling fast and the differentials are getting smaller. In 1970, for example, German women had just over 2 children each, and Turkish women living in Germany had an average of 4.4. By 1996 Germany's Turkish immigrants were having on average only about one more child than German women were.[34] Meanwhile, the Muslim countries that neighbor Europe are developing European-style birthrates. In 2008, the average Algerian woman was estimated to have had 1.82 children, the average Turkish woman, 1.87, and the average Moroccan woman, 2.57.[35] There is no reason to believe that these numbers won't continue to diminish.

To be sure, the proportion of Muslims in Europe is going to grow, but Europe is not on the verge of being swamped. It will, however, have to better learn how to incorporate immigrants—including immigrant women—into its culture and society. Religion, after all, is just one factor leading to higher fertility; poverty and illiteracy are also significant.[36] As the United States has shown, these need not be immutable parts of the Muslim immigrant experience. The more than two million Muslims in the United States are much more likely to be middle class than those in Europe, and they are significantly less supportive of Islamic radicalism.[37]

In the decades to come, Europeans are going to make up a smaller percentage of the world's people. In 1900, a quarter of the people on the planet were European. In 2000, only 12 percent were, and the UN estimates that by 2100 Europe's share of the world population will be 5.9 percent.[38] When the twentieth century began, the population of Europe was three times that of Africa. In 2050, the population of Africa will be three times that of Europe.[39] The future world will be increasingly dominated by Asians and Africans. Western conservatives may not like it, may even try to curtail women's rights in furious reaction to it, but that doesn't make it any less inevitable.

However, one can accept and even welcome the prospect of this new world and still want to see European birthrates increase enough to keep European societies functioning, and developing country birthrates decrease enough so that population growth doesn't keep outstripping development. It need not be about maintaining Western hegemony, though that is surely how it will seem to some. The point, rather, should be to give women the freedom they need to find some kind of reproductive equilibrium, so that when societies do shrink or grow, they do so in a manageable way.

Beyond questions about economics, national security, and the future of Europe, there is a simpler reason for concern over very low birthrates. In most European countries women tell pollsters that they want more children than they are having, although not as many as the right would like them to have. If German women were having as many children as they say they want, the country's birthrate would be 1.75, close to Scandinavia's.[40] Even as Italian fertility fell to around 1.2, people told pollsters their ideal family had, on average, just over 2 children.[41]

Reproductive rights include the right to reproduce, and when huge numbers of women want to but cannot, it means their freedom is being curtailed.

Their societies are not enabling their choices the way they can and should be. That's both the cause of the problem—as it is the cause of almost every demographic imbalance—and a problem in and of itself.

The association between women's rights and higher fertility is relatively recent. Until the 1980s, when the first generation raised with second-wave feminism came of age, conservative Mediterranean countries had more children than more progressive Nordic countries. Between 1970 and 1974, Italy's average fertility rate was 2.35, and Sweden's was 1.89. Italy fell behind Sweden in 1980 and has never come close to catching up. The noted French demographer Jean-Claude Chesnais tried to explain why in a 1996 paper. "There has been an extraordinary improvement in female educational attainment in Italy during recent decades," he wrote. "In the younger birth cohorts, girls now have higher average levels of schooling than boys. As a consequence, young women's expectations and ambitions are very different from those that characterized earlier generations of women. The age-old division of labor between man (the provider) and woman (the mother tending the home) is no longer accepted."

At least not by women. "Italian males, even the young, are ill-adapted to this new equality of genders," wrote Chesnais. "Even those who shared school classes with girls from early childhood are not prepared for family life in which women are on equal footing with men.... The link between these attitudes and fertility behavior is direct. A woman who engages in repeated childbearing runs the risk of being relegated to roles from which young Italian women struggle to escape."

Italian social policy has made the situation worse. Financial support for families has dwindled, and there's little public day care. "Consequently," Chesnais wrote, "the standard of living of a family is markedly reduced with the arrival of each additional child."[42]

Similar dynamics are at work in very different countries, from Germany to Japan, that don't accommodate women's desire to have both a career and a family. Germany, which had an estimated fertility rate of 1.41 children per woman in 2008, sometimes seems like a fairly liberal society, but it has evolved policies that tend to force women to choose between children and careers. In the 1960s, a labor shortage in Sweden led to the mass recruitment of women into the workforce. West Germany also had a labor shortage, but the state, committed to the defense of the traditional family, responded by importing temporary guest workers from Turkey and Yugoslavia instead. Meanwhile, German unions opposed the expansion of part-time work, partly because they feared it would subvert their demands to pay men a "family wage" that could support a homemaking wife.[43] (Interestingly, Allan Carlson and other World Congress of Families conservatives also call for the institution of a "family wage.")

Germany's tax system, like Italy's, favors families in which women don't work by heavily taxing second incomes. Few deductions are allowed for child care, but the government pays women who take care of their own small children several hundred euros a month, what the German Association of Working Mothers calls a "stay-at-home subsidy." Outside child care is also hard to find. There is very little public day care for preschoolers in Germany, and where it does exist it is provided for only a few hours in the morning. Most elementary schools follow the same pattern, dismissing children before lunch.[44]

Exacerbating the problem, the country has retained a deep cultural suspicion of mothers who work. "Few developed countries are more resistant to the idea of working mothers, and the hostility can be summed up in one word: *Rabenmutter*," reported Mark Landler in the *International Herald Tribune*. "It means raven mother, and refers to women who leave their children in an empty nest while they fly away to pursue a career. The phrase, which sounds like something out of the Brothers Grimm, has been used by Germans for centuries as a synonym for bad parent." Even today, wrote Landler, "women who work while rearing children meet disapproval from colleagues and bosses. Rather than vault the hurdles and shoulder the guilt, many German women skip having children. In 2005, 42 percent of those with academic careers were childless. That is double the percentage in France, which has one of Europe's highest birth rates."[45]

Developed countries with relatively high birthrates have a range of family policies, but they are distinguished by systems that allow, and in fact encourage, women to combine families and careers. This is easiest to see in Sweden and France, countries with a rich array of public policies to assist parents. French mothers receive nearly four months of paid maternity leave at around 84 percent of their former salaries. Those with one child can take an additional six months off at a flat rate of five hundred euros a month, while those with two or more can collect the same benefit until their children turn three. Perhaps more significant, France has the best public day care in the world. All three-year-olds in France are guaranteed a place in all-day preschool, and an increasing number of two-and-a-half-year-olds are in these programs as well. Fourteen percent of children are in government-provided after-school programs.[46]

Even more than France, Swedish social policy, engineered to address a shortage of workers, is designed to keep mothers in the labor force. "Swedish policy makers effectively legislated the demise of the male-breadwinner family in the late 1960s and early 1970s, making it financially onerous for one parent to be home full-time," wrote political scientist Kimberly Morgan. "Of particular importance was a tax reform that essentially eliminated the full-time homemaker from Swedish society." Swedes are taxed individually; men can't claim their wives as dependents. Social attitudes have tracked these changes. The number of Swedes who believe mothers of small children should stay home full time is much smaller than in other countries: 29.5 percent in one 1994 survey, compared to 54.7 percent in the United States and 68.5 percent in West Germany.[47]

Society is structured to help parents balance work and home. There is widespread access to public child care and after-school programs. Paid parental leave has expanded continuously, from six months in 1974 to sixteen months today. At least two months must be taken by fathers or they are forfeited. Because payments are based on previous wages, women have an incentive to build up their careers before having children. Once they return to work, parents are entitled to 120 paid days off a year to care for a sick child, and those with kids younger than eight have a right to work a six-hour day.[48]

American women can scarcely dream of such supports. In the United States, the 1993 Family and Medical Leave Act was hailed as a major accomplishment because it required some employers to grant women twelve weeks of *unpaid* leave. And yet women in the United States have the highest fertility rates in the developed world. On the surface, then, America seems like an exception to everything scholars say about the links between progressive societies and higher fertility. Along with Ireland, where fertility is also near replacement, it suggests that social traditionalism is still important in keeping birthrates high. In some ways that's true. But it's not that simple, because in the United States women's rights, despite appearances, probably play a role as well.

American fertility rates hit a low of 1.7 in 1976 but have risen steadily since then, and in 2006 the United States surpassed replacement fertility for the first time in twenty-five years.[49] Population-wise, America has one indisputable advantage over Europe—immigration. Part of America's increase is due to Hispanics, who have more children—an average of 2.9 per woman—than either whites or African Americans. Without Mexican immigrants, Peter McDonald told me, American fertility rates would be more like 1.8 or 1.9. (By comparison, France's Muslim immigrants add less than a tenth of a percentage point to that country's total fertility rate, McDonald said.)

Even without the influence of immigrants, though, birthrates in the United States are very high for a developed country. People on the right are quick to attribute American fecundity to religion, and they are partly correct. Utah, after all, has the highest birthrate in the United States.[50] As demographer Nicholas Eberstadt, a fellow at the conservative American Enterprise Institute, wrote, "The main explanation for the U.S.-Europe fertility gap may lie not in material factors but in the seemingly ephemeral realm of values, ideals, attitudes and outlook.... It is not hard to imagine how the religiosity gap between America and Europe translates into a fertility gap."[51]

Religion may translate into increased fertility in another way as well. America has the dubious advantage of exceptionally high teen pregnancy rates—four times as many as in France or Sweden, representing a tenth of all births.[52] This may well be connected to the absence of sex education and reliable contraceptive access in many American schools. Few countries would want to emulate this part of the American experience, no matter how envious they are of the country's healthy birthrate.

For now, discussion about the connection between religiosity and fertility is largely interesting conjecture. As Eberstadt acknowledged,

[T]here are virtually no official national data for the United States that would permit a rigorous testing of the hypothesis that America's religiosity is directly related to its childbearing. Attempts to connect those two factors on the basis of broad, aggregate observations and trends run the risks of committing what statisticians call the "ecological fallacy"—mistakenly associating two unrelated phenomena for want of examining relationships at the individual level. For the time being, at least, this proposition must remain a speculation.[53]

Even if Eberstadt's speculation is true—and it may well be—it doesn't provide an answer to Europe's demographic dilemma. Setting up Scandinavian-style social welfare systems may be difficult and expensive, but forcing wholesale religious revival on secular populations would surely be even more so. (Nor would it necessarily encourage childbearing. In 2008, the total fertility rate in theocratic Iran was 1.71, despite President Mahmoud Ahmadinejad's stated desire for more people.)[54]

Besides, the entire United States cannot be defined by the values of social conservatives, despite their dominance during Republican administrations. America, after all, is a country of hyperbolic extremes. The United States is *both* very pious *and* very untraditional. Religious conservatives have more influence in America than they do in any highly developed rich country, and yet women's rights are, by many measures, incredibly advanced. The United States is the country of Adrienne Germain *and* Allan Carlson, the nation that brought safe abortion to much of the world and the one that tried to take it away. Feminism and fundamentalism have risen in tandem and exported themselves around the world in similar ways. The reasons for America's demographic exceptionalism are complicated, but in the end they almost certainly incorporate both phenomena.

Seen from some angles, after all, American women have more in common with Swedish and French women than with Italians or Germans. Female employment rates in the United States are, comparatively, quite high—65.6 percent, well above the 56.1 percent average for developed countries. Only four nations—Denmark, Sweden, Norway, and Iceland—have more children under three in day care.[55] Nor are Americans uniquely child-centered. According to the National Marriage Project, "In a cross-national comparison of industrialized nations, the United States ranked virtually at the top in the percentage disagreeing with this statement: 'the main purpose of marriage is having children.'"[56] Despite the influence the American antiabortion movement has had abroad, and its ever present activism at home, abortion laws in the United States remain among the world's most liberal.

Meanwhile, the labor market in the United States is actually one of the least gender-segregated in the world—far more so than in Sweden, where women are concentrated in the public sector. Oddly enough, it turns out that the extreme volatility of American-style hypercapitalism has certain benefits for women, because it works to neutralize the advantages men in other countries accrue by being able to work without interruption. "Ironically, women are advantaged by men's job insecurity, at least in the sense that a woman's career interruptions for childbearing are relatively less disadvantageous.... Her job insecurity becomes less of a liability when everyone is insecure," wrote Rosenbluth, Light, and Schrag. In fact, they argue that because job continuity is less important in the United States, "[H]aving children is less damaging to a woman's career in America than it would be in Germany or Sweden."[57]

While the United States has no public provision of day care, middle-class working women in America can rely on a large pool of poorly paid immigrants to watch their kids. According to Rosenbluth et al., "The wage differentials among women allow wealthier women to benefit from cheap household and child care labor supplied by poorer women, thus subsidizing the fertility among middle-class and affluent women."[58] The free market does, in a much more haphazard, unfair, and anxiety-provoking way, what the state does in Scandinavia and France. Unlike Europe, America does offer support for the notion that religiosity and birthrates are positively linked. But for all its aggressive conservatism, it *also* conforms to the rule that in developed countries higher fertility goes hand in hand with freedom for women. Disentangling the two is difficult; in all likelihood, in America's heterogeneous population, different factors affect different groups of women.

None of these systems are perfect. The French and Scandinavian systems are expensive—public day care accounts for 2 percent of Sweden's GDP.[59] When recession came to Sweden in the 1990s, family support had to be cut. "Even though the resulting levels were still generous by international standards, families with children experienced a considerable reduction in their standard of living," wrote Swedish researcher Britta Hoem. Unemployment rose rapidly, hitting women especially hard because of cuts in the public sector, where many women worked. More and more young people decided to stay in school, postponing childbearing. Just as fertility had increased with female employment, the two fell in tandem. After hitting 2.1 in the early nineties, the fertility rate declined to 1.5 in 1997, though it soon edged back up.[60] One could draw two diametrically opposite conclusions from this. The dip in birthrates could challenge the notion that the Swedish model offers a sustainable solution to Europe's demographic crisis. But because the drop was tied so closely to government policy, it also reaffirms the link between generous help for working families and the perpetuation of society.

In the future the costs of population aging are likely to mean that there will be even less money available to fund the kind of social supports that encourage higher fertility in France and northern Europe. It's a catch-22. Governments need to invest in programs that will help women combine work and children, and thus ensure a steady supply of new citizens. The systematic failure to do so is creating intractable problems that will eventually make such investment almost impossible. The window for governments to act is closing.

The drawbacks of America's laissez-faire family policy are equally clear. The United States is one of only four countries in the world that doesn't guarantee paid leave for mothers in any segment of the workforce, the others being Liberia, Papua New Guinea, and Swaziland.[61] More than a fifth of American children live in poverty, the highest rate in the developed world. (Compare that to Nordic countries like Sweden, where less than 5 percent of children live below the poverty line.)[62] American conservatives are proud that their country produces so much human capital but are oddly content to throw much of it away.

To point out that American women are relatively successful in combining work and family is not to defend everything about the system in which they do so. No doubt economic compulsion, not empowerment, is what ties many American mothers to the workplace. Women in the United States do their jobs and raise their children in the face of tremendous challenges, and many people fall through the cracks—far more than most civilized countries would tolerate. A slightly higher birthrate certainly isn't a justification for America's inequities or a sign of national moral superiority.

But it is advantageous, and it is being deployed as rhetorical ammunition by one side in an international culture war in which motherhood is understood as the key to national and spiritual survival. There is a real danger that as countries become increasingly desperate for babies, women will find their life options curtailed in the face of a desperate, coercive pronatalism. That's why it's so important to remember that right now there's a single common denominator among rich countries with healthy fertility rates, and that is women's liberty. Contrary to Pat Buchanan, Mark Steyn, and the rest of them, all reveling in visions of a godless Europe finding its comeuppance in depopulation, feminism doesn't portend the death of the West. It is the West's best hope.

CONCLUSION: **SEX AND CHAOS**

There is one thing that unites cultural conservatives throughout the world, a critique that joins Protestant fundamentalists, Islamists, Hindu Nationalists, ultra-Orthodox Jews, and ultramontane Catholics. All view women's equality and self-possession as unnatural, a violation of the established order.

Yet in one society after another we can see the *absence* of women's rights creating existential dangers. Overpopulation, with all its pernicious consequences for human development and environmental sustainability; underpopulation, and its threat of economic decline and cultural stasis; sex ratio imbalances, which may someday threaten the security of Asia; even the AIDS pandemic tormenting Africa—all are tied up with gender inequality, and none can be addressed successfully without increasing women's freedom. Women's rights must not be treated as trivial adjuncts to great questions of war and peace, poverty and development. What's at stake are not lifestyles but lives.

For much of the world in the not too recent past, large families equaled group survival. There was land to be subdued and worked by those with enough children to do so, and rewards accrued to those who could harness women's fertility. Subsistence and defense often depended on physical strength. Male dominance might have made evolutionary sense, even if individual women suffered because of it. The year 2008, though, was a fulcrum in history. It marked the first time that more than half the human population lived in cities.[1] Humanity's future is urban, crowded. In such societies large families are more likely to contribute to poverty than to wealth. Everyone fares best when parents can make bigger investments in fewer children, something best accomplished when women are educated and in control of their own bodies. In our new world, patriarchy isn't only unjust. It is maladaptive.

The HIV/AIDS pandemic has been the most deadly demonstration of this yet. A detailed exploration of the disease, and its effect on Africa and the world, is well beyond the scope of this book. But in the story of the struggles over biology, culture, and politics being waged on the turf of women's bodies, it also can't be ignored. All the forces at work in the global battle over reproductive rights are also at play with HIV/AIDS. The most important lesson of the great cold war expansion of family planning was that real change has to begin by giving women more power, not just better prophylactic technology. Exactly the same lesson applies to HIV/AIDS in Africa, though it has been consistently overlooked.

Many people across the political spectrum agree that dealing with the pandemic is one of the great moral challenges of the current generation. What has been insufficiently understood, though, is that in sub-Saharan Africa HIV/AIDS has been feminized, and women's lack of control over their own sexual lives has been enormously important in its spread. Trying to address the disease without reference to gender hierarchies is as counterproductive now as attempts to curb overpopulation without paying attention to the status of women were decades ago.

Women make up 57 percent of adults living with the virus in sub-Saharan Africa, and in some parts of the continent young women are three times more likely than young men to be infected.[2] The reasons for these disparities have as much to do with patriarchy as biology. "The subordinate position of women and girls—politically, socially and in sexual encounters—is ingrained in every aspect of the pandemic," wrote Alex de Waal in *AIDS and Power*.[3] Stephen Lewis, the former United Nations special envoy for AIDS in Africa, went further, telling me, "The struggle for gender equality is the single most important struggle on the face of the planet."

A daughter of Uganda's elite, physician Lydia Mungherera knew, in a vague and academic way, how bad things were for many women in her country. Her mother, after all, was a feminist who attended the Beijing women's summit. Yet it wasn't until she discovered that she was HIV-positive that the depth of women's suffering became visceral to her.

Mungherera was wracked with HIV-related dementia when she was brought home to Uganda from South Africa, where she'd been living and working, in 1997. Her CD4 count—a measure of immune system functioning that's between 500 and 1,500 in healthy adults—was 1. Most people in her condition would have been dead the next day, but somehow Mungherera's family nursed her back to health. She'd been so sick in South Africa that she was barely aware of her diagnosis, but in Uganda she learned to live with it, eventually going on antiretroviral drugs. Soon she joined the Network of People Who Are Living With HIV and AIDS, training others in the use of the drugs. She quickly noticed that the pandemic was hitting women harder than men, and not just for biological reasons.

"Culturally, in African countries, men dominate women, and so I found myself [asking], how can we tackle this disease if we don't fight for women's rights?" she said. "Women don't have rights in deciding when to have sex, and how to have sex—whether to use a condom or not. Men can have as many partners as they want—there's a lot of polygamy here, and women don't have a choice. You find that women are locked up in marriages where they're not happy, and they don't have the financial and educational empowerment to leave those marriages. There's a lot of domestic violence, and I believe that violence drives the pandemic." When it comes to HIV in Africa, marriage is a primary risk factor for young women.[4] At the same time, some poor single women, desperate for food, clothes, and school fees, find themselves forced into sex with older men in exchange for gifts, a survival strategy so common that billboards in Kampala, Uganda's capital, warn against "sugar daddy" relationships.

Looking for a way to make a difference, Mungherera, herself a mother of two, decided to focus on HIV-positive mothers, the cohort she saw as most vulnerable, and in 2004 she formed a support group called the Mamas Club, which now has branches in several Ugandan cities. Today the club, based in Kampala, draws women every day to its two-room headquarters, where they practice money-making skills like tailoring and embroidery, pool their money to make small investments, and share their burdens with each other. They also learn about family planning and their legal rights regarding property and child custody. Despite all their unfathomable miseries, the atmosphere is jovial—

some of the women sing as they work on their crafts, or make jokes and erupt in knowing laughter. It's hard to spend time with them without being a little awed by their resilience. But their stories offer a microcosmic view of the systematic discrimination that is killing so many.

Annet, an astonishingly cheerful young woman with chin-length braids and a wry sense of humor, was fourteen when she was raped by a thirty-five-year-old, the brother of a friend. She got pregnant and, terrified about how her harsh father would react, she ran away to the only place she could—the home of her rapist, who became a kind of common-law husband. "I was so young, and every year I'd get pregnant, because I didn't know any better—I didn't know about family planning," she said. The man had a safe, and Annet knew he kept his money there. What she didn't know is that that's also where he kept his antiretroviral drugs. He never thought to tell her that he was HIV-positive.

A widowed friend of hers who had moved to Kampala from Uganda's remote northwest urged Annet to accompany her to get tested, but Annet was too scared to ever pick up the results. Then her friend passed away, and with nowhere else to go, her three kids went to live with Annet. When Annet's sister died, her two children joined the household as well.

She finally found out she had HIV after giving birth to a baby who tested positive. Three months later her husband died. Four of her five children turned out to be infected. Now she's trying to keep ten children healthy and fed, but the only income she has comes from the Mamas Club.

Her story sounds extreme in its desolation, but many of the women had similar ones. Some were pulled out of school when money ran tight and were forced into early marriages with men who beat them when asked to use condoms. Some, after being tested, were chased away from home by the men who had infected them. Their bodies were taxed by frequent childbirth, which wasn't always voluntary. "The men continue saying that you must have children," said Mungherera. "I have a number of mothers who say the men say they must have more and more and more until their eggs are finished."

And yet, even as the AIDS crisis is fueled by the lack of women's rights, some in Africa blame female promiscuity for the pandemic. One sign of this was the spread of virginity-promotion programs directed solely at girls. In

2001, the king of Swaziland decreed a five-year ban on sex for young women, which included a prohibition on women wearing pants, a garment said to incite men to rape. Virginity testing became a kind of craze in several countries hard hit by HIV/AIDS; one chain of factories in South Africa reserved employment for virgins only, a policy enforced with monthly tests. "Strictly monitoring and controlling women's sexuality is being promoted as a solution to containing the growth of the HIV/AIDS pandemic," wrote the South African anthropologist Suzanne Leclerc-Madlala. In many African societies, she added, "HIV/AIDS has meaning as a disease linked to the moral transgressions of modern women."[5]

The kind of abstinence-only prevention policies promoted by the Bush administration were based on similar reasoning, as if the epidemic could be checked with an injection of spiritual fortitude. Under the President's Emergency Plan for AIDS Relief, or PEPFAR (which was justly praised for its role in providing lifesaving medicines to Africans), a full two thirds of American aid for the prevention of the sexual spread of HIV went to abstinence and faithfulness programs, often run by religious groups. American money influenced Uganda to abandon its successful, home-grown approach to curbing HIV in favor of one that fit the preconceptions of the religious right, with deadly results.

Uganda's initial response to AIDS encouraged people to limit their sexual partners, a policy called "zero grazing," which was not the same as abstinence. Condoms played a role as well. "HIV infection rates fell most rapidly during the early 1990s, mainly because people had fewer casual sexual partners," wrote journalist Helen Epstein in her groundbreaking book *The Invisible Cure: Africa, the West, and the Fight Against AIDS*. "However, since 1995, the proportion of men with multiple partners had increased, but condom use increased at the same time, and this must be why the HIV infection rate remained low."[6]

American abstinence-only policies threatened these gains. "[B]illboards advertising condoms, for years a common sight throughout the country, were taken down in December 2004," Epstein wrote. "Radio ads with such slogans as 'LifeGuard condoms! Ribbed for extra pleasure!' were to be replaced with messages from the cardinal of Uganda and the Anglican archbishop about the importance of abstinence and faithfulness within marriage."[7]

"The policy is making people fearful to talk comprehensively about HIV, because they think if they do, they will miss funding," Canon Gideon, an HIV-positive Anglican minister from Uganda who has been a leader in the clerical response to the pandemic, told me. "Although they know the right things to say, they don't say them, because they fear that if you talk about condoms and other safe practices, you might not get access to this money."

On July 5, 2007, Beatrice Were, the founder of Uganda's National Community of Women Living with HIV and AIDS, stood before hundreds of other HIV-positive women in the vaulted city hall in Nairobi, Kenya, and denounced the Bush administration's AIDS policies. "We are now seeing a shift in recent years to abstinence-only," she said. "We are expected to abstain when we are young girls and to be faithful when we are married to men who rape us, who are not necessarily faithful to us, who batter us." The women in the audience, several waiting to share their own stories of marital rape, applauded.

Were exhorted her audience to "denounce programs that are not evidence-based, that view AIDS as a moral issue, that undermine the issues that affect us, women's rights. I want to be very clear—the abstinence-only business, women must say no!" Again, there were hollers and applause.

Of course, not all women reject the abstinence-only business—far from it. In Africa as well as in America there are always women among the staunchest social conservatives. The owner of the virgins-only factories in South Africa is a woman, and there are many women just as eager to police the behavior of their gender. Feminists worldwide are working to reform not just laws but deeply ingrained traditions and religious strictures as well, institutions in which many women *and* men find the only security and meaning that they know. Sexual hierarchies are literally essential to how most cultures reproduce themselves. Traditional gender roles are being challenged at a time when so much of life is in flux and so many verities are slipping away. No one knows what a world of gender equality would really look like, and so with each step toward it, people move from comforting certainty toward the unknown. To some it no doubt feels like being pushed toward an abyss.

Yet as long as women don't have control of their own sexual and reproductive lives, we're all heading toward possible disaster. HIV/AIDS has added to the Everest of evidence showing how deadly sexism can be. It is not the role of outsiders, either Western governments or foundations, to dictate new sexual norms to others. It should be their role, however, to bolster those trying to make positive, responsible change from within. In almost every society on earth there are women doing heroic work to remake their cultures. They are every bit as authentic as the self-appointed guardians of tradition, and we all have an interest in their success.

"Right now, women are coming to realize that they've been vulnerable for some time, and they are trying to fight to get out of that vulnerability," said Esther Kalule, a Ugandan midwife-turned-district councilor in heavily rural Nakasongala province. "Some women's organizations have come up, to advocate for their rights. Women are trying to participate in politics like I did, to ensure that we fight for our own rights. Very many activities are going on."

I first met Kalule at a conference about women and HIV held in Nairobi during the summer of 2007, and I later visited her in her village. She was forty-nine, a broad-shouldered woman with close-cropped hair and a radiant smile. The men in her village, she said, call her a "rebel woman" and try to keep their wives away from her, lest she turn them into rebels, too.

Having seen AIDS decimate her community, she was defiant about the need to reject old traditions, including polygamy and female economic dependence. "Right now we are in the modern world," she said emphatically. "Some women have gone to school. When they come back and they look at certain things, they say, 'I don't think this is something that should be practiced in my community,' so they try to sensitize others. They're changing the community, changing the society. We need to change! Whether you want it or not, everything has to change."

During the cold war, solidarity inspired liberals in the West to support those trying to profess humanistic ideas in hostile countries. Some Western governments also backed foreign dissidents with liberal views, though they were motivated by realpolitik rather than idealism. Despite being driven by different agendas, both groups recognized a powerful moral and strategic interest in helping those who propagated values in line with their own. Today, everyone concerned with a more just, peaceful, and healthy future has a similar investment in the world's largest and most critical human rights struggle, the struggle for gender equality. The work of Mungherera and Kalule—and of women like them all over the globe—is of epochal importance. From HIV/AIDS to overpopulation to sex ratio imbalances to declining birthrates, the health of entire societies depends on the liberation of women. Over and over again, we see that sexism creates deadly disequilibria.

Which brings us back to where we started. Almost a half century after the great cold war population panic, the ghost of Thomas Robert Malthus once again hovers over the planet. For years, talk of too rapid population growth has been politically incorrect both on the feminist left and on the socially conservative right, but the issue is poised to reappear.

The year 2008 saw food riots in at least a dozen countries, including Egypt, Mexico, Haiti, Indonesia, and Senegal. The price of rice had doubled within four months, even as the costs of other kinds of foods continued a steady climb. In the previous five years world prices for corn and wheat had doubled, as did prices for chicken, while the cost of butter and milk had tripled.[8] Experts warned of widespread hunger and political instability. It was as if all the disasters the Malthusians predicted in the 1960s and 1970s were on the horizon, only a few decades behind schedule. After many years in which caloric abundance seemed the new norm, food was becoming a bit like other coveted energy resources, an ever scarcer commodity in an insatiable global marketplace. The future of food prices, said John Bongaarts, vice president of the Population Council, are "on a long-term upward curve with an occasional spike."

Water shortages loomed as well. At the World Economic Forum the chairman of Dow Chemical called H_2O "the oil of this century."[9] The United Nations Intergovernmental Panel on Climate Change reported that by 2020 between 75 and 250 million people would be "exposed to increased water stress."[10] And decreased supplies of fresh water would further threaten food production.

The world's resources appeared overtaxed. Suddenly, people in the big international institutions and aid agencies started talking about population with more urgency than they had in years. Steven Sinding, the former head of both the International Planned Parenthood Federation and of the population division at USAID, saw a real possibility that family planning and reproductive health would soon see a higher priority in aid budgets. "Even in Europe there's more of a discussion about these issues today than there was two or three years ago," he said.

Meanwhile, there's been renewed interest in the national security implications of population growth. In April 2008, CIA director Michael V. Hayden gave a lecture at Kansas State University in which he spoke of the profound geopolitical significance of demographics. "Today, there are 6.7 billion people sharing the planet," he said. "By midcentury, the best estimates point to a world population of more than 9 billion. That's a 40 to 45 percent increase—striking enough—but most of that growth is almost certain to occur in countries least able to sustain it, and that will create a situation that will likely fuel instability and extremism—not just in those areas, but beyond them as well."[11]

As concern about escalating human numbers moves back into the mainstream, it could be that the entire cycle of the population movement is about to replay itself. "We're going to see all the same debates as we saw before," Sinding said. "But can we proceed more intelligently this time around, on the basis of what we have learned about those debates?"

For global women's rights activists, the reemergence of the population question might seem like a defeat, a return to a discourse in which women's welfare is seen as merely instrumental. But it can also be an opportunity, if it's used to force the world to pay attention to reproductive justice. An unhappy lesson of the last few decades is that men in power will rarely work to advance women's rights for their own sake, but they will do so in the service of some other grand objective, be it demographic or economic. One can decry this reality and try to change it, while also taking advantage of it.

We met Sara Seims in chapter 2, when she was working for USAID in Africa and was troubled by population programs that neglected other aspects of women's health. Now she's the director of the population program at the Hewlett Foundation, overseeing a $60 million budget. Her primary concern has always been to use population initiatives to help improve women's lives. With anxiety about population on the upswing, she sees a renewed opportunity to get development economists and government ministers to take reproductive rights seriously. "If we can help them with a framework where they can better understand how the status and role of women is so fundamentally connected with issues like food security, like education, like breaking through the poverty trap, then I'm more optimistic that we can get the resources to help women," she said.

There's a danger, in talking about demographics, of appearing to blame the world's problems on the fecundity of poor women. The escalating food shortages of 2008, for example, were attributable more to overconsumption in the rich world than to overpopulation in developing countries. High energy prices both drove up agricultural production costs and encouraged the diversion of crops into biofuels—in the United States, as much as a third of the corn harvest went to ethanol production.[12] Meat consumption remained high in the United States, while it grew in Asia, which meant that more grain was being used for livestock feed. Global warming, a phenomenon that is largely the fault of industrialized countries, disrupted ecosystems.

To say that poor countries aren't responsible for resource scarcity, though, doesn't change the fact that it is going to make it even more difficult for them to absorb millions of new people. Despite falling fertility rates in many parts of the world, the global population is still increasing by seventy-eight million people a year, and will probably keep growing by seventy or seventy-five million a year through 2020.[13] Almost all of that growth will be in third world cities—or, rather, in the slums of third world cities.[14]

To feed all these new people will require some combination of major lifestyle changes in the developed world, a new green revolution to increase global agricultural productivity, and the transformation of some of the world's remaining forests into farmland. The first will be excruciatingly difficult but can be done with enough political will; the second, no one can guarantee; and the third will have harmful environmental impacts that could, among other things, eventually negatively affect the food supply.

Nor is food the only problem. "You can't escape when you go and you look at schools and you see these masses of little kids just desperate for an education, and there's even larger numbers waiting at the door to get in," said Seims. "You just can't help but make that connection. I'm seeing more statements come out from African finance ministers that are connecting their efforts on poverty alleviation and economic growth to population growth."

Malthusian pessimists, of course, have in the past been humiliated by history, and perhaps new innovations will come and, once again, erase any memory of scarcity, at least in the first world. Still, the future of humanity should not be staked on hope alone.

We face a range of possible demographic futures, and global policies will help determine which one comes to pass. The United Nations has created several forecasts of what the world's population is going to look like in 2050. In the medium variant, which assumes that fertility rates decline to just over 2 children per woman by 2050, the population will reach 9.2 billion. If fertility remains half a child higher, there will be 10.8 billion people in the world by 2050. Half a child lower, and there will be 7.8 billion.[15]

A massive investment in women's education, birth control access, and income generation would lessen the danger that the world's population would outstrip the planet's resources. Efforts to simply help women have the number of children that they want would make a huge difference. In some very poor areas women desire large families—in Niger, for example, surveys show that they want an average of seven children.[16] But data from others show a wish to limit fertility, coupled with an inability to do so.

In developing countries overall, 15 percent of married women and 7 percent of unmarried women have what researchers call an unmet need for contraception, meaning that they are sexually active, do not want to become pregnant, and yet are not using birth control. In sub-Saharan Africa, the number of married women with an unmet need for contraception is 24 percent.[17] Women in a great many places are having more children than they say they want. According to a Guttmacher Institute paper, more than 40 percent of recent births were unwanted in all Latin American countries except Guatemala (where the number was 29 percent), as well as in the African nations of Gabon, Ghana, Kenya, Lesotho, Namibia, South Africa, and Togo. The actual number of unwanted pregnancies is even higher, since it includes those that end in abortion.[18]

Seims said that in some ways contraceptive access is worse now than it was when she entered the field in 1979. "In the last year I have visited clinics in major capital cities, including places like Jo'burg [Johannesburg] and Nairobi, and they don't have the full array of methods," she said. "If the situation is dire in Nairobi, what on earth is it like in Kisumu and Mombassa and these other towns that are growing very rapidly?" When she entered the field, she said, "[USAID] was vibrant and strong and in the middle of things." Working for the agency in Senegal, she could get whatever she needed. The Centers for Disease Control was skilled in managing supplies and logistics. "Those resources aren't available anymore," she said. "They've been allowed to deteriorate as the politics have become so much worse over time."

A reinvestment in such resources would pay multiple dividends. If the danger of overpopulation turns out to be overstated, programs to educate girls and give women choices about their family size would still advance the causes of social justice, public health, and human development.

In a perfect world the prospect of Malthusian doom would not be required to make international institutions take women's needs seriously. Still, it is heartening to see so many areas where the interests of feminists, environmentalists, economists, and development bureaucrats overlap. They coincide because there is no force for good on the planet as powerful as the liberation of women.

There are also few things as radical. The history of our species is, by and large, a history of male domination. The subordination of women, and their reduction to their reproductive function, has been such a constant that it can appear somehow normal and right, while the upending of old roles seems to cause a disorientating chaos. All over the planet people are reacting to the confusing, bumptious world wrought by globalization by clinging ever more tightly to tradition, or to the illusion of tradition. Emancipated women become a symbol of everything maddening and unmooring about modernity. To tame them seems a first step to taming an unruly world.

But the oppression of women doesn't create order; it creates profound social deformities. It is universal the way violence is universal; both are atavisms that successful societies must contain and transcend. Liberty, ultimately, is something women in every society will have to win for themselves. It cannot be bequeathed by donors or mandated by treaties or courts. It can, however, be either supported or thwarted by international forces, which is why we all share some responsibility, some stake. Women's rights alone will not solve our massive problems, but none of them can be solved unless women are free.

ACKNOWLEDGMENTS

Throughout the writing of this book, so many people all over the world helped me in so many crucial ways. Indeed, in trying to thank them here, I'm slightly terrified that I'm going to unintentionally leave out people who are deserving of my profuse and public gratitude. Nevertheless, here goes:

Thank you, first of all, to the extraordinary women in Latin America, Africa, India, Europe, and the United States who shared the intimate details of their lives with me and who astonished and inspired me with their strength. Thank you particularly to Manju Rani, whose name doesn't appear in this book but who did much to help me understand the situation of women in Haryana, as well as to Sunita Rajput, Lydia Mungherera, Esther Kalule, and Agnes Pareyio, Anne K., and Alicja Tysiąc.

Thank you to the many experts and activists who were so generous with their time, insights, and contacts, including, in no particular order, Frances Kissling, Marta María Blandón, Manmohan Sharma, Eunice Brookman-Amissah, Adrienne Germain, Joan Dunlop, Rei Ravenholt, Sandra Kabir, Nafis Sadik, Saba Kidanemariam, Stirling Scruggs, Ranjana Kumari, Hellen Masama, Sanda Ojiambo, Ligia Altamirano, Ena Singh, Agnieszka Graff, Marianne Møllmann, Kirsten Sherk, Abubakar Dungus, Sharon Camp, Elizabeth Westley, Ravinder Kaur, Ellen Chesler, Wanda Nowicka, Saroj Pachauri, Malcolm Potts, Puneet Bedi, John Bongaarts, Taina Bien-Aimé, Steven Sinding, Sara Seims, Antonie DeJong, Karen Kampwirth, and Wendy Chavkin. Thank you also to my virtual colleagues, the members of the WAM! listserv, who constantly came through with leads, advice, and encouragement.

Thank you to my friends and relatives who read various sections of the manuscript and offered enormously helpful suggestions, including Cassi Feldman, Rick Perlstein, Beth Frederick, and my father, Gerald Goldberg.

Thank you to my amazing on-the-ground fixers and translators—really colleagues and coreporters—including Eliette Cabezas, Anne Christian Largaespada Fredersdorff, Shaikh Azizur Rahman, and Dominika Suwik. Thank you to Nicole Lisa for her work translating documents, and to my friend Jessica Heyman for translating e-mails.

Thank you to my fabulous research assistant, Rose Lichter-Marck, and to the Columbia Hertog Research Assistant Program, which matched us up and paid her stipend.

Thank you to the Lukas Prize Project, created in memory of the towering journalist and author J. Anthony Lukas, for honoring me with the 2008 Work-in-Progress Award, which gave me the support, moral and material, that I needed to finish this book.

Thank you to the creators of the Population and Reproductive Health Oral History Project, which was an invaluable resource, and to the librarians at Smith College who helped me access it.

Thank you to Larry Weissman, my wonderful agent, friend, and occasional amateur therapist.

Thank you to my brilliant editor, Vanessa Mobley. Shortly after she acquired this book, one of her authors, an acquaintance of mine, e-mailed me to congratulate me on signing with the best editor in New York. It didn't take long for me to see what he meant. Thank you to Vanessa's assistant, Nicole Hughes, who was endlessly patient and helpful with my requests throughout the editing process. And thank you to my diligent copy editor, Rachel Burd, who saved me from a number of potentially mortifying mistakes.

Above all, thank you to Matt Ipcar, my husband and favorite person on earth, who for two years spent all of his vacation time visiting me in far-flung corners of the world. When people say marriage is hard work, I still don't know what they mean. For that and everything else, thank you, thank you, thank you.

INTRODUCTION: THE GLOBAL BATTLE FOR REPRODUCTIVE RIGHTS

1. World Health Organization, *Unsafe Abortion: Global and Regional Estimates of the Incidence of Unsafe Abortion and Associated Mortality in 2003*, report, 2007.
2. Ibid.
3. John Cleland, Stan Bernstein, Alex Ezeh, Anibal Faundes, Anna Glasier, and Jolene Innis, "Family Planning: The Unfinished Agenda," *The Lancet*, Sexual and Reproductive Health Series (October 2006).
4. Jonathan Zimmerman, "Son of Africa or Ugly American?" *International Herald Tribune*, June 17, 2008.
5. Philip Jenkins, *The Next Christendom: The Coming of Global Christianity* (New York: Oxford University Press, 2002), p. 199.
6. Germaine Greer, *Sex & Destiny: The Politics of Human Fertility* (New York: Harper Colophon Books, 1985), p. 23.
7. Ibid., p. 123.
8. Ibid., p. 247.
9. UNICEF, *Women and Children: The Double Dividend of Gender Equality*, report, 2007.
10. Thoraya Ahmed Obaid, "Delivering for Women," *The Lancet*, October 13–19, 2007.
11. Apollo Mubiru, "Address Denial of Sex— MPS," *New Vision*, November 26, 2004.
12. World Health Organization, *WHO Multicountry Study on Women's Health and Domestic Violence Against Women*, Summary Report, 2005.
13. Katherine Mayo, *Mother India*; available online at www.gutenberg.org.
14. Katherine Mayo, *Selections From Mother India*, Mrinalini Sinha, ed. (New Delhi: Kali for Women Press, 1998), p. 2.
15. Ibid.
16. Cleland et al., "Family Planning: The Unfinished Agenda."
17. The 16 Decisions of Grameen Bank; available on the Grameen Bank Web site, www .grameen-info.org.

CHAPTER 1: SANDINISTA FAMILY VALUES

1. Indira A. R. Lakshmanan, "Nicaragua Abortion Ban Called a Threat to Lives," *Boston Globe*, November 26, 2006; N. C. Aizenman, "Nicaragua's Total Ban on Abortion Spurs Critics," *Washington Post*, November 28, 2006.
2. Jack Hitt, "Pro-Life Nation," *New York Times Magazine*, April 9, 2006.
3. This figure comes from unpublished community data collected by the Department of Reproductive Health and Research at the World Health Organization.
4. World Health Organization, *An Assessment of Reproductive Health Needs in Ethiopia*, report, 1999.
5. BBC Monitoring Service, "Kenya: Shock After 15 Foetuses Are Dumped in Nairobi Estate." Excerpt from report by Kenyan Nation TV on May 26; Shelley Page, "Birth of a Crisis," *Ottawa Citizen*, October 23, 2004; "Dumped Babies Were Born Dead, Pathologist Tells Court," *East African Standard*, April 19, 2005; "Dr. Nyamu's Charge Was Improper," *The Nation*, June 27, 2005.
6. World Health Organization, *Unsafe Abortion: Global and Regional Estimates of the Incidence of Unsafe Abortion and Associated Mortality in 2000* (Geneva: World Health Organization, 2004), pp. 13–14.
7. Karen Kampwirth, "Arnoldo Aleman Takes On the NGOs: Antifeminism and the New

Populism in Nicaragua," *Latin American Politics and Society* (Summer 2003).

8. Scott Anderson and Jon Lee Anderson, *Inside the League* (New York: Dodd, Mead & Company, 1986), pp. 206–11.

9. Hitt, "Pro-Life Nation."

10. Heathe Luz McNaughton, Ellen M. H. Mitchell, Emilia G. Hernandez, Karen Padilla, and Marta María Blandón, "Patient Privacy and Conflicting Legal and Ethical Obligations in El Salvador: Reporting of Unlawful Abortions," *American Journal of Public Health*, March 29, 2006.

11. This estimate was provided to me by the World Health Organization's Department of Reproductive Health and Research. It was based on hospital data collected from the Ministry of Health Web site for 2002.

12. McNaughton et al., "Patient Privacy."

13. María López Vigil, *Historia de una Rosa* (Managua, Nicaragua: Impresiones Helios, 2003), p. 27.

14. Interview with Marta María Blandón, *Women's Health Journal,* January 1, 2003.

15. Ibid.

16. *Rosita,* directed by Barbara Attie and Janet Goldwater (2005).

17. Steve Bradshaw, *Sex and Holy City*, originally aired on BBC One on October 12, 2003. Produced by Chris Woods for BBC Panorama.

18. Karen Kampwirth, *Women & Guerrilla Movements* (University Park, PA: Pennsylvania State University Press, 2002), p. 2. Timothy P. Wickham-Crowley has written that he thinks the 30 percent figure is exaggerated but says, "I am still persuaded that a quantum leap occurred in women's participation in Latin American revolutionary movements, roughly between 1965 and 1975." Wickham-Crowley, *Guerrillas and Revolution in Latin America* (Princeton, NJ: Princeton University Press, 1992), pp. 216–17.

19. Giocanda Belli, *The Country Under My Skin: A Memoir of Love and War* (New York: Anchor Books, 2003), p. 262.

20. Ibid., p. 272.

21. Katherine Isbester, *Still Fighting: The Nicaraguan Women's Movement, 1977–2000* (Pittsburgh: University of Pittsburgh Press, 2001), p. 147.

22. Kampwirth, "Arnoldo Aleman Takes On the NGOs."

23. Ed Vulliamy, "Nicaragua's Daniel Ortega in the Lion's Den Again," *Observer of London,* September 2, 2001.

24. Sara Miller Llana, "Evangelicals Flex Growing Clout in Nicaragua's Election," *Christian Science Monitor,* November 2, 2006.

25. Héctor Tobar, "Nicaragua Poised to Outlaw All Abortions," *Los Angeles Times,* October 26, 2006.

26. Miller Llana, "Evangelicals Flex Growing Clout."

27. Jenkins, *The Next Christendom,* p. 142.

28. Ann Barger Hannum, "Sex Tourism in Latin America," *ReVista: Harvard Review of Latin America* (Winter, 2002).

29. *El Nuevo Diairo,* "Votos vergonzantes," October 27, 2006.

30. Roberto Collado, "'Rosita' revictimizada," *El Nuevo Diario,* August 9, 2007

31. Ernesto García, "Declaran culpable a padrastro de 'Rosita,'" *El Nuevo Diario,* November 16, 2007; Eloísa Ibarra and Luis Alemán, "Fiscalía va tras red de Mujeres contra la Violencia," *El Nuevo Diario,* November 24, 2007.

32. Ibarra and Alemán, "Fiscalía va tras red de Mujeres."

33. Ibid.

34. Lance Lattig and Angela Heimburger, "Abortion Ban Killing Women," *Miami Herald,* October 22, 2007.

35. Associated Press, "Women Die After Nicaragua's Ban on Abortions," November 6, 2007; Human Rights Watch, *Over Their Dead Bodies: Denial of Access to Emergency Obstetric Care and Therapeutic Abortion in Nicaragua,* report, October 2007.

36. Human Rights Watch, *Over Their Dead Bodies.*

37. Catholic News Service, "Pope Praises Nicaragua's Recent Ban on Therapeutic Abortions," September 25, 2007.

CHAPTER 2: THE GREAT POPULATION PANIC, OR FIGHTING COMMUNISM WITH CONTRACEPTION

1. Lisa Cronin Wohl, "Would You Buy an Abortion from This Man? The Harvey Karman Controversy," *Ms.* (September 1975).

2. Ibid.

3. Ibid.

4. Malcolm Potts, interview by Rebecca Sharpless, transcript of audio recording, October 8–9, 2002. Population and Reproductive Health Oral History Project, Sophia Smith Collection, Smith College, Northampton, MA, p. 74.

5. Cronin Wohl, "Would You Buy an Abortion from This Man?"

6. Ibid.

7. From National Security Study Memorandum 200, reprinted in Stephen D. Mumford, *The Life and Death of NSSM 200: How the Destruction of Political Will Doomed a U.S. Population Policy* (Research Triangle Park, NC: Center for Research on Population and Security, 1996), p. 550.

8. Andrzej Kulczycki, *The Abortion Debate in the World Arena* (New York: Routledge, 1999), p. 30.

9. Reimert Thorolf Ravenholt, interview by Rebecca Sharpless, transcript of audio recording, July 18–20, 2002. Population and Reproductive Health Oral History Project, Sophia Smith Collection, p. 122.

10. Phyllis Tilson Piotrow, *World Population Crisis: The United States Response* (New York: Praeger Publishers, 1973); foreword by George H. W. Bush, p. ix.

11. Ellen Chesler, *Woman of Valor: Margaret Sanger and the Birth Control Movement in America* (New York: Anchor Books, 1993), p. 436.

12. Malcom Potts, oral history, p. 22.

13. Center for Reproductive Rights, "The World's Abortion Laws, May 2007." Available on the center's Web site, www.reproductiverights.org.

14. Joseph Chamie, "Coping with World Population Boom and Bust—Part I," YaleGlobal, August 19, 2004.

15. Amy Ong Tsui, "Population Policies, Family Planning Programs, and Fertility: The Record," *Population and Development Review,* vol. 27, Supplement: Global Fertility Transition (2001), pp. 184–204.

16. David Bloom, David Canning, and Jaypee Sevilla, *The Demographic Dividend: A New Perspective on the Economic Consequences of Population Change* (Santa Monica, CA: Rand Corporation, 2003), p. 34.

17. United Nations International Conference on Population and Development, "Programme of Action of the Conference," Cairo, September 19, 1994. Available at www.unfpa.org/ispd/ispd-programme.cfm.

18. Cited in Chesler, *Woman of Valor,* p. 209.

19. Hugh Moore, *The Population Bomb,* self-published booklet, 1957. Rockefeller Archives, Pop Council IV3B4.2, General File Acc. 1, Box 22, File 344.

20. Thomas Robert Malthus, *An Essay on the Principle of Population* (Whitefish, MT: Kessinger Publishing, 2004), pp. 44–45.

21. Ibid., p. 27.

22. Chesler, *Woman of Valor,* p. 196.

23. Matthew Connelly, *Fatal Misconception: The Struggle to Control World Population* (Cambridge, MA: Belknap Press, 2008), p. 77.

24. Chesler, *Woman of Valor,* p. 216.

25. Ibid., p. 215.

26. Connelly, *Fatal Misconception,* p. 8; Chesler, *Woman of Valor,* p. 215.

27. Connelly, *Fatal Misconception,* p. 53.

28. Chesler, *Woman of Valor,* p. 216.

29. Ibid., p. 215.

30. Piotrow, *World Population Crisis,* pp. 3–5.

31. Chesler, *Woman of Valor,* pp. 421–22.

32. Joan Dunlop, interview by Rebecca Sharpless, transcript of audio recording, April 14–15, 2004. Population and Reproductive Health Oral History Project, Sophia Smith Collection, p. 23.

33. Ibid., p. 44.

34. Phyllis Tilson Piotrow, interview by Rebecca Sharpless, transcript of audio recording, September 16, 2002. Population and Reproductive Health Oral History Project, Sophia Smith Collection, p. 27.

35. Piotrow, *World Population Crisis,* pp. 37–38.

36. Ibid., p. 38.

37. William H. Draper Jr., interview by Jerry N. Hess, transcript of audio recording, January 11, 1972. Truman Presidential Museum and Library. Available at trumanlibrary.org/oralhist/draperw.htm.

38. Piotrow, *World Population Crisis,* p. 39.

39. Ibid., p. 38.

40. Arthur Krock, "The Most Dangerous Bomb of All," *New York Times,* October 2, 1959.

41. *Time,* "Flood of Babies," March 2, 1959.

42. Reuters, "Pakistan to Push Population Curb," *New York Times,* January 17, 1960.

43. George Dugan, "Christian Use of Birth Control Backed in World Church Study," *New York Times,* October 7, 1959.

44. *Time,* "The Birth Control Issue," December 7, 1959

45. Ibid.

46. James Reston, "Kennedy Opposes Advocacy by U.S. of Birth Control," *New York Times,* November 28, 1959.

47. Piotrow, *World Population Crisis,* p. 70.

48. Ibid.

49. Ibid., p. 46.

50. Jonathan Spivak, "Birth Control Push: U.S. Is Moving to Make Family-Planning Help Available to Everyone," *Wall Street Journal,* October 21, 1965.

51. Piotrow, *World Population Crisis,* p. 89.

52. Joseph Califano, *The Triumph & Tragedy of Lyndon Johnson: The White House Years* (College Station, TX: A&M University Press, 2000), pp. 154–55.

53. Ibid., p. 155.

54. Ibid., p. 156.

55. Piotrow, *World Population Crisis,* p. 106.

56. Robert McClory, *Turning Point: The Inside Story of the Papal Birth Control Commission, and How* Humanae Vitae *Changed the Life of Patty Crowley and the Future of the Church* (New York: Crossroad, 1997), p. 27.

57. Ibid., pp. 4–5.

58. Ibid., p. 26.

59. Ibid., pp. 73, 90, 92.

60. Ibid., pp. 96–97.

61. Ibid., p. 97.

62. Ibid., pp. 176–77.

63. Garry Wills, *Papal Sin: Structures of Deceit* (New York: Image Books, 2001), p. 95.

64. Ibid., p. 79.

65. McClory, *Turning Point,* p. 1.

66. Ibid., p. 132.

67. Wills, *Papal Sin,* pp. 95–96.

68. Reimert Thorolf Ravenholt, interview by Rebecca Sharpless, transcript of audio recording, July 18–20, 2002. Population and Reproductive Health Oral History Project, Sophia Smith Collection, p. 85.

69. Ibid.

70. Ibid., p. 94.

71. Ibid., p. 2.

72. Ibid., p. 36.

73. Ibid., p. 97.

74. Stephen F. Minkin, "Abroad, the U.S. Pushes Contraceptives Like Coca-Cola," *Los Angeles Times,* September 23, 1979.

75. Donald P. Warwick, *Bitter Pills: Population Policies and Their Implementation in Eight Developing Countries* (Cambridge, England: Cambridge University Press, 1982), p. 10.

76. Ibid., p. 11.

77. Ravenholt oral history, pp. 108–109.

78. Dunlop oral history, pp. 41–42.

79. Ernest B. Fergurson, "Baby-making vs. Vote-getting," *Chicago Tribune,* March 25, 1972.

80. Paul Ehrlich, *The Population Bomb* (New York: Ballantine Books, 1968), p. xi.

81. Duff Gillespie, interview by Rebecca Sharpless, transcript of audio recording, May 19–20, 2003. Population and Reproductive Health Oral History Project, Sophia Smith Collection, pp. 34–35.

82. Ravenholt oral history, p. 111.

83. Gillespie oral history, p. 41.

84. Ibid., p. 38.

85. Ravenholt oral history, p. 129.

86. Piotrow, *World Population Crisis,* p. 211.

87. Richard Nixon, "Statement About the Report of the Commission on Population Growth and the American Future," May 5, 1972. Available at the American Presidency Project: www.presidency.ucsb.edu.

88. Clayton Fritchey, "Don't Overlook A.M.A. Issues," *Chicago Tribune,* September 19, 1972.

89. Clayton Fritchey, "The Nixon-McGovern Campaign," *Washington Post,* May 20, 1972.

90. Ravenholt oral history, p. 95.

91. Potts oral history, p. 79.

92. Reprinted in Stephen D. Mumford, *The Life and Death of NSSM 200: How the Destruction of Political Will Doomed a U.S. Population Policy* (Research Triangle Park, NC: Center for Research on Population and Security, 1996), p. 61.

93. Ibid., pp. 65, 70.

94. Ibid., pp. 510–511.

95. Ibid., p. 504.

96. Ibid., p. 76.

97. Sara Seims, interview by Rebecca Sharpless, transcript of audio recording, September 17, 2004. Population and Reproductive Health Oral History Project, Sophia Smith Collection, p. 25.

98. Ibid., pp. 23–24.

99. Ibid., pp. 32–33.

CHAPTER 3: SISTERHOOD IS INTERNATIONAL

1. Adrienne Germain, interview by Rebecca Sharpless, transcript of audio recording, June 19–20, 2003. Population and Reproductive Health Oral History Project, Sophia Smith Collection, Smith College, Northampton, MA, p. 18.

2. Ibid., p. 34.

3. Ibid., p. 22.

4. *Family Planning,* Walt Disney, 1967.

5. Phyllis Tilson Piotrow, interview by Rebecca Sharpless, transcript of audio recording,

September 16, 2002. Population and Reproductive Health Oral History Project, Sophia Smith Collection, pp. 70–71.

6. Cicely Marston and John Cleland, "Relationships Between Contraception and Abortion: A Review of the Evidence," *International Family Planning Perspectives*, vol. 29, no. 1. (March 2003), pp. 6–13.

7. Bernard Berelson, "Beyond Family Planning," *Studies in Family Planning*, vol. 1, no. 38 (February 1969), p. 12.

8. Germain oral history, p. 58.

9. Ibid., p. 59.

10. Adrienne Germain, "A Major Resource Awaiting Development: Women in the Third World," *New York Times*, August 26, 1975.

11. Germain oral history, pp. 38–39.

12. Amartya Sen, *Development as Freedom* (New York: Anchor Books, 1999), p. 194.

13. John C. Caldwell, "Cultural and Social Factors Influencing Mortality Levels in Developing Countries," *Annals of the American Academy of Political and Social Science*, vol. 510, *World Population: Approaching the Year 2000* (July 1990), pp. 44–59.

14. Ibid.

15. Ibid. Caldwell writes, "There is convincing evidence that the achievement of a small family, or even the intention of having one by employing birth control, is associated with declines in child mortality." See also John C. Caldwell, "Routes to Low Mortality in Poor Countries," *Population and Development Review*, vol. 12, no. 2 (June 1986), pp. 171–220.

16. Sen, *Development as Freedom*, p. 225.

17. Dunlop oral history, p. 51.

18. Ibid., p. 5.

19. Ibid., pp. 5–6.

20. Ibid., p. 7.

21. Ibid., pp. 41–42.

22. Germain oral history, p. 52.

23. Barbara Ehrenreich, Mark Dowie, and Stephen Minkin, "The Charge: Gynocide," *Mother Jones* (November/December 1979).

24. "China Raps U.S., Soviet Union for Raising Alarm on Population," *Los Angeles Times*, August 22, 1974.

25. Marvine Howe, "Brazil is Seeking a High Birth Rate," *New York Times*, June 3, 1974.

26. Gladwin Hill, "Marx vs. Malthus: Ideas Stir Rancor at Population Meeting," *New York Times*, August 26, 1974.

27. Memo from Joan Dunlop dated September 24, 1974, Rockefeller Archive Center, Sleepy Hollow, NY, Rockefeller Family, Rec. Group 17, Series Joan Dunlop, Box 8, folder Post Bucharest.

28. Copy of speech in the Rockefeller Archives, Collection: Rockefeller Family, Rec. Group 5, Series 2, Box 10, folder 106.

29. Bill Peterson, "Battling the Birth Boom: Small Wins—Big Failures," *Washington Post*, May 18, 1978.

30. Duff Gillespie, interview by Rebecca Sharpless, transcript of audio recording, May 19–20, 2003. Population and Reproductive Health Oral History Project, Sophia Smith Collection, p. 33.

31. Davidson R. Gwatkin, "Political Will and Family Planning: The Implications of India's Emergency Experience," *Population and Development Review*, vol. 5, no. 1 (March 1979), pp. 29–59.

32. Ibid.

33. Muhammad Yunus, *Banker to the Poor: Micro-Lending and the Battle Against World Poverty* (New York: Public Affairs, 2003), p. 71.

34. Ibid., p. 72.

35. Ibid., p. 134.

36. John C. Caldwell, Barkat-e-Khuda, Bruce Caldwell, Indrani Pieris, and Pat Caldwell, "The Bangladesh Fertility Decline: An Interpretation," *Population and Development Review*, vol. 25, no. 1 (March 1999), pp. 67–84.

37. William K. Stevens, "Poor Lands' Success in Cutting Birth Rate Upsets Old Theories," *New York Times*, January 2, 1994.

38. Sen, *Development as Freedom*, p. 201.

39. Susan Brownmiller, *Against Our Will: Men, Women, and Rape* (New York: Fawcett, 1975), p. 82.

40. Ibid., p. 84.

41. Bella Stumbo, "Bangladesh War Toll: Mass Abortions," *Los Angeles Times*, March 31, 1972.

42. Ibid.

43. Ibid.

44. Sandra Kabir, interview by Deborah McFarlane, transcript of audio recording, March 13–14, 2004. Population and Reproductive Health Oral History Project, Sophia Smith Collection, p. 19.

45. Randall Balmer, *Thy Kingdom Come: An Evangelical's Lament* (New York: Basic Books, 2006), pp. 12–15.

46. Kabir oral history, p. 17. (I also heard the tape of this interview, hence my italics to indicate how Kabir emphasized her outrage.)

47. Ibid., p. 23.
48. Ibid., p. 24.
49. Germain oral history, p. 82.
50. Dunlop oral history, p. 68.
51. Ibid., p. 78.
52. Gregg Easterbrook, "Forgotten Benefactor of Humanity," *Atlantic Monthly* (January 1997).
53. Norman Borlaug, "The Green Revolution, Peace, and Humanity." Delivered at the Nobel Institute, Oslo, Norway, December 11, 1970. Available at the Nobel Foundation Web site, www.nobelprize.org.
54. Julian Simon, *The Ultimate Resource* (Princeton, NJ: Princeton University Press, 1981), p. 197.
55. Ibid., p. 149
56. Sharon L. Camp and Craig R. Lasher, *International Family Planning Policy—A Chronicle of the Reagan Years* (February 1989), Population Crisis Committee, unpublished manuscript.
57. Ibid.
58. Ibid.
59. Ibid.
60. American Life Lobby, "SPECIAL WARNING TO ALL ISLAMIC PRO-LIFERS: *These men are dangerous to your health!*" Article found in documents requested from the Ronald Reagan Presidential Library, Simi Valley, CA.
61. "A Population Aide Tells of Attacks," *New York Times*, August 16, 1984.
62. Rowland Evans and Robert Novak, "The Population Policy Battle," *Washington Post*, June 13, 1984.
63. Mary Vallis, "Barack Obama, the New Prince: One of These Men Represents Democrats' Hope for Future," *National Post (Canada), October 21, 2004.*
64. Phil Gailey, "White House Urged Not to Bar Aid to Countries Supporting Abortion," *New York Times*, June 19, 2004.
65. Jason L. Finkle and Barbara B. Crane, "Ideology and Politics at Mexico City: The United States at the 1984 International Conference on Population," *Population and Development Review*, vol. 11, no. 1 (March 1985), p. 1.
66. U.S. Policy Statement given at the International Conference on Population by Ambassador James L. Buckley, August 8, 1984. Reagan archives.
67. Cristine Russell, "End Urged to Aiding Population Control," *Washington Post*, June 11, 1984.
68. Note from William Westmoreland to James Baker, found in documents requested from the Reagan archives
69. "Population, Resources, and Politics in the Third World: The Long View," Directorate of Intelligence (January 1984). Reagan archives.
70. Camp and Lasher, *International Family Planning Policy.*
71. Susan F. Rasky, "Reagan Restrictions on Foreign Aid for Abortion Programs Lead to a Fight," *New York Times*, October 14, 1984; Camp and Lasher, *International Family Planning Policy.*
72. Camp and Lasher, *International Family Planning Policy.*
73. Rasky, "Reagan Restrictions on Foreign Aid."
74. Matthew Connelly, *Fatal Misconception: The Struggle to Control World Population* (Cambridge, MA: Belknap Press, 2008), p. 343.
75. Bernard D. Nossiter, "Population Prizes from U.N. Assailed," *New York Times*, July 24, 1983.
76. Dunlop oral history, p. 80.

CHAPTER 4: CAIRO AND BEIJING

1. John Hooper, "Pope And Tehran Do Abortion Deal," *The Guardian*, August 9, 1994.
2. Deutsche Presse-Agentur, "Cairo: Abortion Row Gets Fresh Emotional Charge," September 8, 1994.
3. Francis Fukuyama, *The End of History and the Last Man* (New York: Avon Books, 1992), p. 126.
4. Paul Kennedy, *The Parliament of Man: The Past, Present, and Future of the United Nations* (New York: Random House, 2006), p. 169.
5. Margaret Mead, *Male & Female* (New York: Perennial, 2001), p. 7.
6. Ronald Inglehart and Pippa Norris, *Rising Tide: Gender Equality and Cultural Change Around the World* (New York: Cambridge University Press, 2003), p. 10.
7. Joel Achenbach, "At Summit, Dueling Hemispheres; North-South Rift Over Overpopulation," *Washington Post*, June 5, 1992.
8. Joan Dunlop, interview by Rebecca Sharpless, transcript of audio recording, April 14–15, 2004. Population and Reproductive Health

Oral History Project, Sophia Smith Collection, p. 95.

9. Ibid., p. 115.

10. Sandra Kabir, interview by Deborah McFarlane, transcript of audio recording, March 13–14, 2004. Population and Reproductive Health Oral History Project, Sophia Smith Collection, p. 52.

11. Nafis Sadik, interview by Rebecca Sharpless, transcript of audio recording, July 24, 2003. Population and Reproductive Health Oral History Project, Sophia Smith Collection, pp. 31–32.

12. Sharon Camp, interview by Rebecca Sharpless, transcript of audio recording, August 20–21, 2003. Population and Reproductive Health Oral History Project, Sophia Smith Collection, p. 52.

13. Ibid., p. 53.

14. George Weigel, *Witness to Hope* (Cliff Street Books: New York, 1999), p. 717.

15. Ibid.

16. Ibid., p. 720.

17. Carl Bernstein and Marco Politi, *His Holiness: John Paul II and the History of Our Time* (New York: Penguin Books, 1996), p. 524.

18. Ibid.

19. "Vatican Pleas to Islam Raise Fears in West," *International Herald Tribune,* August 19, 1994.

20. Ibid.

21. Donna Lee Bowen, "Abortion, Islam, and the 1994 Cairo Population Conference," *International Journal of Middle East Studies,* vol. 29, no. 2 (May 1997), p. 164.

22. Akbar Aghajanian and Amir H. Merhyar, "Fertility, Contraceptive Use and Family Planning Program Activity in the Islamic Republic of Iran," *International Family Planning Perspectives,* vol. 25, no. 2 (June 1999).

23. Ilana Landsberg-Lewis, ed., *Bringing Equality Home: Implementing the Convention on the Elimination of All Forms of Discrimination Against Women,* UNIFEM, 1998. Available at the UNIFEM Web site, www.unifem.org.

24. United Nations Population Fund, *State of the World Population,* 1999. Available at the UNFPA Web site, www.unfpa.org.

25. Thomas C. Fox, "Vatican OKs Most of U.N. Document After Cairo Tactics Stir Bitterness—United Nations Population Conference, Egypt, 1994," *National Catholic Reporter,* September 23, 1994.

26. Ibid.

27. Weigel, *Witness to Hope,* p. 727.

28. Adrienne Germain, interview by Rebecca Sharpless, transcript of audio recording, June 19–20, 2003. Population and Reproductive Health Oral History Project, Sophia Smith Collection, p. 170.

29. Conor Cruise O'Brien, "A Great Defeat for the Vatican," *The Independent,* September 16, 1994.

30. "More Words Than Deeds," *The Economist,* September 9, 1995.

31. Barbara Crossette, "U.S. Upholds Role at Talks on Women," *New York Times,* August 6, 1995.

32. Nancy Pelosi, Letter to the Editor, *New York Times,* August 18, 1995.

33. R. W. Apple Jr., "An Obstacle Removed; China's Ouster of Wu Helps Make Route to Better Relations a Little Less Bumpy," *New York Times,* August 25, 1995.

34. Laurie Goodstein, "Women's Work: New Options; Debating Focus of Conference; Traditionalists Want Motherhood Stressed," *Washington Post,* August 27, 1995.

35. Patrick E. Tyler, "Hillary Clinton, in China, Details Abuse of Women," *New York Times,* September 6, 1995.

36. Carl Bernstein, *A Woman in Charge* (New York: Knopf, 2007), p. 438.

37. Quoted in ibid.

38. Quoted in Carroll Bogert, "We Turned This Around," *Newsweek,* September 18, 1995.

39. Sonia Correa, "What Beijing Means." International Women's Health Coalition; available at the coalition Web site, www.iwhc.org.

CHAPTER 5: RIGHTS VERSUS RITES

1. Richard A. Shweder, "When Cultures Collide: Which Rights? Whose Tradition of Values? A Critique of the Global Anti-FGM Campaign," originally prepared for the Joint Princeton University/Central European University Conference on "Universalism and Local Knowledge in Human Rights" (October 24–25, 2003), Princeton, New Jersey.

2. Bettina Shell-Duncan and Ylva Hernlund, "Female 'Circumcision' in Africa: Dimensions of the Practice and Debates," published in *Female 'Circumcision' in Africa: Culture, Controversy, and Change,* Bettina Shell-Duncan

and Ylva Hernlund, eds. (Boulder, CO: Lynn Rienner Publishers, 2000), p. 9.

3. World Health Organization, "Classification of Female Genital Mutilation." Available at the WHO Web site, www.who.int.

4. UNICEF Innocenti Digest, *Changing a Harmful Social Convention: Female Genital Mutilation/Cutting*, Alexia Lewnes, ed., 2005.

5. Report on Female Genital Mutilation as Required by Conference Report (H. Rept. 106-997) to Public Law 106-429 (Foreign Operations, Export Financing, and Related Programs Appropriations Act, 2001). U.S. Department of State, Office of the Senior Coordinator for International Women's Issues.

6. World Health Organization, "Female Genital Mutilation and Obstetric Outcome: WHO Collaborative Prospective Study in Six African Countries," *The Lancet* (2006):367:1835–41.

7. Ibid.

8. Shweder's comments were published on John Tierney's *New York Times* TierneyLab blog on December 5, 2007. The blog is located at www.tierneylab.blogs.nytimes.com.

9. Gerry Mackie, "Ending Footbinding and Infibulation: A Convention Account," *American Sociological Review*, vol. 61, no. 6 (December 1996), pp. 999–1017.

10. Ibid.

11. Ibid.

12. Hanny Lightfoot-Klein, *Prisoners of Ritual: An Odyssey into Female Genital Circumcision in Africa* (New York: Harrington Park Press, 1989), pp. 48–49.

13. Elizabeth Heger Boyle, *Female Genital Cutting: Cultural Conflict in the Global Community* (Baltimore, MD: Johns Hopkins Press, 2002), p. 31.

14. Lightfoot-Klein, p. 39.

15. Ibid., pp. 38–40.

16. Ibid., p. 42.

17. Lynn M. Thomas, *Politics of the Womb: Women, Reproduction, and the State in Kenya* (Berkeley and Los Angeles: University of California Press, 2003), p. 22.

18. Ibid., p. 1.

19. Ibid., p. 34.

20. Ibid., p. 41.

21. Jomo Kenyatta, *Facing Mount Kenya* (New York: Vintage Books, 1965), p. 128.

22. Shweder, "When Cultures Collide."

23. Joseph P. Kahn, "Fran P. Hosken, 86; Activist for Women's Issues Globally," *Boston Globe*, February 12, 2006.

24. Alex de Waal, *AIDS and Power: Why There Is No Political Crisis—Yet* (London: Zed Books, 2006), p. 120.

25. Ibid., p. 57.

26. Judy Mann, "When Journalists Witness Atrocities," *Washington Post*, September 23, 1994.

27. Associated Press, "Four Arrested Over Female Circumcision Televised by CNN," September 12, 1994.

28. Eileen Alt Powell, "Long-Taboo Subject Hits Headlines, Seen as Chance for Change," Associated Press, September 19, 1994; Nadia Abou Al-Magd, "Egyptian Lawyer Sues CNN Over Female Circumcision Film," Associated Press, November 5, 1994.

29. Boyle, *Female Genital Cutting*, p. 4.

30. Ibid.

31. Ibid., pp. 4–5.

32. Fauziya Kassindja, *Do They Hear You When You Cry?* (New York: Delta, 1998), p. 3.

33. Ibid., p. 152.

34. Ibid., p. 5.

35. Spice News Services, "Jammeh Says His Government Will Not Ban FGM," January 22, 1999; Demba Jaw, "Women Disappointed by Jammeh's Pro-Mutilation Stance," Panafrican News Agency, January 22, 1999.

36. Boyle, *Female Genital Cutting*, p. 91.

37. See Center for Reproductive Rights briefing paper, "The Protocol on the Rights of Women in Africa: An Instrument for Advancing Reproductive and Sexual Rights," February 2006.

38. *Daily Observer*, "Gambia; NAMS Ratify Women's Rights Protocol," April 28, 2006.

39. Alice Walker, *Possessing the Secret of Joy* (New York: Harcourt, 1992), p. 63.

40. Fuambai Ahmadu, "Ain't I a Woman Too? Challenging Myths of Sexual Dysfunction in Circumcised Women," in *Transcultural Bodies: Female Genital Cutting in Global Context*, Bettina Shell-Duncan and Ylva Hernlund, eds. (Piscataway, NJ: Rutgers University Press, 2007), pp. 281–83.

41. Ibid., p. 283.

42. Fuambai Ahmadu, "Rites and Wrongs: An Insider/Outsider Reflects on Power and Excision," in *Female 'Circumcision' in Africa: Culture, Controversy, and Change*, Bettina Shell-

Duncan and Ylva Hernlund, eds. (Boulder, CO: Lynne Rienner Publishers, 2001), p. 287.

43. Ibid.

44. *New York Times*, "Sierra Leone Women's Group Mutilates 600 Girls," January 13, 1997; IRIN News, "In-Depth: Razor's Edge—The Controversy of Female Genital Mutilation," UN Office for the Coordination of Humanitarian Affairs (March 2005).

45. Mariama Kandeh, "Sierra Leone: FGM Back on the Agenda," *Concord Times* (Freetown), February 4, 2008.

46. Agence France-Presse, "Sierra Leone Women Demonstrate for 'Traditional' Mutilation," March 4, 2008.

47. Ahmadu, "Rites and Wrongs," p. 290.

48. Ibid., pp. 291–92.

49. Ibid., p. 292.

50. Ibid., p. 293.

51. Kipchumba Kemei, "Kenya Protest Violence Spreads to South," Reuters, January 18, 2008; Paul Salopek, "On Road to Kenya's Past, Future Looks Bleak," *Chicago Tribune*, February 10, 2008.

52. Jonathan Clayton, "Masai Girls Flee Cruelties of Tribal Traditions," *Times* (London), May 7, 2004.

53. Cathy Jenkins, "Kenya: Changing Attitudes to Female Circumcision," BBC Online, Monday, September 6, 1999.

54. "A Safe Haven for Girls Escaping Harm in Kenya," September 9, 2005, UNFPA News. Available at the UNFPA Web site, www .unfpa.org.

55. BBC News Online, "Kenyan Girls Flee Mutilation," February 7, 2003.

56. Inter Press Service, "Disturbing Trend in Female Genital Mutilation," June 9, 2004.

57. *The Nation*, "Man on the Run After Forced Circumcision Saga," September 20, 2004.

58. Equality Now, press release, "Two Maasai Girls in Kenya Forced to Undergo Genital Mutilation. Equality Now Urges Kenyan Authorities to Hold Perpetrators Accountable," September 14, 2004.

59. IRIN News, "In-Depth: Razor's Edge," UN Office for the Coordination of Humanitarian Affairs, March 2005.

60. Inter Press Service, "Disturbing Trend in Female Genital Mutilation," June 9, 2004.

61. "Kenya: Creating a Safe Haven, and a Better Future, for Maasai Girls Escaping Violence," UNFPA. Available at www.unfpa.org.

CHAPTER 6: THE GLOBALIZATION OF THE CULTURE WARS

1. Human Rights Watch, *Kosovo: Rape as a Weapon of Ethnic Cleansing*, report, March 21, 2000.

2. Manuel Carballo, "Report of a UNFPA Mission to Albania and Macedonia," April 5–13, 1999. Privately provided to the author.

3. D. Serrano Fitament. "Assesment Report on Sexual Violence in Kosovo." Written for the UNFPA, April 27–May 8, 1999. Privately provided to the author.

4. Austin Ruse, "UN Pro-life Lobbying: Full Contact Sport," *Human Life Review* (Winter 2000).

5. Ibid.

6. Ibid.

7. Michelle Goldberg, "The Zealots Behind President Bush's U.N. Family Planning Sellout," Salon.com, June 13, 2002.

8. Rod Dreher, "U.N. Opens Kosovo to Anti-family Zealots," *New York Post*, August 22, 1999.

9. Reprinted in Paul Marx, *Confessions of a Prolife Missionary* (Gaithersburg, MD: Human Life International, 1988), p. 48.

10. Ibid., p. 1.

11. Quoted by the Anti-Defamation League in "ADL Investigation Reveals Strain of Anti-Semitism in Extreme Factions of the Anti-Abortion Movement," press release, October 30, 1998.

12. Marx, *Confessions of a Prolife Missionary*, p. 269.

13. Ibid., p. 136.

14. Jennifer Gonnerman, "The Terrorist Campaign Against Abortion," *Village Voice*, November 3–9, 1998.

15. "HLI's Population Group Gains Financial Independence," Human Life International press release, July 5, 2000.

16. Jay Mathews, "Stanford Expels Student Faulted on China Study," *Washington Post*, February 25, 1983.

17. Fox Butterfield, "Secrecy in a Dismissal by Stanford Fuels Academic Freedom Dispute," *New York Times*, June 7, 1983.

18. Steven Mosher, "United in Opposing People," Population Research Institute Weekly Briefing, November 14, 2000.

19. Steven Mosher, "Ten Great Reasons to Have Another Child," Population Research Institute Weekly Briefing, July 2, 2001.

20. Catholics for a Free Choice, *Bad Faith at the UN: Drawing Back the Curtain on the Catholic Family and Human Rights Institute,* report, 2001.

21. Ibid.

22. Ibid.

23. Jennifer S. Butler, *Born Again: The Christian Right Globalized* (Ann Arbor, MI: Pluto Press, 2006), pp. 105–6.

24. Susan Whitney and Jennifer Toomer, "Family Advocates Find Common Thread—Hope," *Deseret News,* March 25, 1997.

25. Peggy Fletcher Stack, "Health Official: Western Sexuality Ruining Africa; Western Ideas About Sex Hurt Africa," *Salt Lake Tribune,* November 16, 1999.

26. Butler, *Born Again,* pp. 1–2.

27. Ibid., p. 2.

28. Deutsche Presse-Agentur, "Disillusion in Women's Politics Five Years After Beijing," June 4, 2000.

29. Ruse, "UN Pro-life Lobbying."

30. Desikan Thirunarayanapuram, "Envoys to Probe Use of U.S. Funds for Forced Abortions," *Washington Times,* May 12, 2002.

31. Ibid.

32. Michelle Goldberg, "A $34 Million 'Political Payoff,'" Salon.com, July 23, 2002.

33. Ibid.

34. Michael M. Phillips and Matt Moffett, "Brazil Refuses U.S. AIDS Funds, Rejects Conditions," *Wall Street Journal,* May 2, 2005.

35. Michelle Goldberg, "A Disastrous Appointment," Salon.com, January 5, 2006.

36. Susan A. Cohen, "The Global Contraceptive Shortfall: U.S. Contributions and U.S. Hindrances," *Guttmacher Policy Review,* vol. 9, no. 2 (Spring 2006).

37. *Access Denied: The Impact of the Global Gag Rule in Kenya, 2006 Update,* collaborative report by International Planned Parenthood Federation, Ipas, Population Action International, Pathfinder, EngenderHealth, and Planned Parenthood; Marion Edmunds, "A Bitter Political Pill," *The Guardian,* September 28, 2004.

38. Federal Democratic Republic of Ethiopia Ministry of Health, "Technical and Procedural Guidelines for Safe Abortion Services in Ethiopia" (June 2006).

39. James Dao, "Over U.S. Protest, Asian Group Approves Family Planning Goals," *New York Times,* December 18, 2002; Vijay Joshi, "U.S. Loses Vote at Population Conference," Associated Press, December 17, 2002.

40. Marwaan Macan-Markar, "Population: Asians Rebuff U.S. at Population Parley," Inter Press Service, December 18, 2002.

41. Ibid.

42. Brian Whitaker, "Fundamental Union," *The Guardian,* January 25, 2005.

43. See www.yearofthefamily.org/Doha.htm.

44. Colum Lynch, "Islamic Bloc, Christian Right Team Up to Lobby U.N.," *Washington Post,* June 17, 2002.

45. Sarah Boseley, "Britain Comes to Aid of UN Family Planning Agency Snubbed by Bush," *The Guardian,* March 5, 2004.

46. Joyce Mulama, "A New Report Fires Up the Abortion Debate," Inter Press Service, May 7, 2004.

47. "Ngilu: Hospitals to Get Abortion Kits," *East African Standard,* May 7, 2004.

48. BBC Monitoring Service, "Kenya: Shock After 15 Foetuses Are Dumped in Nairobi Estate." Excerpt from report by Kenyan Nation TV, May 26, 2004; Shelley Page, "Birth of a Crisis," *Ottawa Citizen,* October 23, 2004.

49. "Horror of Killed Babies," *East African Standard,* May 27, 2004.

50. "Tears as the Babies in Bags Laid to Rest," *The Nation,* June 4, 2004.

51. Ibid.

52. "Kenya: Dr. Nyamu's Charge Was Improper," *The Nation,* June 27, 2005.

53. *Republic v. John Nyamu, Merion N Kibathi and Mercy K Mathai,* Republic of Kenya in the High Court of Kenya at Nairobi, Criminal Division. Criminal Case No. 81 of 2004, June 14, 2005.

54. "Dumped Babies Were Born Dead, Pathologist Tells Court," *East African Standard,* April 19, 2005.

55. "Awori Roots for Safe Abortion," *The Nation,* June 27, 2007

56. Address of His Holiness Pope Benedict XVI to the Diplomatic Corps Accredited to the Holy See for the Traditional Exchange of New Year Greetings. January 8, 2007. Available at the Vatican's Web site, www.vatican.va.

57. Dinesh D'Souza, *The Enemy at Home: The Cultural Left and Its Responsibility for 9/11* (New York: Doubleday, 2007), p. 279.

CHAPTER 7: MISSING GIRLS

1. Barbara D. Miller, *The Endangered Sex* (Ithaca, NY: Cornell University Press, 1981), pp. 50–51.

2. Ibid., p. 58.

3. Christophe Z. Guilmoto, "Characteristics of Sex-Ratio Imbalance in India, and Future Scenarios," United Nations Population Fund. Presented at the Fourth Asia Pacific Conference on Reproductive and Sexual Health and Rights, Hyerabad, India, October 29–31, 2007.

4. United Nations Population Fund, *Missing: Mapping the Adverse Child Sex Ratio in India,* November 2003.

5. Prabhat Jha, Rajesh Kumar, Priya Vasa, Neeraj Dhingra, Deva Thiruchelvam, and Rahim Moineddin, "Low Male-to-Female Sex Ratio of Children Born in India: National Survey of 1.1 Million Households," *The Lancet,* vol. 367, iss. 9506 (January 21, 2006), pp. 211–18.

6. Sabu George, "Sex Selection/Determination in India: Contemporary Developments," *Reproductive Health Matters,* vol. 10, no. 19, *Abortion: Women Decide* (special issue, May 2002), pp. 190–92.

7. Christophe Z. Guilmoto, "Sex-ratio Imbalance in Asia: Trends, Consequences and Policy Responses," United Nations Population Fund. Available at the UNFPA Web site, www .unfpa.org

8. "Vernacular Dailies Pulling NRIs Back Home for Sex Tests," *Times of India,* August 19, 2007.

9. Douglas Almond and Lena Edlund, "Son-Biased Sex Ratios in the 2000 United States Census," Proceedings of the National Academy of Science, March 31, 2008.

10. Valerie M. Hudson and Andrea M. den Boer, *Bare Branches: The Security Implications of Asia's Surplus Male Population* (Cambridge, MA: MIT Press, 2004), pp. 164–67.

11. *Missing: Mapping the Adverse Child Sex Ratio in India.*

12. Tulsi Patel, "The Mindset Behind Eliminating the Female Foetus," in *Sex-Selective Abortion in India: Gender Society and New Reproductive Technology,* Tulsi Patel, ed. (New Delhi: Sage Publications, 2007), p. 170.

13. Ibid., pp. 161–62, 170–71.

14. "Dowry 'Kills' Her on 1st Anniversary," *Times of India,* May 1, 2008.

15. "Sample Registration System Statistic Report 2005," Office of the Registrar General, India.

16. Data available on the Kerala government Web site, www.kerala.org.

17. Ibid.

18. Ishwar C. Verma, Rose Joseph, Kusum Verma, Kamal Buckshee, and O. P. Ghai, "Prenatal Diagnosis of Genetic Disorders," *Indian Pediatrics* (May 1975).

19. Forum Against Sex Determination and Sex Pre-selection, "Using Technology, Choosing Sex, the Campaign Against Sex Determination and the Question of Choice," *Development Dialogue,* vol. 1, no. 2 (1992), pp. 91–102.

20. John Ward Anderson and Molly Moore, "Born Oppressed: Women in the Developing World Face Cradle-to-Grave Discrimination, Poverty," *Washington Post,* February 14, 1993.

21. Guilmoto, "Characteristics of Sex-Ratio Imbalance in India."

22. Ravi Duggal and Vimala Ramachandran, "The Abortion Assessment Project—India: Key Findings and Recommendations," *Reproductive Health Matters,* vol. 12, no. 24, Supplement: Abortion Law, Policy, and Practice in Transition (November 2004), pp. 122–29.

23. Ibid.

24. "Punjab Village Cries for Unborn Girls," *Times of India,* January 19, 2006.

25. According to the World Health Organization, a survey in the state of Madhya Pradesh showed that 49 percent of women thought abortion was illegal, and 36 percent did not know its legal status. *Unsafe Abortion: Global and Regional Estimates of the Incidence of Unsafe Abortion and Associated Mortality in 2003,* World Health Organization, 2007. Available at the WHO Web site, www.who .int.

26. Manisha Gupte, "Declining Sex Ratio, The Two Child Norm, and Women's Status," in *Coercion Versus Empowerment: Perspectives from the Peoples Tribunal on India's Coercive Population Policies and Two-Child Norm,* Shruti Pandey, Abhijit Das, Shravanti Reddy, and Binamrata Rani, eds. (New Delhi: Human Rights Law Network, 2006), p. 55. See also, "Defeat Because Hindutva Agenda Abandoned: VHP," *Times of India,* October 17, 2004.

27. Douglas A. Sylva, "The Lost Girls," *Weekly Standard,* March 21, 2007.

28. Gita Aravamudan, "Who Killed the Girls?" *Deccan Herald,* August 5, 2007.

29. Guilmoto, "Sex-Ratio Imbalance in Asia."

30. Scott J. South and Katherine Trent, "Sex Ratios and Women's Roles: A Cross-National Analysis," *American Journal of Sociology*, vol. 93, no. 5 (March 1988).

31. Hudson and den Boer, *Bare Branches*, p. 261.

32. Ibid., pp. 134–36.

33. Ibid., p. 140.

34. Ibid., pp. 208–11.

35. Woojin Chung and Monica Das Gupta, "Why Is Son Preference Declining in South Korea? The Role of Development and Public Policy, and the Implications for China and India," Policy Research Working Paper, the World Bank Development Research Group, Human Development and Public Services Team (October 2007).

36. Ibid.

37. Ibid.

38. Ibid.

39. Ibid.

40. *Times of India*, "Save the Girl Child, Says Manmohan Singh," April 29, 2008.

41. Maria Cheng, "Next Test Tells Fetus Sex After 6 Weeks," Associated Press, May 15, 2007; "Easy Availability of Gender ID Kits on Net a Threat: Minister," Indo-Asian News Service, March 15, 2008.

CHAPTER 8: THE BIRTH STRIKE

1. "Europe's Last Best Hope in the Battle for the Family." Available at the World Congress of Families Web site, www.worldcongress.org.

2. Agnieszka Graff, "We Are (Not All) Homophobes: A Report from Poland," *Feminist Studies* (Summer 2006); Nicholas Watt, "Polish Rightwingers Stoke Israeli Concern: Party Is Anti-Semitic, Diplomat Tells Warsaw; MEPs to Attend Gay March Amid Homophobia Claims," *The Guardian*, June 5, 2006.

3. Judy Dempsey, "Letter from Europe: Shaping the Agenda of Poland's Drift to the Far Right," *International Herald Tribune*, July 26, 2007.

4. Casey Sanchez, "The Latvian Connection," *Intelligence Report* (Fall 2007).

5. Quoted in Philip Jenkins, *God's Continent: Christianity, Islam, and Europe's Religious Crisis* (New York: Oxford University Press, 2007), p. 6.

6. Mark Steyn, *America Alone: The End of the World As We Know It* (Washington, D.C.: Regnery Publishing, 2006), pp. 12, 108.

7. CIA, *The World Factbook*, available on the CIA Web site, www.cia.gov.

8. Peter McDonald, "Gender Equity, Social Institutions, and the Future of Fertility," *Journal of Population Research*, vol. 17, no. 1 (May 2000).

9. Richard Jackson and Neil Howe, *The Graying of the Great Powers: Demography and Geopolitics in the 21st Century* (Washington, D.C.: Center for Strategic and International Studies, 2008), p. 5.

10. Ibid.

11. Francis G. Castles, "The World Turned Upside Down: Below Replacement Fertility, Changing Preferences and Family-Friendly Public Policy in 21 OECD Countries," *Journal of European Social Policy*, vol. 13, no. 3 (2003).

12. Frances Rosenbluth, Matthew Light, and Claudia Shrag, "The Politics of Low Fertility: Global Markets, Women's Employment, and Birth Rates in Four Industrialized Countries," Leitner Working Paper. Available at the Yale University Web site, www.yale.edu.

13. David Willett, *Old Europe? Demographic Change and Pension Reform*, Centre for European Reform, report, 2003.

14. Kirsty Scott, "Pensions Crisis? Just Have Babies," *The Guardian*, September 24, 2003.

15. Willetts, *Old Europe?*

16. Reuters, "Russian Province Tells Couples: Skip Work, Have Sex, Make Babies . . . Win Prizes!" September 13, 2007.

17. Yasha Levine, "Incentivized Birth: How Russia's Baby-Boosting Policies Are Hurting the Population," Slate.com, July 10, 2008.

18. Seth Mydans, "A Different Kind of Homework for Singapore Students: Get a Date," *New York Times*, April 29, 2008.

19. European Court of Human Rights, Fourth Section. Case of *Tysiąc v. Poland* (Application no. 5410/03), Judgement, Strasbourg, March 20, 2007.

20. Polish Federation for Women and Family Planning, "Contemporary Women's Hell: Polish Women's Stories," Warsaw (2005).

21. Ibid.

22. Beata Pasek, "Will Poland Say No to Abortion?" *Time*, March 30, 2007.

23. Ian Traynor, "Court Censures Poland for Denying Abortion Rights," *The Guardian*, March 21, 2007.

24. Adam Easton, "Social Change Slows Polish Birth Rates," BBC News online, March 29, 2006.

25. Ronald D. Bachman, ed., *Romania: A Country Study* (Washington, D.C.: Government Printing Office for the Library of Congress, 1989), available online at countrystudies. us/romania/; Charlotte Hord, Henry P. David, France Donnay, and Merrill Wolf, "Reproductive Health in Romania: Reversing the Ceauşescu Legacy," *Studies in Family Planning*, vol. 22, no. 4 (July–August 1991), pp. 231–40.

26. "World Population Prospects: The 2006 Revision," Executive Summary, United Nations Department of Economic and Social Affairs, Population Division, New York, 2007.

27. Willetts, *Old Europe?*

28. Ibid.

29. "Krekar Claims Islam Will Win," *Aftenposten*, March 13, 2006.

30. Quoted in Ian Buruma, *Murder in Amsterdam* (New York: Penguin Press, 2006), pp. 56–57.

31. Dan Bilefsky and Ian Fisher, "Across Europe, Worries on Islam Spread to Center," *New York Times*, October 11, 2006.

32. Philip Jenkins, *God's Continent: Christianity, Islam, and Europe's Religious Crisis* (New York: Oxford University Press, 2007), p. 15.

33. Charles Westoff and Tomas Frejka, "Religiousness and Fertility Among European Muslims," *Population and Development Review*, vol. 33, no. 4 (December 2007), pp. 785–809.

34. Ibid.

35. CIA. *The World Factbook*, accessed online May 20, 2008.

36. Westoff and Frejka, "Religiousness and Fertility Among European Muslims."

37. Pew Research Center, *Muslim Americans: Middle Class and Mostly Mainstream*, report, May 22, 2007.

38. United Nations Population Division, *The World at Six Billion* (1999); United Nations Population Division, *World Population to 2300* (2004). Both available at the UN Population Division Web site, www.un.org/esa/population.

39. United Nations Population Division, *The World at Six Billion* (1999).

40. Elizabeth Leahy, with Robert Engelman, Carolyn Gibb Vogel, Sarah Haddock, and Tod Preston, *The Shape of Things to Come—Why Age Structure Matters to a Safer, More Equitable World*, Population Action International report, April 11, 2007.

41. Jean-Claude Chesnais, "Fertility, Family and Social Policy in Contemporary Western Europe," *Population and Development Review*, vol. 22, no. 4 (December 1996), pp. 729–39.

42. Ibid.

43. Frances Fosenbluth, Matthew Light, and Claudia Schrag, "The Politics of Gender Equality: Explaining Variation in Fertility Levels in Rich Democracies," *Women & Politics*, vol. 26, no. 2 (2004).

44. Rana Foroohar, "Myth and Reality," *Newsweek*, February 27, 2006; Andrea Brandt, Steffen Kraft, Cordula Meyer, and Conny Neumann, "Women Face an Unfair Choice: Career or Children," *Spiegel Magazine*, May 5, 2006; Mary Daly and Katherine Rake, *Gender and the Welfare State* (Cambridge, UK: Polity Press, 2003), p. 139.

45. Mark Landler, "Germany Fights Stigma Against Working Mothers," *International Herald Tribune*, April 24, 2006.

46. Kimberly Morgan, *Working Mothers and the Welfare State: Religion and the Politics of Work-Family Policies in Western Europe and the United States* (Stanford, CA: Stanford University Press, 2006), p. 123.

47. Ibid., pp. 114–15.

48. Ibid., p. 113.

49. Rob Stein, "U.S. Fertility Rate Hits 35-Year High, Stabilizing Population," *Washington Post*, December 21, 2007.

50. Philip Longman, *The Empty Cradle: How Falling Birthrates Threaten World Prosperity and What to Do About It* (New York: Basic Books, 2004), p. 100.

51. Nicholas Eberstadt, "Born in the USA," *American Interest*, April 19, 2007.

52. Ibid.; Jacqueline E. Darroch, Jennifer J. Frost, and Susheela Singh, *Teenage Sexuality and Reproductive Behavior in Developed Countries*, Alan Guttmacher Institute, November 2001.

53. Eberstadt, "Born in the USA."

54. CIA, *World Factbook*, accessed online May 17, 2008; Robert Tait, "Ahmadinejad Urges Iranian Baby Boom to Challenge West," *The Guardian*, October 23, 2006.

55. Data available at the Organization for Economic Co-Operation and Development Web site, www.oecd.org.

56. David Popenoe, *The State of Our Unions: The Social Health of Marriage in America*, National Marriage Project, 2007.
57. Rosenbluth, Light, and Schrag, "The Politics of Low Fertility."
58. Ibid.
59. Ibid.
60. Britta Hoem, "Entry into Motherhood in Sweden: The Influence of Economic Factors on the Rise and Fall in Fertility, 1986–1997," *Demographic Research*, vol. 2, Art. 4 (April 17, 2000). Fosenbluth, Light, and Schrag, "The Politics of Low Fertility."
61. Jody Heymann, Alison Earle and Jeffrey Hayes, *The Work, Family, and Equality Index: How Does the United States Measure Up?*, report of The Project on Global Working Families at Harvard University and McGill University, 2007.
62. UNICEF, *Child Poverty in Perspective: An Overview of Child Well-being in Rich Countries*, report, 2007.

CONCLUSION: SEX AND CHAOS

1. United Nations Population Fund, *State of the World Population 2007: Unleashing the Potential of Urban Growth*. Available at www.unfpa.org.
2. UNICEF, *The State of the World's Children, 2008*, available at www.unicef.org.
3. Alex de Waal, *AIDS and Power: Why There Is No Political Crisis—Yet* (London: Zed Books, 2006), p. 20.
4. Lawrence K. Altman, "H.I.V. Risk Greater for Young African Brides," *New York Times*, February 29, 2004.
5. Suzanne Leclerc-Madlala, "Protecting Girlhood? Virginity Revivals in the Era of AIDS," *Agenda 56* (2003).
6. Helen Epstein, *The Invisible Cure: Africa, the West, and the Fight Against AIDS* (New York: Farrar, Straus and Giroux, 2007), p. 193.
7. Ibid.
8. International Food Policy Research Institute (IFPRI) policy brief, *High Food Prices: The What, Who, and How of Proposed Policy Actions*, May 2008.
9. Mark Clayton, "Is Water Becoming 'the New Oil?'" *Christian Science Monitor*, May 29, 2008.
10. UN Intergovernmental Panel on Climate Change, *Climate Change 2007*, Synthesis Report: "Summary for Policymakers." Available on the panel's Web site, www.ipcc.ch.
11. Transcript of Remarks by Director of the Central Intelligence Agency, General Michael V. Hayden, at the Landon Lecture Series, Kansas State University, April 30, 2008. Available at the CIA Web site, www.cia.gov.
12. IFPRI, "High Food Prices."
13. Jeffrey D. Sachs, *Common Wealth: Economics for a Crowded Planet* (New York: Penguin Press, 2008), pp. 163–64.
14. UNFPA, *State of the World Population, 2007*.
15. United Nations Population Division, *World Population Prospects, The 2006 Revision Highlights*. United Nations, New York, 2007.
16. Gilda Sedgh, Rubina Hussain, Akinrinola Bankole, and Susheela Singh, *Women with an Unmet Need for Contraception in Developing Countries and Their Reasons for Not Using a Method*, Guttmacher Institute Occasional Report, no. 37 (July 2007).
17. *Facts About the Unmet Need for Contraception in Developing Countries*, Guttmacher Institute fact sheet, July 2007.
18. Sedgh et al., *Women with an Unmet Need for Contraception*.